W9-BVA-339

Persuasion and Politics
The Social Psychology
of Public Opinion

Michael A. Milburn
University of Massachusetts–Boston

Brooks/Cole Publishing Company
Pacific Grove, California

EMERSON COLLEGE LIBRARY

HM
261
.M517
1991

I dedicate this book to my friend,
lover, and partner, Deborah

Brooks/Cole Publishing Company
A Division of Wadsworth, Inc.

© 1991 by Wadsworth, Inc., Belmont, California 94002. All rights reserved.
No part of this book may be reproduced, stored in a retrieval system, or transcribed,
in any form or by any means—electronic, mechanical, photocopying, recording, or
otherwise—without the prior written permission of the publisher,
Brooks/Cole Publishing Company, Pacific Grove, California 93950,
a division of Wadsworth, Inc.

Printed in the United States of America
10 9 8 7 6 5 4 3 2 1

Library of Congress Cataloging-in-Publication Data

Milburn, Michael A., [date]
   Persuasion and politics : the social psychology of public opinion
 / Michael A. Milburn.
      p.   cm.
   Includes bibliographical references and index.
   ISBN 0-534-15948-6
   1. Public opinion. 2. Political psychology. 3. Social
psychology.
   HM261.M517   1991
   303.3'8—dc20   90-22404
                                                        CIP

Sponsoring Editor: *Philip L. Curson, Marianne Taflinger*
Marketing Representative: *John Moroney*
Editorial Assistant: *Heather L. Riedl*
Production Editor: *Marjorie Z. Sanders*
Manuscript Editor: *Carol Beal*
Permissions Editor: *Mary Kay Hancharick*
Interior and Cover Design: *Sharon L. Kinghan*
Art Coordinator: *Lisa Torri*
Interior Illustration: *John Foster*
Typesetting: *Kachina Typesetting, Inc.*
Printing and Binding: *Malloy Lithographing, Inc.*

Preface

This book is about political psychology. In it I have attempted to apply theories and research from various areas within psychology, primarily social psychology, to the analysis of why people feel the way they do about political issues, how individuals' thinking about politics influences their opinions, how people's political attitudes change, and what role the mass media play in influencing individuals' opinions and political reasoning.

This book is thus relevant to a variety of academic disciplines, including *social psychology, political science,* and *communication.* For individuals interested in social psychology, I discuss various political applications of research on socialization, values, attribution theory, and social cognition. In addition, a detailed discussion of various theories of attitudes and attitude change is included; and a frequent topic in social psychology, the effects of the mass media, is examined.

For those interested in public opinion, this book provides an alternative perspective to other treatments of this topic. First, I examine the psychological bases of opinions, including the effects of personality, cognitive complexity, and social cognition processes. This psychological approach is contrasted to the more traditional approach of examining differences in opinion between members of different social groups. Then, I review social psychological theories of attitude change and apply them to the analysis of political communication. Finally, an important source of public opinion, the mass media, is examined in some detail.

For those who are particularly interested in the mass media, this book also provides a unique perspective. The chapter on the mass media is in many ways the focal point of the book. The earlier chapters on the psychological bases of public opinion and theories of attitude change provide the foundation for considering the nature of the political messages in the media and what effects the mass media have on individuals' political thinking and political opinions.

As I said earlier, this is a book in political psychology. Political psychology is an emerging field with interdisciplinary roots in psychology, political science, history, and psychiatry. This field also has its own professional association, the International Society of Political Psychology, to which a great many of the scholars whose work is reviewed in this volume belong.

Throughout my academic life I have tried to maintain a focus on the disciplines of psychology and political science. As an undergraduate, I shifted majors between these two departments. During this time, two instructors were very influential on my thinking, James March and Daryl Bem. Later, I applied to both disciplines for graduate work, before choosing the social psychology program at Harvard. It was there I had the opportunity to study under Thomas Pettigrew, whose course on the social psychology of public opinion provided the inspiration for much of my later research in this field and, consequently, for this book.

I have many people to thank for this book. I want to express my appreciation to the first political psychologist I encountered in my life, my dad, Thomas Milburn. My wife, Deborah Kelley-Milburn, a reference librarian at Widener Library, assisted greatly in assembling information that went into this book. In addition, various others have read the manuscript and given me tremendously helpful feedback on it, including Daryl J. Bem, Cornell University; Earl R. Carlson, California State University, Long Beach; Jon A. Krosnick, Ohio State University; Ann McGrail, State University of New York, Buffalo; Thomas Pettigrew, University of California, Santa Cruz, and University of Amsterdam; Eliot Smith, Purdue University; and Michael L. Wyckoff, Northern Illinois University. Barbara Robertson worked diligently to help clean up a variety of loose ends and gave comments on all the chapters. I particularly want to thank Janice Fine, Massachusetts Institute of Technology, who read the entire volume, giving many helpful comments for changes, and whose insistent question "What are you trying to say here?" compelled me to improve the book substantially. I want also to thank Phil Curson of Brooks/Cole, whose confidence in this project has been a continuing source of support and encouragement. Additionally, the writing of this book was supported with funds from grant number SES-8921327 from the National Science Foundation.

I want to add an additional note of thanks to all the students in my *social attitudes* and *public opinion classes* at the University of Massachusetts–Boston. They read earlier versions of the manuscript, giving me much helpful feedback and spotting various errors. Any remaining errors are, of course, my responsibility.

But beyond spotting typos and identifying passages that were unclear, my students have helped me maintain my enthusiasm for this endeavor. Students typically come into my class with some general knowledge about psychological principles and are familiar with some psychological research. Additionally, students generally have some awareness of the political world but do not have any way of integrating their background in psychology with their experience (generally through the mass media) of political events. Students often have finished my class with a greatly enhanced awareness of how important psychology is for understanding political events, how these political events are portrayed in the mass media, and how these television portrayals influence the way citizens think about politics. Seeing my students grow in this way has been particularly gratifying to me. I hope readers of this book will encounter the same increased awareness of and excitement in political psychology that I and my students have experienced.

Michael A. Milburn

Contents

■ CHAPTER ONE

**Introduction and Overview: The Psychological
Foundations of Public Opinion**   **1**

Why Political Psychology?   1

Focus and Organization of This Book   2

    The Nature and Sources of Public Opinion   2

    Political Cognition   3

    Persuasion and Opinion Change   4

■ SECTION ONE

The Nature and Sources of Public Opinion   **5**

■ CHAPTER TWO

Attitudes and Public Opinion   **7**

The Dynamic Nature of Attitudes   7

The Attitude Concept   8

    The Theory of Reasoned Action   8

    Situational Influences   10

    Applying the Theory of Reasoned Action to Voting Behavior   11

    Attitude Generation in Polls   13

Public Opinion   13

    The State-of-Consciousness Fallacy   14

    The Situational Perspective on Public Opinion   15

    Defining Public Opinion   15

Some Cautionary Notes about Surveys   16

    Types of Samples   17

Errors Due to Response Rate and Sample Selection   17
Sampling Error   19
The Effects of Question Wording   19

■ CHAPTER THREE
Social Factors and Public Opinion   **21**

Background Characteristics and Their Influence on
Public Opinion   21
Separating the Effects of Different Variables   21
Explanations for the Relationship Between Social Factors and
Public Opinion   23
The Relationship of Individual Social Factors to Public Opinion   24
Social Class and the Crisis in Political Participation   32
Putting the Variables Together   34
Political Socialization   36
Transmission of Political Attitudes   37
Content of Political Learning   38
A Caveat   38
Conclusion   39

■ CHAPTER FOUR
Personality and Public Opinion   **40**

Personality Needs Affect Opinion   40
Holistic Approaches   41
Lasswell's Theory of Personality Development   41
The Authoritarian Personality   43
Authoritarianism of the Left?   45
Eysenck's Two-Factor Theory of Attitude Structure   45
Rokeach's Value Pluralism Model   46
Tomkins's Polarity Theory   49
Tomkins's Polarity Theory Scale   50
Left and Right Ways of Seeing   51
Roots of Ideological Differences   51
Empirical Support for Tomkins's Polarity Theory   52
Conclusion   53

■ SECTION TWO
**The Relationship Between Political Thinking
and Public Opinion**   **55**

■ CHAPTER FIVE
The Nature of Political Thought   57

Political Ideology   58
  The Belief Systems Approach to Political Ideology   58
  The Situational Perspective on Ideological Consistency   60
  Ideological Consistency and Political Sophistication   60
Political Reasoning   61
  Piaget's Model of Cognitive Development   61
  Rosenberg's Application of the Piagetian Model   62
  Tetlock's Approach to Cognitive Complexity   63
  Comparing Rosenberg and Tetlock   63
Attribution Theory and Dialectical Thinking   65
  Attribution Theory   65
  Dialectical Thinking   65
  Cognitive Complexity and Explanations for Terrorism   68
  Pragmatic-Reasoning Schemas   69
Conclusion   70

■ CHAPTER SIX
Political Schemas   72

The Schema Concept   72
  Person Schemas   73
  Self-Schemas   74
  Role Schemas   75
  Political Schemas   75
Schema Accessibility: Expert-Novice Differences   76
Schema Activation   78
  Effects of Schema Activation on Schema Accessibility   78
  Schema Activation and Emotion   80
  Schema Activation and Cognitive Complexity   80
Cognitive Heuristics   82
  Representativeness   82
  Law of Small Numbers   82
  Availability   83
  Political Implications of Cognitive Heuristics   83
Conclusion   85

■ SECTION THREE
Theories of Persuasion and Opinion Change   87

■ CHAPTER SEVEN

Belief Consistency   89

Balance Theory   90

Cognitive Dissonance Theory   92

  The Original Demonstration of Dissonance   93

  Additional Aspects of Dissonance   93

  The Importance of Personal Responsibility   94

Resolution of Belief Dilemmas   95

  Four Ways of Resolving Belief Dilemmas   95

  An Example of Political Persuasion   97

  Additional Examples of Belief Dilemma Resolution   102

  Dissonance versus Belief Dilemma Resolution   103

Conclusion   104

■ CHAPTER EIGHT

Persuasive Communications and
Attitude Change   106

The Yale Model of Persuasion   107

  Source Characteristics   107

  Message and Audience Characteristics   109

  Political Implications of Persuasive Communication Research   110

Social Judgment Theory   110

  The Physiological Basis of the Social Judgment Effect   111

  Cognitive Anchoring   111

  Attitude Intensity and Importance   112

  An Experimental Demonstration of the Social Judgment Effect
    for Attitude Change   113

  Applications of the Social Judgment Effect   115

  Comparing Dissonance Theory and Social Judgment Theory   117

Fishbein and Ajzen's Model of Persuasive
  Communication Effects   119

  Message Discrepancy and the Probability of
    Message Acceptance   119

  Facilitating Factors   120

  Attitude Change   121

  Using the Fishbein and Ajzen Model to Predict the Outcome
    of Aronson et al. (1963)   123

The Elaboration Likelihood Model   123

  Two Routes to Persuasion   123

The Cognitive Response to a Persuasive Message   124
Differences Between Individuals in Their Interest in Thinking
  about Issues   126
Affect and Persuasion   127
Self-Schemas and Message Perception   127
The Personal Relevance of the Persuasive Communication   128
The Political Implications of the ELM Model   129
Conclusion   129

CHAPTER NINE
The Mass Media and Public Opinion   131

The Structure and Content of the Mass Media   131
  The Definition of *News*   132
  Ideology and the Mass Media   133
  A Liberal Bias?   134
  Another Perspective   136
  Ideological Bias in Newspapers' Coverage of Foreign Events   136
  The Ideological Orientation of Television News   137
  The Critical Media Studies Approach to the Mass Media   138
Effects of the Mass Media   139
  Political Effects of the Mass Media   141
  The Mass Media and Agenda Setting   142
  The Effect of Negative Political Campaign Advertisements   144
  Mass Media Effects on Policy Attitudes, Affective Responses, and
    the Complexity of Thinking   146
  Additional Negative Effects of Television   150
  Media Credibility   150
Conclusion   151

CHAPTER TEN
Conclusion   152

The Political Psychology of Public Opinion—a Summary   152
Political Psychology and Political Analysis   155

References   159

Index   177

■ ■ ■ ■ ■

CHAPTER ONE

Introduction and Overview: The Psychological Foundations of Public Opinion

Following the Democratic National Convention in July 1988, some public opinion polls indicated that Michael Dukakis, the nominee for the Democratic party, led George Bush, the likely Republican presidential nominee, by almost 20 points. Four months later, Dukakis lost the race for president by a spread of almost ten points. What happened? Is public opinion so volatile that huge swings in citizens' attitudes are inevitable, or did George Bush just run an outstanding campaign? Is the public liberal or conservative; or given the swing from left to right, do we assume that the public is left one moment and right the next? And whichever it is, how could the public support candidates so different? How do these election results make sense, given that the same electorate voted in an overwhelmingly Democratic House and Democratic Senate at the same time they voted in a Republican president?

■ Why Political Psychology?

The dynamics of public opinion are not straightforward and can be difficult to fathom at first. Research in social psychology, however, can help explain many of the complexities of attitudes and opinions. Because social psychology has always been particularly concerned with the application of theory and research, it has always been the most politically oriented area of psychology. Theoretically, social psychology views behavior as an interaction between personality characteristics and situational influences. This perspective is also fundamental to an understanding of public opinion. The emerging discipline of political psychology takes the insights of social psychology and applies them to politics.

   The aim of this book is to apply a social psychological perspective to the analysis of public opinion and politics. My contention is that one cannot even begin to understand where political attitudes come from and how they change unless one understands this fundamental truth: Attitudes and behavior are a function of an interactive process between the internal—or what people carry around with them: personality, knowledge, and belief structures—and the external—or what is brought to them from the outside: the influence exerted by other individuals in conversations

1

and through the mass media. Thus there is a dialectical and ongoing interactive process between internal and external forces. Overemphasis or sole emphasis on either the internal or the external forces leads to an incomplete analysis of the dynamics of public opinion.

■ Focus and Organization of This Book

An examination of some of the apparent contradictions involved in social attitudes and public opinion is the focus of this book, and three primary questions are addressed: (1) What are opinions and where do they come from? (2) How are opinions related to political thinking? (3) How do opinions change? Thus there are three primary sections to this book: The first section covers *the nature and sources of opinions*. The second section describes *the relationship between political thinking and public opinion*. The third section discusses *theories of persuasion and opinion change*.

These three central aspects of public opinion can best be understood in the context of what political scientist Walter Dean Burnham (1982) has called "the current crisis in American politics." This crisis refers to the declining level of political interest and political participation, particularly voting, that has developed in the United States during the second half of this century. There has been a substantial increase in feelings of political alienation in recent years and a questioning of the government's legitimacy in an increasing proportion of the public. Where political opinions come from, how they relate to political thinking, and how they change are all influenced by the social, historical, and political processes that led to this crisis in American political participation.

The Nature and Sources of Public Opinion

What are attitudes and opinions? Where do they come from? The first section provides a review of the research addressing these questions. Chapter Two defines attitudes and opinions and their measurement, Chapter Three considers the influence of broad social categories on opinions, and Chapter Four analyzes the relationship of personality to public opinion.

Chapter Two presents the model of the relationships between beliefs, attitudes, and behavior proposed by Martin Fishbein and Icek Ajzen that they call the theory of reasoned action (Fishbein & Ajzen, 1975, 1981). The relationship of public opinion to political attitudes is then considered, and a major conceptual approach to public opinion, the situational perspective on public opinion (Bennett, 1980), is reviewed. Finally, since opinion polling is a major source of information about public opinion, the nature of polling and its potential errors are discussed.

Chapter Three takes the traditional approach to understanding public opinion, focusing on the effects of broad social differences upon individuals' attitudes (for instance, race, gender, age, social class). For example, what are the opinion differences between Blacks and Whites, or between older individuals and younger persons? Factors such as race, gender, age, and social class do, in fact, influence opinion; differences in the socialization that members of different groups receive—as well as the effects of belonging to different groups—affect their political opinions. Although social factors are essential to the analysis of public opinion, on their own they have limited explanatory power. We must look further for explanations of differences in opinion and political ideology. A psychological perspective is essential to the generation of explanations in this realm.

Personality, considered in Chapter Four, is a fundamental psychological concept. An individual's personality represents the cumulative influence of that individual's socialization and life experiences. These experiences can have a considerable impact on the current attitudes and opinions the individual expresses. For example, a person's rigidity or flexibility can have, as we shall see, important implications for his or her political attitudes.

Political scientists have tended to minimize the importance of personality factors on political opinions and behaviors, preferring an examination of the impact of social factors. Greenstein (1975) observes, however, that since personality characteristics are largely determined by various social environmental factors, the question of whether personality or social factors is more important for political behavior is irrelevant. Chapter Four discusses the way certain personality structures, particularly authoritarianism and dogmatism, are related to individuals' political attitudes. The research we discuss that relates background experiences to both personality characteristics and political attitudes clarifies and extends the analysis in Chapter Three of the effects of social characteristics on public opinion.

Political Cognition

Chapter Five examines political ideology and various theories of the complexity of political thinking, and Chapter Six reviews current research on cognitive structures called schemas and how they affect political attitudes and political thinking.

From the beginning, research and theory in political science has focused on political ideology. Chapter Five first examines political ideology and then discusses several theories that seek to describe and account for differences between individuals in the way that they think about political issues and the causes of political events. As we shall see, results from these different perspectives all point to a coherent view of the various ways that different people think about politics. One important aspect of individuals' ideological thinking is the complexity with which they view political events. A person's political ideology implies or states directly a model of the way events in the world are causally related. Some people have only vague notions of the causes of particular events (such as a terrorist's attack), and others think in terms of a complex system of interacting and reciprocally influencing forces. The research described in Chapter Five suggests a mechanism to explain the influences that specific situational factors have upon the complexity of individuals' political thinking.

Implicit in a discussion of cognitive complexity is a consideration of the different ways individuals hold information about politics in their minds—that is, the "cognitive structures" of political knowledge that people have. Social psychologists in recent years have devoted considerable attention to research on *schemas*, a term referring to a hierarchically organized structure of information related to a particular person, object, or area. Chapter Six presents social psychological research on the schema concept and its application to the way individuals process political information.

Persuasion and Opinion Change

Chapter Seven surveys several theories of cognitive consistency and applies this approach to the analysis of political communication; Chapter Eight deals with several important social psychological theories of persuasion; and Chapter Nine analyzes the most important source of political information and persuasion, the mass media.

A critical aspect of public opinion research is to understand how individuals' opinions change. Social psychological research on attitudes and attitude change has provided a wealth of information about how different factors can influence the opinions that individuals hold and under what conditions these opinions can change. Chapters Seven and Eight review research on attitudes and attitude change from a variety of perspectives. Chapter Seven examines research under the general heading of "consistency theories"—that is, theories that start from the assumption that individuals are motivated to maintain consistency among their attitudes, beliefs, and behavior. Chapter Eight continues this discussion with an examination of attitude change theories that focus on how individuals respond to persuasive communications—that is, messages intended to change the receivers' attitudes.

There is wide consensus that one of the most important factors in politics in the latter half of the 20th century, if not *the* most important, is the mass media. Chapter Nine examines research on the nature of the mass media and their effects on political attitudes, drawing from the previous chapters on cognitive complexity, schematic processes, and theories of attitude change. We shall see that the mass media affect individuals' thinking as well as the political process itself. Such influence appears to have some very damaging effects on the U.S. political system. These negative effects are particularly important in the context of the crisis in American politics of voter apathy and nonparticipation (Burnham, 1982).

The Nature and Sources of Public Opinion

CHAPTER TWO

Attitudes and Public Opinion

■ The Dynamic Nature of Attitudes

If you want to ask an individual what his or her attitude is on a particular topic, your question assumes that the person has an attitude that can be measured. For some people, particularly for attitudes that are central for them, this assumption is likely to be true. With many other people, however, attitudes cannot be measured, because they have not made a verbal statement of them, even in their own minds. It is only when confronted with the object of this attitude, or being asked what their attitude is, that they may *generate* their attitude following a cognitive review of their knowledge, information, and beliefs about that object.

An awareness of the dynamic nature of attitudes is important to keep in mind throughout this book. In the next section of this chapter we will discuss the Fishbein and Ajzen model of the belief/attitude relationship that underlies the generation process. In Chapters Three and Four we discuss the bases of many of the beliefs that generate attitudes and opinions: social group membership and personality. Then in Chapters Five and Six we discuss the cognitive processes central to attitude generation: cognitive complexity and schema activation—that is, what determines the information and beliefs that will be used to construct a particular attitude. An application of viewing political communication from the perspective of schema activation is considered in Chapter Seven with an analysis of President Reagan's speech to the nation following the Tower Board Report on the Iran-Contra revelations. Finally, a major source of schema activation, often called *priming,* is discussed in Chapter Nine on the mass media.

All the research we will be discussing about the dynamic nature of attitudes can be understood from what Bennett (1980) has called the "situational perspective" on public opinion, discussed in some detail later in this chapter. Political scientists have had a tendency to view opinions as either fixed or nonexistent—that is, as "non-attitudes," according to Converse (1970). A more appropriate model of attitudes conceptualizes them instead as cognitions generated in response to various situational factors (such as the mass media) that interact with existing personal differences (such as political sophistication). To begin this consideration, we turn now to a discussion of the attitude concept.

■ The Attitude Concept

Gordon Allport (1985) has called the concept of attitude "probably the most distinctive and indispensable concept in contemporary American social psychology" and "the keystone in the edifice of American social psychology" (p. 35). An individual's attitude toward some object or public policy has historically been defined in social psychology as his or her general feeling of like or dislike toward that object. Attitudes toward some object, person, or behavior can thus be distinguished in terms of the *direction* of the attitude (positive or negative) and the *strength* of the attitude (strong or weak).

Psychologists have typically measured attitudes with a variety of different attitude scales (Lemon, 1973). These scales may include a list of items related to the object of the attitude to which a respondent agrees or disagrees (Thurstone, 1928), individual items on which an individual indicates the extent of his or her disagreement on a five- or seven-point scale (Likert, 1932), or the semantic differential scale (Osgood, Suci, & Tannenbaum, 1957), a set of adjective pairs of opposites (for example, good/bad, active/passive, strong/weak), each pair with seven intermediate points between them that an individual uses to describe a particular object.

For a long period in the 1960s and 1970s, social psychological books on the nature of attitudes (such as Oskamp, 1977) stated that there are three components of attitudes: cognitive (what a person believes about an object), affective (how the person feels toward the object), and behavioral (how the person expects to behave toward that object). Oskamp gives the example of an individual's attitudes toward Martians. The cognitive component might be "Martians look strange"; the affective component could be "I don't like Martians"; and the behavioral component might be "I wouldn't want my daughter to marry one." Although these distinctions made some intuitive sense, there was a lack of evidence supporting these differentiations. McGuire (1969) argued that these three components had proved to be so highly intercorrelated that it might not be useful to continue making these distinctions.

During this same period some social psychologists began to question the usefulness of the attitude concept altogether. For decades, studies had produced evidence that attitudes were not predictive of behavior (LaPiere, 1934; Wicker, 1969). If a person's attitude could not predict how that person would behave toward another individual, then what use was it?

The Theory of Reasoned Action

In this context of theoretical uncertainty, Fishbein and Ajzen (1975, 1981) proposed their theory of reasoned action. Figure 2-1 displays Fishbein and Ajzen's model of the relationship among beliefs, attitudes, and behavior. Fishbein and Ajzen were particularly interested in demonstrating that attitudes are predictive of behavior. Their model specifies elements that correspond to the three components of attitudes: beliefs (cognitive), attitudes (affective), and behavioral intentions (conative). These elements are linearly related to the behavior in which a person engages.

In Fishbein and Ajzen's model, beliefs combine with evaluations of the consequences of those beliefs to produce attitudes. This means that beliefs about the consequences of a particular behavior are linked to the value that a person puts on

Figure 2-1   Fishbein and Ajzen's theory of reasoned action

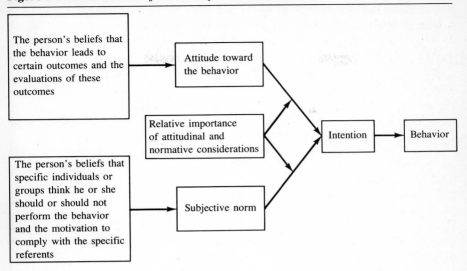

Note: Arrows indicate the direction of influence.
Source: From Icek Ajzen/Martin Fishbein, *Understanding Attitudes and Predicting Social Behavior,* © 1980, pp. 8, 181. Reprinted by permission of Prentice-Hall, Inc., Englewood Cliffs, New Jersey.

each outcome. In Fishbein and Ajzen's model, the probability of each outcome occurring, multiplied by how positive or negative the person feels about that outcome occurring, and with these products summed, results in a positive or negative attitude toward the behavior of some specific magnitude. They represented the belief/attitude relationship with the following formula:

$$A = \Sigma \; b_i \cdot e_i \qquad\qquad (1)$$

In this formula, A represents a person's attitude toward a particular object or behavior, each b_i represents a belief related to the object or behavior, and each e_i is the evaluation or value that the person attaches to that belief, either positive or negative.

Thus, in Fishbein and Ajzen's model, a person may have the *beliefs* that voting for George Bush versus Michael Dukakis would mean increased likelihood of both restrictions on abortion rights and increased defense spending, and a decreased probability of new taxes. The Fishbein and Ajzen model would multiply the strength of these beliefs by the *value* that the person places on each belief; for example, the person is in favor of restricting abortion rights (a positive outcome of voting for George Bush), opposed to more defense spending (a negative outcome), and opposed to new taxes (another positive outcome). The product of the belief and value combinations will predict the person's attitude.

To present a numerical example, suppose Jim is asked to express his agreement with the following beliefs about the death penalty by rating the probability that each belief is true on a scale from 0 to 1:

1. The death penalty deters crime.
2. The death penalty may result in the execution of innocent people.
3. The death penalty obtains revenge for wrongs against society.
4. The death penalty is more likely to be applied to Blacks than to Whites.

Jim doesn't believe that the death penalty is likely to deter crime, so he rates belief 1 with the low probability of .20. In contrast, Jim is quite sure that the death penalty will end up executing innocent people, so he rates belief 2 with a probability of .95. He also agrees that the death penalty will obtain revenge, so he gives that a probability of .90. Finally, Jim thinks that the death penalty is more likely to be applied to Blacks than to Whites, so he gives that a high probability of .80.

Jim is then asked to rate the consequences of each belief (the e_i) on a scale ranging from +5 (very positive) to −5 (very negative). Even though he doesn't think it very likely that the death penalty will deter crime, he views deterring crime as very desirable, so he evaluates belief 1 as +4. Jim considers the execution of innocent people as extremely bad, so he evaluates belief 2 as −5. Finally, Jim views both taking revenge and inequitably applying the death penalty to Blacks as wrong, so he evaluates 3 and 4 as −4. Multiplying the probabilities Jim associates with the different beliefs by the evaluation Jim gives to the consequences of each belief and then adding all those products gives Jim's attitude toward the death penalty. Table 2-1 presents the calculations to determine Jim's attitude toward the death penalty, using the Fishbein and Ajzen model. As you can see, the result is a very negative attitude toward the death penalty.

Situational Influences

The attitude a person has toward a particular behavior is an important influence on the corresponding behavioral intention. As you can see in Figure 2-1, however, there is another set of influences that Fishbein and Ajzen refer to as "subjective norms." This component of their model includes situational influences. If a person's social situations (for instance, parents, spouse, co-workers) all favor a particular behavior, and if the person often acquiesces to social pressure or wants to comply in this situation for various reasons (in Figure 2-1, the "motivation to comply"), then these elements will contribute to the likelihood of that person's behavioral intention. Fishbein and Ajzen argue that this intention will be strongly predictive of the person's actual behavior.

Table 2-1 Determining attitude (A) from beliefs (b_i) and evaluations (e_i)

Belief about the Death Penalty	Belief		Evaluation		$b_i \cdot e_i$
1. Deters crime	.20	×	+4	=	.80
2. Executes innocent people	.95	×	−5	=	−4.75
3. Obtains revenge	.90	×	−4	=	−3.6
4. Applied more to Blacks	.80	×	−4	=	−3.2
Total (Attitude)					−10.75

$$A = \Sigma \, b_i \cdot e_i = -10.75$$

For example, if one is measuring a person's attitude toward voting for George Bush, then this attitude will be predictive of the person's behavioral intention ("I intend to vote for George Bush"). The subjective norms that the person perceives ("How do other people in my social environment feel about my voting for George Bush?") and the person's motivation to comply ("How strongly do I feel that I want to comply with their wishes?") will also predict the person's intention to vote for George Bush. Research has shown that behavioral intentions are highly predictive of actual behavior.

Applying the Theory of Reasoned Action to Voting Behavior

Ajzen and Fishbein (1980) applied their model to political attitudes and voting behavior in the 1976 U.S. presidential election. They conducted a small survey of voting-age residents in Champaign County, Illinois, at various points shortly prior to the 1976 election. Because an election is a choice situation, they measured individuals' "differential" beliefs, attitudes, intentions, and behavior, although the underlying model of attitude/behavior relationships is basically the same. A differential belief, for example, is the difference between one's belief that a particular outcome (such as a $5 to $7 billion cut in defense spending) would occur if Carter were elected president and the belief that it would occur if Ford were elected president.

Ajzen and Fishbein's first task was to assess the beliefs that respondents held about the likely actions of the two candidates, Jimmy Carter and Gerald Ford, were they to become president. There was general agreement among respondents that Carter would be more likely to grant amnesty to draft evaders and deserters and to cut the defense budget. Where respondents varied was in their *evaluation* of that particular outcome. Respondents who saw these as good outcomes tended to favor Carter; individuals who opposed these policies in general preferred Ford. The sum of all a person's differential beliefs combined with the evaluations was highly correlated with differential attitude (see Figure 2-2). This attitude in turn was highly predictive of the intention to vote for either Ford or Carter.

Fishbein and Ajzen also include in their model the effect of situational pressures, which they refer to as "subjective norms." These norms are a function of the individuals' beliefs about whether the important people in his or her life want him or her to engage in the relevant behavior ("normative beliefs"), and the extent to which the person wants to conform to the expectations of these other people ("motivation to comply"). In their study of the 1976 presidential election, Fishbein and Ajzen found that their estimates of individuals' perceptions of whether significant people in their social environment wanted them to vote for Ford or Carter ("differential subjective norms") were almost exclusively a result of differences in beliefs about whom they should vote for. There were no differences between Ford and Carter voters in how motivated they were to comply with others' beliefs.

Figure 2-2 displays the effects of both attitudes that individuals hold toward voting for Ford or Carter and their beliefs about the expectations of those in their

Figure 2-2 The theory of reasoned action applied to the 1976 presidential election

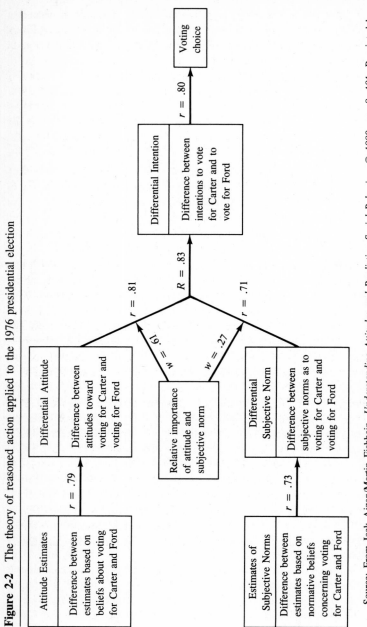

Source: From Icek Ajzen/Martin Fishbein, *Understanding Attitudes and Predicting Social Behavior*, © 1980, pp. 8, 181. Reprinted by permission of Prentice-Hall, Inc., Englewood Cliffs, New Jersey.

social environment. As you can see, by itself, each variable is highly correlated with intentions (attitudes: $r = .81$; subjective norms: $r = .71$). What is important to consider, however, is what effect each variable has on holding the effect of the other constant. Fishbein and Ajzen found that the relative weights told a very different story: Attitudes remained highly predictive (weight $= .61$), while the effect of subjective norms was much smaller (weight $= .27$).

We noted earlier McGuire's (1969) question about the soundness of making distinctions between the three components of attitudes. Breckler's (1984) more recent examination of the validity of the tripartite model of attitudes with cognitive, affective, and behavioral components confirms the importance and validity of the conceptual distinctions Fishbein and Ajzen make. The importance of individuals' attitudes for predicting their behavior strengthens our interest in the focus of this book: what effect individuals' cognitions (political attitudes, schemas, cognitive complexity) have on their political behavior, and what factors influence the development of those cognitions.

Attitude Generation in Polls

For many people, the expression of attitudes is a dynamic process. Many attitudes are actively produced, rather than simply recalled when a question is asked about them. For political attitudes, considerable research has supported the conclusion of differences in stability and consistency between "elite" attitudes (the opinions of those who deal with politics on a daily basis) and those of the "mass public" (Converse, 1964, 1970). Converse (1970) has argued that the opinions offered by most respondents to opinion surveys reflect "non-attitudes," responses simply generated at the time. Converse's model of attitudes reflects the dynamic process of attitude production.

Recent research also takes this perspective. Tourangeau and Rasinski (1988) argue that when individuals are asked about their attitude on a particular issue, their response is a result of a four-stage cognitive process involving interpretation of the meaning of the question and the accessing of relevant beliefs and feelings in order to make a judgment about the issue. Recalling Fishbein and Ajzen's model that attitudes are a result of the combination of relevant beliefs and evaluations related to a particular issue, we see that *which beliefs* are recalled obviously has a significant effect on the nature of the resulting attitude. In Chapter Six, when we discuss schematic effects upon attitudes, we will see that this dynamic model of attitude production underlies the process of political thinking. We turn now to a discussion of public opinion.

■ Public Opinion

The study of public opinion has a long history, and there are many definitions of it. Writing in the early 1500s, Niccolo Machiavelli (1975) was one of the first political thinkers to use the term *public opinion*. In his *Discourses*, he observes that "a wise man will not ignore public opinion in regard to particular matters, such as the distribution of offices and preferment." In 1762, the philosopher Jean Jacques Rousseau expressed the belief that governments rest ultimately upon public opinion and that social change is difficult without the support of popular opinion (Rousseau, 1913). In the late 18th century, James Madison wrote in *The Federalist Papers* that the opinions of the public could serve to set limits on the actions of leaders, although he felt it preferable for a political elite to construe the concerns of the general population rather than have a direct democracy.

Early in this century, writers such as Abbott Lawrence Lowell (1913) and Walter Lippmann (1922) began the scientific study of public opinion. Measuring public opinion is now big business, both for scientists and pollsters. Every national election year, using millions of dollars from the National Science Foundation, the Survey Research Center at the University of Michigan administers its National Election Study surveys. These data are made available to researchers around the country. Additionally, the polling industry now has revenues in the millions of dollars annually, and any actual or potential political candidate is virtually required to have poll data to direct his or her campaign.

The State-of-Consciousness Fallacy

While there is extensive research available now on the nature of public opinion, W. Lance Bennett (1980) has observed that many research studies in past years have fallen victim to what he calls the "state of consciousness" fallacy. Many researchers, he argues, have implicitly viewed the public as a fixed entity whose composition remains the same over time and for different issues.

Thus, from the state-of-consciousness perspective, it appears to make sense to ask whether public opinion is informed, stable, or consistent. It is from a state-of-consciousness perspective that a journalist can question whether the public has changed its mind. Bennett argues, however, that these are not good questions. He cites research that shows that the public is ill informed, inconsistent in its attitudes, and highly changeable over time, but he also discusses evidence that finds just the opposite result. How can this be? Bennett suggests that it is because the question (such as whether the public's attitudes are stable) is a poor one.

It is important to recognize that *public opinion* is a theoretical construct, not a characteristic of an actual entity that can be measured. How much a person weighs is an attribute that can be measured, so a researcher could weigh Bob at different times and comment on the stability of Bob's weight. Public opinion is different. Unlike the composition of Bob, who remains the same person over time, the composition of the public that holds opinions may vary from issue to issue. Additionally, opinion can be influenced by features in the environment, such as ease of access to political information and the content of communication from political elites. Asking whether opinion is stable overlooks the interactive nature of individuals' opinions and the political environment.

The Situational Perspective on Public Opinion

Bennett (1980) argues that these disagreements over the stability and consistency of the public's attitudes are a result of the state-of-consciousness fallacy and that a quite different perspective, a "situational perspective," on public opinion should be utilized. This alternative perspective views the public as an aggregation of people who actually develop and express opinions on a particular issue at a specific time. Thus, different political situations may affect the formation and expression of public opinion. For example, because identifying important political information costs time and money, it will be difficult for many individuals to gather the information necessary to develop and crystallize opinions, unless a government is particularly interested in maintaining two-way communication with members of the public. Considering the nature of political systems, it is not likely that important information will generally be available to all citizens. As Bennett (1980) notes, information is politically valuable, and government officials or political candidates will not make it widely available unless it is in their own political interest to do so.

Viewing public opinion from this situational perspective, we can see that different people may be active (that is, articulating their opinions) at different times and on different issues; the content of political communication, particularly that presented in the mass media, may have a pivotal effect on the opinions that individuals hold; and political institutions may also influence the attitudes that people hold and the political actions that they take. From this perspective, questions such as "Is public opinion consistent?" lose their relevance, because opinion at any one time is a reflection of the political environment and the electorate's exposure to different kinds of political communication.

This controversy is important, because the perspective one takes on public opinion has significant implications for democracy. Early political thinkers such as John Madison and Alexander Hamilton (*The Federalist Papers*) were suspicious of direct democracy and favored a more limited representational form of government. They distrusted the public, viewing it as uninformed and inconsistent in its opinions. Viewing public opinion from the situational perspective, Bennett (1980) writes that "it is meaningless to argue that government can only be as democratic as the consciousness of the people allow, if the consciousness of the public depends in large part on how the structure of government affects opinion situations" (p. 38).

This situational perspective on public opinion is particularly important to keep in focus when we consider the crisis of political nonparticipation in the United States (Burnham, 1982), discussed in some detail in Chapter Three. We shall see that we cannot simply view the high rates of nonparticipation as the result of a politically unsophisticated electorate; an examination of the message content of the political environment and the values held by political elites in this country indicates important reasons for the low participation and for its likely continuation.

Defining Public Opinion

How should we define public opinion? Political scientist V. O. Key (1967) defined public opinion as "those opinions held by private persons which governments find it prudent to heed" (p. 14). This definition is quite broad and contains an important element: Public opinion is policy oriented and has political consequences. Governments and politicians who ignore the constraints of public opinion do not long remain in power. Beginning in the 1930s, the use of public opinion surveys grew extensively, in part because of the advances in social psychology at that time in attitude theory and measurement. There has been a close relationship between the concepts of attitude and opinion. Crotty (1970) suggested that "opinions represent expressions of attitudes." Oskamp (1977) defined opinions more narrowly, equating them with beliefs, seeing them as more cognitive than emotional. For an extensive discussion, see Hennessey (1981).

The position taken in this book is that opinions are best viewed as attitudes rather than beliefs. Consider a specific opinion—for example, "The government should give aid to disadvantaged minorities." As with attitudes (in Fishbein and Ajzen's model), there is clearly a set of beliefs that underlies this judgment (for instance, years of discrimination have put minority groups at a disadvantage; the government's role should be to ensure a good life for all its citizens; government action will help those who are disadvantaged). These opinions will often have an affective component as well; a person may feel passionately for or against a particular policy. If a person agrees with the policy statement "Abortion should be banned," the words *I feel that* (abortion should be banned) are implicit.

Having said all this, I concede that there are some opinions that are best viewed as beliefs. For example, the answer to the question "Do you think the Soviet Union will fall apart within the next five years?" is not evaluative. When we examine a particular opinion statement, we should pay attention to whether there are implicit evaluations imbedded in the statement. Most of the opinions we consider in this volume are more like attitudes than beliefs.

Public opinion thus reflects the policy-related attitudes of different individuals across a variety of issues. Some individuals may hold these attitudes strongly and express them often. Others may articulate their attitudes only when asked about them or in the context of an election campaign, when specific beliefs are made salient to them. Fishbein and Ajzen's theory of reasoned action provides a model for understanding the dynamic nature of attitude development. This dynamic model of attitude production furnishes a psychological foundation for Bennett's (1980) theory of the situational influences of the political environment on public opinion. In reading the chapters ahead, you'll develop an understanding of these processes.

■ Some Cautionary Notes about Surveys

Researchers often attempt to measure public opinion through surveys. However, when we obtain survey results through a newspaper or television report, we should avoid accepting the report's conclusions at face value. Attention should be paid to a number of characteristics of a survey that affect the validity of its findings, including the sample size of the survey, the response rate, the way the sample was selected, and the wording of the survey questions. This section reviews some important information about conducting and interpreting surveys. For more detailed information, see Fowler (1988), Bradburn and Sudman (1988), or Bainbridge (1989).

Types of Samples

The point of a *sample survey* is to estimate how the larger *population* from which the sample is drawn feels about a particular issue. In many national surveys, the population of interest might be the voting public, and a researcher would want to select a sample that is representative of this larger population.

There are a variety of ways of drawing a sample. The easiest way is to collect a **haphazard sample.** This survey technique involves selecting respondents in an unsystematic way, simply at the whim of the interviewer. Stopping passersby for person-on-the-street interviews is an example of a haphazard survey. This survey is different from a **random survey.** Because a haphazard sample is not representative of any specific population, the results from such a sample have no scientific worth and should be mistrusted.

Selecting a random sample requires identifying a population and choosing individuals randomly from that population to be included in the sample. There is no way of identifying the population to which to generalize the results of a haphazard survey.

A technique used by many commercial polling organizations is **quota sampling**. This technique involves selecting respondents in the same proportion as found in the population. Thus, if a national sample of 100 respondents is planned, a quota sample might require 50 men and 50 women; 82 White, 11 Black, and 7 Hispanic; and so on. The interviewer contacts and interviews people until the quota is fulfilled for each particular group. This procedure avoids the unsystematic biases of the haphazard sample, but more subtle errors may creep in. The interviewer may avoid certain types of people or only call at certain times of the day, thus excluding some groups of people (such as people who work at night) from the sample.

The preferred method of sampling is call a **probability sample**. With this technique, every individual in the population has a known probability of being included in the sample. In a **simple random sample**, each individual has an equal probability of being selected for the sample. An alternative to this type of sample is called a **stratified random sample**, in which the population is broken down into different units (for example, counties). Either probability samples are selected within each unit, or the units are broken down into even smaller units (such as precincts or census tracts), and probability samples are drawn from these units. Probability samples are the preferred scientific method of sampling because the amount of sampling error can be estimated exactly—which cannot be done for haphazard and quota samples.

Errors Due to Response Rate and Sample Selection

A subtle source of error in a survey is the response rate. The proper way to conduct a survey is to identify the population, select a sample from that population, and interview as many individuals in that sample as possible. The number of people from which completed interviews are obtained is called the **response rate** (it's actually a little more complicated than this, but we'll ignore some details). If the response rate in a survey is below about 70%, serious questions about the representativeness of the survey arise, and thus the validity of the results are called into question. Even in a survey with a higher response rate, if one kind of respondent (say older people) refuses at a much higher rate than other kinds, then there is a potential for bias in the survey results.

The most famous example of a nonrepresentative poll is the one taken by the *Literary Digest* for the 1936 presidential election between Franklin Roosevelt and Alf Landon. The *Digest* solicited opinions of candidate preference from millions of potential voters by using names obtained from telephone books, magazine subscription lists, and automobile registration records. On the basis of the reports of those who returned questionnaires, the *Digest* predicted that Landon would win by a comfortable margin. What it had done, however, was draw a sample from a group that was relatively well-off financially, since during the Depression, the only people who could afford phones, magazines, and cars were those who were affluent. When the election results were in, Roosevelt had carried 46 of the 48 states with over 60% of the popular vote. The *Literary Digest* went out of business two years later.

Andrew Kohut (1988), president of the Gallup organization, notes that the current demands for overnight poll results from polling companies and news organizations' in-house polling groups sometimes cause errors in sampling. Pollsters in a rush to get results may miss individuals who are mobile and hard to reach; often, those individuals are well educated and affluent. Kohut noted that in an October 1988 Gallup Poll, if the results based only on those who were reached on the first call had been released, then a 2% Dukakis advantage would have been reported—rather than the 6% Bush advantage that resulted after other respondents

Figure 2-3   Percent error in a survey as a function of sample size

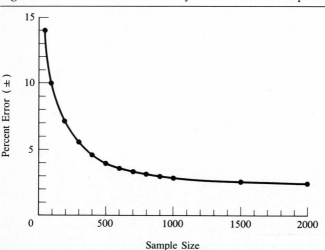

were reached with repeated calling. Those who were harder to reach were more likely to be Bush supporters (Kohut, 1988).

Sampling Error

Sample size is one of the most important features of a survey. The accuracy of the sample estimate is a direct function of the sample size (assuming the population being sampled is very large). For a sample of 1000 people the error is about ±3%. Figure 2-3 shows how the percentage error decreases as the sample size increases. As the sample size gets smaller, the accuracy of the survey results drops rapidly; for a sample of 50, the percentage error is ±14%. If the sample size is not reported, we have no way of judging how precise the estimates are.

The Effects of Question Wording

When you hear or read about the results of a survey, you should notice whether the exact wording of the question respondents were asked is reported. Question wording can make a very big difference in the results. Table 2-2 presents data reported in Schuman and Presser's (1981) extensive examination of the effects on individuals'

Table 2-2 Effect of question wording on respondents' answers

Original Question		Communist Takeover Version	
If a situation like Vietnam were to develop in another part of the world, do you think the United States *should* or *should not* send troops?		If a situation like Vietnam were to develop in another part of the world do you think the United States *should* or *should not* send troops to stop a Communist takeover?	
SRC-74 Fall			
Send troops	18.3%	Send troops	33.2%
Not send troops	81.7	Not send troops	66.8
	100		100
	(459)		(871)
	$X^2 = 34.54$, df = 1, $p <.001$		
SRC-76 Feb.			
Send troops	15.6%	Send troops	27.9%
Not send troops	84.4	Not send troops	72.1
	100		100
	(575)		(549)
	$X^2 = 24.93$, df = 1, $p <.001$		
SRC-78 Fall			
Send troops	18.3%	Send troops	36.7%
Not send troops	81.7	Not send troops	63.3
	100		100
	(885)		(449)
	$X^2 = 52.67$, df = 1, $p <.001$		

Source: From *Questions and Answers in Attitude Surveys,* by H. Schuman and S. Presser. Copyright © 1981 by Academic Press. Reprinted by permission.

Figure 2-4   The subtleties of question wording in a survey

Doonesbury

BY GARRY TRUDEAU

DOONESBURY © 1989 G. B. Trudeau. Reprinted with permission of Universal Press Syndicate. All rights reserved.

responses of question wording and of the context in which survey questions are asked. They employed a methodology called a split-ballot design, asking a different form of the same question to different survey respondents.

In the example presented in Table 2-2 Schuman and Presser, in three different surveys, asked two different groups of respondents the same question about sending U.S. troops somewhere in the world in case of another situation like Vietnam. To test the effect of different question wording, in the question for one of the groups they added the phrase "to stop a Communist takeover." As you can see, the addition of this phrase had a dramatic effect on the answers obtained in the survey. Almost twice as many individuals endorsed sending troops if stopping communism was presented as a justification. Figure 2-4 presents another example of the effect of question wording in a survey. An interesting additional finding Schuman and Presser (1981) obtained is that this effect was fairly consistent across levels of education; that is, individuals with a college education showed about the same support for U.S. military intervention as did individuals with much less education (0–8 years).

Related to question wording is the effect of the context in which a question is asked. Tourangeau and Rasinski (1988) report that the same question gets very different results depending upon what questions are asked before or after it in the survey. Before asking a question on support of or opposition to abortion, they asked respondents either four questions related to women's rights or four questions concerned with traditional values. Individuals asked the women's rights questions voiced greater support for abortion than did those asked the traditional-values questions.

As you can see, we should not use the results of a particular survey without knowing something about how it was conducted. Chapter Six presents research that clarifies the context and question wording effects that can be a significant factor in survey results.

Having considered the nature of attitudes and opinions, we turn, in the next two chapters, to an examination of the sources of public opinion.

CHAPTER
THREE

Social Factors
and Public Opinion

What are the sources of public opinion? To what extent do differences in individuals' backgrounds such as their gender, income, or education influence their political attitudes? In Chapter Two we discussed attitudes and opinions and a primary way of measuring them: opinion surveys. In this chapter, we examine the results of several different surveys for evidence about the sources of political opinions.

A traditional approach to public opinion research has been to explore the relationships between individuals' political attitudes and various social factors such as age, race, education, and gender. These factors are indicators of how individuals' life experiences differ and are thus potentially useful predictors of differences between people in their political attitudes. Individuals from different social groups (for example, men and women) do hold substantially different opinions on various issues. However, individual social factors do not operate in isolation from each other. Thus, men and women tend to differ on a variety of other variables in addition to gender—for example, income, education, and age. As a consequence, to assess the effect of one specific variable (such as gender) on opinion, one must "control" for the effects of the other variables. Statistical control is discussed in the next section.

Social factors are an extremely important part of the story and are essential to any understanding of public opinion. We will examine a number of simple relationships between social factors and opinion, and then we present more complex analyses utilizing statistical controls. We will find that even this sophisticated analysis does not tell us everything about the origins of opinions. The next chapter will add to this chapter's discussion of the sources of public opinion with an analysis of the effects of personality on public opinion. Let us now begin with a discussion of the relationship of social factors to public opinion.

■ Background Characteristics and Their Influence on Public Opinion

Separating the Effects of Different Variables

A political science professor of mine once noted, "One of the major difficulties in working in the social sciences is that God gave the easy problems to the physicists"

21

Table 3-1   Age and listening to religious programs

Listen to Religious Programs	Young Listeners	Old Listeners
Yes	17%	26%
No	83	74
Total	100	100

Source: From *The Language of Social Research,* by F. Paul Lazarsfeld and Morris Rosenberg. Copyright © 1955 by The Free Press, renewed 1983 by Patricia Kendall Lazarsfeld. Adapted with permission of The Free Press, a Division of Macmillan, Inc.

(see Lave & March, 1975). Nothing illustrates the difficulties in social science research more than the study of the extent to which different background characteristics influence political attitudes. Social scientists face this major obstacle: The predictors they use are all highly multicollinear—that is, interrelated. For example, compared with younger people, older people are likely to be poorer and lower in education. Thus, if differences are found between the opinions of young people and old people, the source of the difference might be age, but it also might be income or education.

Let us consider an example of statistical control from Morris Rosenberg's (1968) classic book, *The Logic of Survey Analysis.* Table 3-1 presents the relationship of age (young or old) to whether the individual listens to religious programs on the radio. As you can see, there is a clear association between these two variables, with older people being more likely to listen to religious broadcasts. One explanation of these results might be that as people get older and closer to death, they are more interested in the message of religious programs.

An alternative explanation is possible, however. Since older people tend to be less educated than younger people—that is, there is a negative relationship between age and education—the explanation might be that people with less education tend to listen to religious programs more. To test this alternative explanation, one must do the same comparison between age and religious program listening—but do it separately for individuals high in education and those low in education. Table 3-2 presents this analysis. As you can see in this table, there is now little relationship

Table 3-2   Age and listening to religious programs, by education

Listen to Religious Programs	High Education		Low Education	
	Young	Old	Young	Old
Yes	9%	11%	29%	32%
No	91	89	71	68
Total	100	100	100	100

Source: From *The Language of Social Research,* by F. Paul Lazarsfeld and Morris Rosenberg. Copyright © 1955 by The Free Press, renewed 1983 by Patricia Kendall Lazarsfeld. Adapted with permission of The Free Press, a Division of Macmillan, Inc.

between age and religious listening. Those individuals high in education listen much less to religious programs than those low in education, but the relationship that appeared to exist in Table 3-1 has disappeared—after *controlling* for the effects of education.

When one examines the effect on an opinion of a number of different social variables, one must assess the independent effect of each variable, which requires a statistical procedure such as multiple regression. This method allows a researcher to test the effect of each individual variable while statistically controlling the other variables—that is, holding the effects of the other variables constant. Later in this chapter we shall see how this problem of multicollinearity is handled for individual predictors such as age, race, education, and religion. Our analyses will show that although some factors predict opinion, others do not, and still others appear to influence opinions but, in fact, only reflect the influence of other variables.

Explanations for the Relationship Between Social Factors and Public Opinion

Why should social scientists expect background factors to predict political attitudes at all? Various different processes support this conclusion. Differences in social background affect the people with whom an individual will interact. For instance, people from different religious backgrounds are likely to have different political attitudes. Their attitudes are not necessarily a result of the different theologies they have been exposed to but the different patterns of interpersonal interaction and the range of personal opinions to which they have been exposed. Roman Catholics who attended private Catholic high schools or colleges may show little difference in their religious beliefs from those Catholics who did not, but their interpersonal contacts (and, consequently, their political attitudes) may be very different.

A second important reason why social background factors may predict differences in public opinion is that individuals with similar backgrounds often have social and economic interests in common. Differences in people's economic opportunities will be reflected in income/occupational differences, and these background differences will predict their political attitudes. For instance, one's opinion about changes in the rate of taxing capital gains will generally be a function of whether one has or is likely to have any capital gains to be taxed. However, additional factors can influence attitudes toward taxes, and these will be discussed later in this chapter.

Finally, differences in social background characteristics should be related to different political attitudes, because many of these differences will produce differences in individuals' reference groups. A *reference group* is a social grouping with which an individual identifies. The individual may or may not belong; a reference group is thus not necessarily the same as a membership group, although often it is. Different reference groups may hold very different political attitudes. In an experimental study, Charters and Newcomb (1958) demonstrated how political attitudes can be manipulated by making a person's reference group particularly salient. Catholic students expressed significantly different opinions on a variety of issues related to official positions of the Catholic church when their religious background was made salient to them. Specifically, Catholic students who were reminded of their religious background (membership in the Catholic church)—that is, they were told "everyone here is a Catholic"—were significantly more in favor of parochial school and against birth control than Catholic students who were not presented with such an observation by the experimenter.

Thus, there are various reasons to explain why we would expect differences in social background to produce differences in social and political attitudes. Let us now consider some evidence related to specific social differences in age, education, income, religion, race, and sex. We will also examine the effects of different potential sources of direct political influence such as parents, peers, and schools.

The Relationship of Individual Social Factors to Public Opinion

Age

The older a person is, the more likely it is that the person will be conservative in political attitudes. Older people tend to be more prejudiced, pessimistic, and authoritarian than younger people. For example, Table 3-3 presents the differences between age groups in their opinions about the ability of women to hold important positions in society (data are from the 1984 National Election Study conducted by the Center for Political Studies at the University of Michigan). As you can see, older respondents agree with this statement (generally regarded as a conservative position) significantly more than those who are younger, and agreement increases with age. The same pattern emerges when respondents reported their ideological (liberal/conservative) self-identification. Twenty-seven percent of those aged 17–30 called themselves either a strong or a not very strong liberal; only 19% of those aged 61 or older did so.

Do these findings mean that there is something about the aging process that makes people more conservative? Not necessarily. Age is related to a host of other variables, all of which are likely to influence individuals' attitudes. The old tend to be poorer than those who are younger; they tend to be less educated; they are more

Table 3-3   Attitudes toward women's position in society, by age

Respondents were asked how much they agreed or disagreed with this statement: "Men are just better cut out than women for important positions in society."

Age	Disagree	Neither	Agree
17–30	76%	11%	13%
31–45	77	9	14
46–60	69	9	21
61–older	57	11	32

Source: Data are from the 1984 National Election Study conducted by the Center for Political Studies at the University of Michigan.

likely to live in rural rather than urban areas; they generally have strong ethnic ties; and they are more likely to be separated, divorced, or widowed. All of these factors may contribute to their more conservative attitudes.

Gergen and Back (1966) argue that the personal characteristics of respondents, particularly the age of those interviewed, may significantly influence answers to survey items. Through analysis of a series of Gallup surveys, the authors sought to test Cumming and Henry's (1961) proposition that as people grow older, they "disengage" from other members of society. They found evidence to suggest that the level of opinionation (the number of opinions expressed in response to survey questions) decreases with age. Although there is some empirical support for the disengagement theory, there are many studies inconsistent with its conclusions. Glenn (1969) found that when education was the controlled variable, opinionation actually increased with age. Thus, the apparent finding that older people are less likely to have attitudes was simply a result of older people being less educated. Additionally, a very consistent finding is that the older a person is, the *higher* political participation is, particularly voting (Sigelman, Roeder, Jewell, & Baer, 1985; Wolfinger & Rosenstone, 1980). In fact, Sigelman et al. (1985) found that the strongest predictor of whether a person would register and vote was age. Wolfinger and Rosenstone (1980) also found higher voting rates for those who are older, but they noted that this effect is greatest for those low in education; they found that level of education had the greatest effect on voter turnout. Thus, the findings that disengagement theory sought to explain were simply a result of a failure to control for all the important variables.

Education

The pattern of opinions for individuals with different educational backgrounds parallels that for individuals' with different incomes. This should not be surprising since education and income tend to be fairly highly correlated. Table 3-4 shows

Table 3-4 Opinion on government-guaranteed jobs, by education

Education	Government should see to a job and a good standard of living	↔	Government should let each person get ahead on his own
Less than high school	21%	41%	38%
High school degree	25	57	19
Some college	26	58	17
College degree	29	63	9
Graduate training	29	57	15

Note: The question was answered on a 1-to-7 scale, with "1" labeled "Government should see to a job and a good standard of living," and "7" labeled "Government should let each person get ahead on his own." For display in this table, these responses were collapsed into three columns. The number in the first column is the percentage of respondents answering "1" or "2," the second column is the percentage answering "3," "4," or "5," and the third column reports the percentage answering "6" or "7."

Source: Data are from the 1984 National Election Study conducted by the Center for Political Studies at the University of Michigan.

respondents' opinions on the economic issue of whether the government should guarantee a job for every citizen. Thirty-eight percent of those at the lowest educational level (less than a high school education) favor such a government guarantee. Note that this group is the one most likely to benefit from such a guarantee. Only 15% at the highest educational level (postgraduate training) do so. Those who endorse the position that people should get ahead on their own show the reverse pattern: 29% of those with postgraduate education favor self-reliance over government support; only 21% of those with less than a high school education feel this way. On economic issues, many individuals with high levels of education do not support programs that do not directly benefit them. Why might this be? Later in this chapter we will consider the effect on opinions about economic issues of a variable that is highly correlated with education: income.

Individuals with higher education tend to be more liberal on social issues than people with less education. Table 3-5 presents the differences in attitudes toward women by educational level. The effect of education is dramatic. Although 34% of those with less than a high school education agree that "men are just better cut out than women for important positions in society," only 6% of those with some education beyond college agree. The same pattern emerges for opinions on abortion and whether the government should aid minority groups: the more education, the more liberal the opinions individuals express on social issues.

Many studies (such as Corbett, 1982) have pointed to the liberalizing effects of education. One classic study with this conclusion is the Bennington College study done in the 1930s (Newcomb, 1943). Bennington College attracted young women from fairly well-to-do families that tended to be Republican and conservative. The professors at Bennington, as is often the case, were more liberal in their attitudes and supportive of Roosevelt's New Deal proposals. Studying the same women from freshman year to senior year, Newcomb found that they became more liberal in their political attitudes. These changes appeared to be partially a result of contact with liberal professors but also a result of peer influences, with the older women in the college exerting a liberalizing influence on the younger ones. As we noted at the beginning of this chapter, individuals with different social backgrounds will have different patterns of interpersonal interaction. Newcomb (1971) found that these more liberal attitudes persisted over 25 years.

Table 3-5 Opinion on women's position in society, by education

Respondents were asked how much they agreed or disagreed with this statement: "Men are just better cut out than women for important positions in society."

Education	Disagree	Neither	Agree
Less than high school	52%	13%	34%
High school degree	71	10	19
Some college	79	10	11
College degree	81	8	12
Graduate training	88	6	6

Source: Data are from the 1984 National Election Study conducted by the Center for Political Studies at the University of Michigan.

Religion

Historically, Americans have been a very religious people, and there have been substantial differences in public opinion associated with religious differences. Jews have traditionally been the most liberal group, followed by Catholics, with Protestants being the most conservative. Having said this, I must note now that the effect of religion on attitudes appears to be declining.

This change is illustrated by differences in opinions on abortion between individuals from different religious backgrounds. Table 3-6 presents these data. Although Jews clearly remain the most liberal group on this social issue, there are very few differences between Catholics and Protestants. Virtually the same percentage of both groups supports an outright prohibition on abortion, and a similar percentage supports a prochoice position. The total prohibition of abortion advocated by many antiabortion groups is supported by only a small minority of the public.

An important exception to this decline in religious differences on political issues is the increasing strength of Christian fundamentalists in this country, also called the new Christian right. Paul Watanabe (1987) observes that there are roughly 10 million Americans who are "wholehearted fundamentalists," and the political activists among this group tend to be zealous ultraconservatives who advocate a political agenda ranging from concern about the content of public school textbooks to abortion and defense spending. As we shall see later in this chapter, a person's identification as a Christian fundamentalist exerts a more significant influence on political attitudes than membership in any other religious group.

A variable that may be more important than religious identification in predicting political attitudes is frequency of church attendance. Those who attend church often tend to be conservative in their political attitudes; while those with no ties to an organized religion tend to be more liberal. Opinions on abortion are differentiated much more by frequency of church attendance than by religious group, as Table 3-7 shows. Gordon Allport (1954) observed that there are two types of religiosity, what he called *internalized* and *institutionalized*. Those who have

Table 3-6   Opinions on abortion, by religious group

Respondents were asked: "There has been some discussion about abortion during recent years. Which one of the opinions on this page best agrees with your view? (1) By law, abortion should never be permitted. (2) The law should permit abortion only in case of rape, incest or when the woman's life is in danger. (3) The law should permit abortion for reasons other than rape, incest or danger to the woman's life, but only after the need for the abortion has been clearly established. (4) By law, a woman should always be able to obtain an abortion as a matter of personal choice."

Religious Group	Never	Rape or Incest	Only for Need	Prochoice
Protestant	14%	32%	22%	31%
Catholic	15	34	16	36
Jewish	4	10	21	65

Source: Data are from the 1984 National Election Study conducted by the Center for Political Studies at the University of Michigan.

Table 3-7 Opinions on abortion, by frequency of church attendance

Respondents were asked: "There has been some discussion about abortion during recent years. Which one of the opinions on this page best agrees with your view? (1) By law, abortion should never be permitted. (2) The law should permit abortion only in case of rape, incest or when the woman's life is in danger. (3) The law should permit abortion for reasons other than rape, incest or danger to the woman's life, but only after the need for the abortion has been clearly established. (4) By law, a woman should always be able to obtain an abortion as a matter of personal choice."

Church Attendance	Never	Rape or Incest	Only for Need	Prochoice
Never	10%	26%	16%	50%
Few times a year	7	25	22	47
Once/twice a month	13	27	29	32
Almost every week	14	38	25	23
Every week	26	43	14	17

Source: Data are from the 1984 National Election Study conducted by the Center for Political Studies at the University of Michigan.

internalized religiosity have adopted their religion's values and are generally more tolerant of different opinions and groups. In contrast, those who are religious in an institutionalized way care more for the symbols of the church and the financial and social benefits membership brings than for its values or ideas. These individuals, for example, might see the church as a way of developing contacts to sell insurance.

Race

Differences in opinions between Whites and people of color reflect one of the fundamental cleavages in our society. On virtually every issue measured in the 1984 National Election Study, people of color expressed more liberal attitudes than did Whites. On government-guaranteed jobs, 49% of people of color favor this proposal; only 16% of Whites do. Forty-two percent of people of color say they are "very worried" about a nuclear war; only 28% of Whites report as much worry. A similar pattern emerges for opinions on abortion. Interestingly, the one opinion on which people of color express more conservative opinions than Whites is women's position in society. Table 3-8 displays White and non-White opinion on this issue. Twenty-six percent of the people of color agree with the statement that men are more capable than women, but only 18% of Whites agree.

Table 3-8 Opinions on women's position in society, by race

Respondents were asked how much they agreed or disagreed with this statement: "Men are just better cut out than women for important positions in society."

Race	Agree	Neither	Disagree
White	18%	10%	72%
Non-White	26	12	62

Source: Data are from the 1984 National Election Study conducted by the Center for Political Studies at the University of Michigan.

It is interesting to speculate why there is a difference between Whites and people of color on this question about women's position. We should remember that the predictors of opinion are all highly correlated and that there are significant differences between Whites and people of color in education and income levels. The results in Table 3-12 (presented later in the chapter) indicate that opinions on women's role in society became more liberal as income increased. Similarly, Table 3-5 shows that opinions also became more liberal as education level increased. We can thus hypothesize that the opinion differences between racial groups on women's issues are in part due to their differences in education and income. We will consider this question later in the chapter when we discuss a more sophisticated statistical approach to the relationship of social factors and opinions.

Sex

The "gender gap," the apparent difference in opinions between men and women, has received considerable attention in the past few years. Whether or not it has real political significance, politicians have begun to act as if it does. Poole and Zeigler (1985) point out that in 1983, presidential aspirant Gary Hart promised women's organizations that he would use the power of the presidency to coerce states to pass the Equal Rights Amendment (ERA) by granting or withholding federal funds. In the 1988 presidential election campaign, the gender gap received considerable media attention prior to the election. Presidential candidate George Bush ran even with Michael Dukakis in pre-election polls in some states among men but ran 20 points behind Dukakis among women. Clearly, Dukakis's platform and agenda appealed to women and their issues more than Bush's did.

The actual political importance of the gender gap, however, is open to debate. Lake (1982) found that 9.6% fewer women than men voted for Reagan in 1980. Consistent with this result, preelection surveys for the congressional elections in 1982 indicated that gender would be a factor, but there was only a slight preference among women (3–6 percentage points) for the Democrats. In 1984, preelection polls suggested considerable differences in opinion between men and women on war and peace issues. Table 3-9 presents data from 1984 on the extent of worry that men and women expressed about nuclear war. As the table shows, women express considerably more worry than men. This gap did not translate into an electoral advantage for Mondale, however; in the general election Reagan won an electoral landslide. Mondale was unable to make a nuclear threat a salient issue in the campaign.

Two areas of opinion in which a gender gap consistently appears are nuclear power and environmental concerns. Table 3-10 displays the percentages of men and women among different ideological groups who support building more nuclear power plants. As the table shows, the conservative women are more antinuclear (33% favor more plants) than the liberal men (37% favor building more plants). A similar pattern exists for opinion on environmental regulation (Poole & Zeigler, 1985). As we shall see, however, merely looking at bivariate relationships can be misleading if one tries to use the gender gap in political opinion to predict voting behavior.

Table 3-9   Worry about nuclear war, by sex

Respondents were asked: "How worried are you about our country getting into a nuclear war at this time?"

Sex	Not Worried	Somewhat Worried	Very Worried
Male	46%	30%	24%
Female	28	38	34

Source: Data are from the 1984 National Election Study conducted by the Center for Political Studies at the University of Michigan.

Although there may be differences overall between men and women on some specific issues, this does not necessarily mean these differences are politically important. Differences in these attitudes would be politically important if they influenced the public's approval of a president or other political candidate. The most comprehensive study of the gender gap and its relationship to presidential approval is Martin Gilens's (1988) analysis of the 1982 National Election Study (NES) postelection survey of President Reagan's job performance. Using a sophisticated series of multiple regression analyses, Gilens found that, *controlling for other variables*, environmental concerns played no role in the overall 10.9% gender difference in presidential approval. Two foreign policy variables contributed to the overall gender gap: attitudes toward defense spending (7.8%) and approval of Reagan's handling of the Soviet Union (3%). As Gilens pointed out, women are more liberal than men on defense-related issues. More important, however, women's attitudes toward defense had a bigger effect on their approval of the president than did men's opinions.

It is interesting to consider the implications of these data for the 1988 presidential campaign between George Bush and Michael Dukakis. In July following the Democratic convention, Dukakis led Bush in some polls by 17% of the electorate. Driving this Democratic advantage was a gender gap of major proportions: Dukakis's advantage over Bush among women exceeded 20% in some polls. By September, however, Bush was leading in most polls and the gender gap had disappeared. What happened? Bush's skillful campaign was able to portray Dukakis as naive on defense issues and opposed to "necessary" weapons systems. Thus, the concern that women have about nuclear war and defense-related issues may have worked against Dukakis if he was perceived as naive enough to be unable to handle the Russians.

Table 3-10   Percentages supporting building more nuclear power plants

Sex	Liberal	Moderate	Conservative
Male	37%	48%	63%
Female	15	21	33

Source: Data are from the 1980 National Election Study conducted by the Center for Political Studies at the University of Michigan.

Income

The effect of income differences on public opinion varies depending on the issue. Opinions on economic issues are very different from attitudes on foreign policy issues and other noneconomic issues. Although some attitudes (such as raising or lowering taxes) directly affect a person's life, other issues (such as abortion) are based on morality or values.

On economic issues, poorer people are generally more inclined than affluent people to favor social welfare programs designed to raise standards of living for those with less money. Table 3-11 shows the 1984 NES results for a question about whether the government should guarantee a job for every person. As is apparent, agreement for this policy is highest among those at the lowest income level and drops dramatically as respondents' income increases.

Evidence consistent with this pattern appears in Sears and Citrin's (1982) book on the tax revolt in California. The most enthusiastic supporters of the tax revolt tended to be higher-income, middle-aged Whites living in southern California. Because of this group's high level of homeownership and high perceived tax burden, they clearly had self-interest reasons for supporting the tax revolt. Sears and Citrin (1982) found the self-interest variables—home ownership, perceived tax burden, and not being a government employee—to be statistically significant predictors of support for the tax revolt. There is thus clear support for the proposition that the direct effects of a particular public policy (taxes) have a significant impact on an individual's attitudes toward that policy.

At the same time, however, the tax issue illustrates the difficulty of unraveling causality in public opinion research. Higher-income, middle-aged Whites living in

Table 3-11   Support for a guaranteed job, by income level

Question: "Some people feel the government in Washington should see to it that every person has a job and a good standard of living. Others think the government should just let each person get ahead on his own."

Income	Government should see to a job and a good standard of living	↔	Government should let each person get ahead on his own
0–$10,000	29%	51%	19%
$10,000–$25,000	17	58	25
$25,000–$40,000	11	60	29
$40,000 or higher	5	55	40

Note: The question was answered on a 1-to-7 scale, with "1" labeled "Government should see to a job and a good standard of living," and "7" labeled "Government should let each person get ahead on his own." For display in this table, these responses were collapsed into three columns. The number in the first column is the percentage of respondents answering "1" or "2," the second column is the percentage answering "3," "4," or "5," and the third column reports the percentage answering "6" or "7."

Source: Data are from the 1984 National Election Study conducted by the Center for Political Studies at the University of Michigan.

southern California tended to be politically conservative; so in addition to self-interest, they also had ideological and symbolic reasons for opposing taxes. Sears and Citrin (1982) found that voter turnout in support of reducing taxes and activist behavior promoting the tax revolt campaigns in California was strongly associated with various ideological and attitudinal variables. The strongest predictor of tax revolt support was what they called "symbolic racism." People opposed to government support for minorities jumped on the tax revolt bandwagon regardless of whatever else they supported. In addition, Republican party identification and conservative ideological self-identification also significantly predicted support for the tax revolt. Thus, opposition to taxes is not simply a result of self-interest, though self-interest does play a part.

Although individuals with high incomes tend to hold more conservative opinions on economic issues than low-income individuals do, the opposite pattern emerges for opinions on social issues. For the question on women's position in society, respondents in the upper-income levels give more liberal answers than those in the lower-income brackets (Table 3-12). The same pattern exists for attitudes toward abortion in the 1984 data. Although 18% of the respondents in the lowest-income category (0–$10,000) felt that abortion should never be permitted, only 6% in the $40,000-and-higher category supported total prohibition.

Social Class and the Crisis in Political Participation

In their chapter on the relationship of income to public opinion, Holloway and George (1986) argue that the primary reason that socialism has failed to attract a mass following in the United States is that the American people are affluent and content. This argument has its roots in the "politics of happiness" argument put forth by Lipset (1960) to explain decreased political interest in the United States. Consistent with this argument, Holloway and George go even further to suggest that the elections of 1980 and 1984 indicate that there is emerging public support for a conservative national agenda in the United States. These arguments overlook a number of critically important aspects of U.S. political history.

Walter Dean Burnham (1982) observes that political alienation has increased dramatically in the United States over the past 20 years. He cites Harris survey

Table 3-12 Opinions on women's position in society, by income

Respondents were asked how much they agreed or disagreed with this statement: "Men are just better cut out than women for important positions in society."

Income	Disagree	Neither	Agree
0–$10,000	67%	11%	23%
$10,000–$25,000	74	10	16
$25,000–$40,000	80	9	11
$40,000 or higher	77	11	12

Source: Data are from the 1984 National Election Study conducted by the Center for Political Studies at the University of Michigan.

results that indicate that from 1966 to 1978 public agreement with the statements "The rich get richer and the poor get poorer" and "People running the country don't really care what happens to you" has increased more than 30%. Paralleling these expressions of alienation, voter turnout has declined in every federal election since 1960, and the voter turnout rate has never equaled what it was in 1940.

Income plays an important role in this crisis. Burnham (1982) documents that the United States is unique among Western democracies (such as Sweden and Germany) in its disenfranchisement of the lower classes. Voter turnout in the United States is significantly related to class. Individuals from lower-class backgrounds vote at a substantially lower rate than do those individuals who are more affluent. In other Western democracies, individuals from different class backgrounds vote at the same rate, and participation rates remain stable over time as well.

Burnham (1982) presents a much more compelling explanation for the failure of socialism in this country. The political history of the United States is unique among Western democracies in that the right to vote, at least among White males, was widely available from almost the beginning of the country; in 1821 the requirement of owning property in order to vote was abolished. Thus, in the United States there was never a mass movement, as in European countries, to usurp political power from an entrenched nobility. Since political participation is largely mobilized by political parties, the absence of parties that struggle against entrenched political elites and with which the lower classes can identify has ultimately resulted in much lower political participation in the United States, stratified by social class. The political parties in the United States have not been particularly relevant to the needs of the lower classes since 1900 (Burnham, 1982).

In the absence of the political class struggle that has existed and continues to exist in other Western democracies, what developed in the United States was what Burnham (1982) has called *uncontested hegemony*. *Hegemony* means preponderant influence or authority over others, and in this case Burnham refers to the power or hegemony of the particular ideology or set of ideas that he called "liberal capitalism." By this term he means that among political elites in the United States, from early on, there was general agreement about how the political and economic system should operate. This uncontested ideological hegemony has thus contributed substantially to the decline in political participation in this country. In Chapter Nine we will discuss the role the mass media play in this crisis.

To the extent that the arguments made by Holloway and George (1986)—that Americans are by and large happy and conservative in their opinions—may have some validity, economic developments in the past 20 years point to important changes. Two prominent political economists, Bennett Harrison and Barry Bluestone (1988), have documented what they call "the great U-turn." Specifically, they found that real family income increased following World War II until 1973; since that time, family income measured in real (inflation-adjusted) dollars has *decreased*. If this trend continues, particularly in the context of the absence of political parties that represent the interests of low- and moderate-income people, the most likely result is greater political alienation.

Holloway and George (1986) also argued that the 1984 election of Reagan over

Mondale indicated the continuation of the conservative mood in the country initiated by Ronald Reagan in 1980. Although conservatives might find some reassurance in the 1988 election of George Bush as president, a fundamental aspect of that election was that the Democrats increased the sizes of their majorities in both houses of Congress. No similar event has occurred in the past 150 years. Rather than reflecting a conservative mood in the country, the 1988 election appears to have been a repudiation of Michael Dukakis following an effective Bush campaign that was able to activate greater feelings of confidence in Republican management of the presidency. The psychological impact of the two campaigns is discussed in greater detail in Chapter Six.

Putting the Variables Together

How can we summarize our findings so far? The older that people are, the more conservative they appear to be. The higher the income and education an individual has, the more likely he or she is to be liberal on social issues (such as abortion and women's place in society) and the higher the probability that he or she will be conservative on economic issues. A simple comparison of the attitudes of men and women suggested differences on defense and environmental issues, but a more sophisticated analysis revealed that the two sexes appear to differ primarily on foreign policy issues. We noted similar alternative explanations for differences in opinions between Whites and people of color. Although people of color are the most consistently liberal group as indicated by their concern about nuclear war and their support for government-guaranteed jobs, they were surprisingly conservative in their opinions about women's place in society. We speculated that rather than being a racial difference, this result might instead be a difference due to unequal educational and income levels between the races. As we noted at the beginning of this chapter, one of the biggest difficulties in assessing the effects of different background factors on individuals' opinions is that the variety of predictors are all correlated with each other. People of color tend in general to have lower incomes and lower levels of education than Whites. In order to separate these effects, we need to turn to a more sophisticated kind of statistical analysis called multiple regression.

Multiple regression analysis allows a researcher to examine the influence of one variable on another—for example, the differences between Whites and people of color on their opinions—while *controlling* for the effects of other variables—for example, income and education. Thus, differences between Whites and people of color can be examined separately for people who have low incomes, moderate incomes, and high incomes. Similarly, for education, White/non-White differences can be examined for those with low, moderate, and high levels of education. If there really are racial differences in opinion, then there will be differences in opinions between Whites and people of color at all the various levels of income and education; otherwise, the differences in opinion will disappear.

Table 3-13 presents results of a multiple regression analysis predicting individuals' opinions on the question of women's place in society. As the table shows, there are statistically significant effects of sex, age, education, income, and church attendance. Women feel more positively about women's capabilities than do men. The older a person is, the less capable he or she feels a woman is. The richer and more educated people are, the more positively they thought about women's abilities. Finally, the more frequently a person attends church, the more conservative the attitude is about women's position in society. Interestingly, even after controlling for income and education, a significant effect for race remains: People of color think less positively about women's capabilities than do Whites. Of course, this result does not mean that all people of color are sexist; it simply means that, on the average, people of color feel less positively toward women's position in society than do Whites. There may be some cultural elements present in Black and Hispanic communities related to attitudes toward women that are responsible for this effect. It may also be that the oppression the men in these groups have experienced is passed on to the less powerful group: women.

Table 3-14 reports the significant predictors for the question about whether the government should provide guaranteed jobs. The full wording of the question was: "Some people feel that the government in Washington should see to it that every person has a job and a good standard of living. Others think the government should just let each person get ahead on his own. And of course, some other people have opinions somewhere in between." As you can see, only two variables (race and income) show a significant association with answers to this question. As you might expect, given the historically higher unemployment rates among people of color, they are significantly more in favor of government-guaranteed jobs than are Whites. Additionally, the more well-to-do are also less supportive of such policies. Membership in a Christian fundamentalist group is the only other variable that approaches statistical significance.

Table 3-13   Multiple regression analysis results for opinions on women's position in society

Respondents were asked how much they agreed or disagreed with this statement: "Men are just better cut out than women for important positions in society."

Variable	Regression Coefficient	Significance
Sex	.10	$p < .001$
Age	−.15	$p < .001$
Education	.22	$p < .001$
Income	.09	$p < .001$
Church attendance	−.06	$p < .01$
Race	−.05	$p < .02$
Fundamentalists	−.09	$p < .10$
Protestants	−.08	$p < .10$
$R^2 = .13$		

Source: Data are from the 1984 National Election Study conducted by the Center for Political Studies at the University of Michigan.

Table 3-14 Multiple regression analysis results for opinions on government-guaranteed jobs

Variable	Regression Coefficient	Significance
Race	.26	$p < .001$
Income	$-.08$	$p < .01$
Fundamentalists	$-.10$	$p < .10$
$R^2 = .08$		

Source: Data are from the 1984 National Election Study conducted by the Center for Political Studies at the University of Michigan.

Table 3-15 reports very similar findings about whether a person identifies as a liberal or a conservative. As with opinion on a guaranteed job, race and income significantly influence an individual's ideological identification (people of color and poorer individuals being more liberal). More important than belonging to any specific denomination is the frequency with which a person attends church, with frequent church attenders being more conservative, although being a fundamentalist again shows a small effect.

An important statistic from Tables 3-13 through 3-15 is the R^2 for each regression equation. This number indicates the percentage of variance in the dependent variable (the answers to the attitude question) that is explained by the independent variables (the social predictors). The R^2 figures for the three analyses (.13, .08, and .06) reveal that even though there are a number of statistically significant predictors for opinion on each question, only a very small percentage of variation in these opinions is explained.

Table 3-15 Multiple regression results on respondents' liberal/conservative self-description

Variable	Regression Coefficient	Significance
Race	.14	$p < .001$
Income	$-.14$	$p < .001$
Church attendance	$-.08$	$p < .001$
Education	.05	$p < .10$
Fundamentalists	$-.11$	$p < .10$
$R^2 = .06$		

Source: Data are from the 1984 National Election Study conducted by the Center for Political Studies at the University of Michigan.

■ Political Socialization

Research on political socialization has sought to identify the processes by which social factors contribute to individuals' political attitudes. To say that education or religion influences an individual's attitudes is another way of saying that some elements in childhood and adolescence have contributed to the political attitudes he or she has formed. Researchers in political socialization have attempted to assess the extent to which different potential sources of influence (such as family or peers) shape individuals' attitudes and opinions. Consistent with our earlier discussion, researchers have found evidence of only small effects of attitude transmission from different sources.

Transmission of Political Attitudes

The family is obviously an important potential source of political information and values. Parents have almost exclusive contact with children in their first years, although this contact has diminished in recent years, with an increasing number of children in full-time day care. Frequently, politics is not a topic of discussion in many families. Consequently, despite the monopoly on a growing child's time, one might expect some discontinuities between parents' and children's political attitudes. This is precisely what Jennings and Niemi (1968) found. The average correlation of student's attitudes with their parents' attitudes on four different issues was $r = .20$. Thus on these issues, parents' attitudes explained an average of 4% (equal to the correlation coefficient squared) of the variation in their children's attitudes. Only on party identification was there a substantial correlation ($r = .47$). Hamilton, Knox, and Keilin (1986) found a similarly low correspondence between parents' attitudes and children's attitudes about the threat of nuclear war. If you had to predict, would you expect children's attitudes to be more consistent with their fathers' or their mothers' opinions? Interestingly, studies have consistently found that mothers appear to exert more influence on specific attitudes than do fathers (Campbell, 1980; Jennings & Niemi, 1974). We should note, however, that correlations between parents' attitudes and those of their children do not necessarily reflect a causal effect. Since parents and children often come from similar backgrounds, and thus have many similar experiences, any correspondence between their attitudes may be a result of these factors rather than direct influence.

Research on the effect of a child's peers on political attitudes generally indicates that parents' attitudes have a greater effect than friends' attitudes (Sebert, Jennings, & Niemi, 1974; Tedin, 1980). Studying the effect of a child's peers on his or her attitudes, Sebert et al. (1974) asked high school students to identify their friends; then they compared the students' answers with a series of political attitude questions. They asked for opinions on 18-year-olds' voting (a hypothetical choice in the 1964 presidential election) and included a question on political trust as well. Similar to the findings on the effect of parents' political beliefs, the authors found relatively small relationships between students' and their friends' attitudes, smaller than the correlations with parents' opinions. As Sebert et al. (1974) note, "Political traits are not a frequent, overarching basis for *intimate* friendships" (p. 235). Kandel and Lesser (1972) reiterate this point, observing that politics is rarely the *basis* for adolescent friendships.

Content of Political Learning

Researchers in political socialization have generally differentiated between the kinds of political learning that takes place in early childhood (ages 5 to 9), late childhood (about ages 9 to 13), and adolescence (around ages 13 to 18). The classic studies in this area indicate that political learning in early childhood primarily involves forming attachment to vague political symbols; in late childhood, children substantially increase their amount of political information; and in adolescence, individuals typically change the way they think about politics.

Easton and Hess (1962) have argued that a child's political world begins to take shape even before the child enters elementary school. This political world involves vague feelings and attachments without much cognitive content. At an early age, children begin to assert attachment to a political party. At the earliest age studied, second grade by Easton and Hess (1962) and fourth grade by Greenstein (1965), over half of the children reported some party identification. These attachments were of the form "I am a Democrat," without being able to say what that means. The concept of voting is similarly vague. At the age of 6, my youngest daughter once asked me, "Daddy, do we vote for the Red Sox or the Yankees?"

It is also during early childhood that the child begins to acquire an orientation toward political authorities and roles. Children at this age tend to view authorities as highly personalized and as indiscriminately benevolent and helpful (Greenstein, 1965). Easton and Dennis (1969) found that most children are familiar with the president, whom children see as powerful and as a person who causes good things to be done.

In late childhood, from the ages of about 9 to 13, individuals move away from the highly personalized images of political leaders and greatly increase their level of political knowledge. During this period, children begin to separate the roles of political leaders from the individuals who occupy those positions. They also move away from the image of leaders as purely benevolent and recognize some reasons that political leaders are motivated to act in reasonable ways—for example, so they can be reelected (Dawson, Prewitt, & Dawson, 1977). Levels of political knowledge also increase. Greenstein (1965) found that from fourth grade to eighth grade, correct answers to various questions such as the role of the state legislature increased significantly, from 5% in fourth grade to 37% in eighth grade.

Significant changes in political learning take place in adolescence (ages 13 to 18), paralleling changes in individuals' social, emotional, and cognitive development during this period (Santrock, 1990). Adolescents develop the capacity for abstract thought, become less authoritarian in their thinking, and become capable of ideological thinking (Dawson et al., 1977). The relationship of cognitive development to political thinking, particularly the structural developmental approach advanced by Rosenberg (1987, 1988a, 1988b), is discussed in detail in Chapter Five.

A Caveat

The development of political attitudes has been the focus of researchers studying political socialization. It is important to be aware, though, that not all researchers see political socialization in as benign a context as the research reviewed in this chapter. Charles Lindblom in his 1981 presidential address to the American Political Science Association convention, observed:

> Many conventional scholars see political socialization as a lifelong process . . . in which citizens "mature." Socialization helps the citizen to "comprehend" and "evaluate." . . . Such a view slights the possibility that socialization is intellectually confining, is sometimes crippling, may reduce understanding and may obstruct the development of skill in evaluation. But which of these it does, or in what mixture, is as important a question for political science as can be examined.

Some scholars have argued that schools, rather than develop in their students the capacity for critical thinking, instead dull their minds with unintegrated sets of facts and serve mainly to prepare individuals for mindless factory jobs (Bowles & Gintis, 1976). Others (Bradshaw, 1988; Miller, 1983) have contended that the family, through the parents' use of shame, helps children develop a tremendous capacity for the use of denial, a defense mechanism that has considerable personal and political implications. We turn in the next chapter to an examination of the relationship of personality to politics, and we find that the nature of the family environment, irrespective of the overt political attitudes that are communicated, can have a substantial impact on an individual's political ideology.

■ Conclusion

So what can we conclude about the effect of social background characteristics upon political attitudes? It is clear that social factors are important for some kinds of opinions (such as attitudes toward the position of women in society) but not others (such as whether government should provide guaranteed jobs). In addition, some predictors significant for explaining some attitudes are not useful for explaining other attitudes, as was revealed with sex, age, and education in the multiple regression analysis. Finally, some characteristics are not predictive at all. Overall in this chapter, we saw that social factors combined explained only a relatively small proportion of the variation in the public's attitudes.

It is important to keep in mind that the process of opinion formation and change is a dynamic process that is difficult to explain, given fairly static background characteristics. As we shall see in later chapters, elements of the political environment, particularly messages and political images emphasized in the mass media, can shape the nature of political attitudes and thinking. These media influences, though, occur in the context of existing political attitudes developed over a period of years, reflecting the influence of a variety of social factors.

CHAPTER
FOUR

Personality and Public Opinion

In the previous chapter, we examined the relationship between individuals' political opinions and different background characteristics. The differences between individuals that we considered, however, were very broad—for example, between women and men, or between Whites and people of color—without a discussion of specific life experiences. In this chapter, we consider factors that influence the development of an individual's personality and how these personality differences are related to political attitudes and political ideology.

Ideological differences, whether individuals are politically left wing or right wing, generally reflect underlying differences in individuals' personalities. These personality differences reflect, in large part, differences in the patterns of childhood socialization, particularly patterns of child rearing. Harsh socialization by parents using physical punishment and emotional shaming tends to be associated with rigidity, intolerance of ambiguity, and authoritarianism. These personality characteristics can be found among individuals of both the left and the right, although the overwhelming majority are politically conservative.

■ Personality Needs Affect Opinion

How did Ronald Reagan maintain such a high level of popularity among the American public while advocating policies that a majority of the public opposed? Aid to the Nicaraguan contras who were fighting to overthrow the Sandinista government was one of his central passions; but a majority of the public has almost without exception opposed aid to the contras (Bowen, 1989). Reagan also favored a variety of programs labeled collectively as the "right-wing social agenda," including the prohibition of abortion, opposing handgun control, and so on, policies that a majority of the public did not support.

One answer to this question is to argue that despite public opposition to some of his policies, the public did support a number of his positions, including permitting prayer in public schools, reducing the size of government, and cutting taxes. However, this explanation misses a central element of Reagan's popularity: that he

40

made people feel good again about being Americans. Political leaders can build support by fulfilling the emotional needs of the public as well as through their policies. Reagan, making use of slogans and symbols with which many Americans had quite positive associations (such as "It's Morning in America!"), was much better at this than was former president Jimmy Carter.

In July of 1979 President Jimmy Carter, seeing his popularity declining, retreated to Camp David and emerged to give what many considered his finest political speech. In it he described the "malaise" affecting the American people, a characterization that many regarded as quite accurate. Nevertheless, his popularity continued to decline. The impact of the energy crisis and the tighten-your-belt attitude that Carter communicated may have contributed to the public's insecurities. What the people wanted was not to be lectured at but to feel better. This is what Reagan was able to accomplish, to address some basic personality needs of a great many people in the United States.

This example demonstrates how individuals' personality needs have a considerable influence on their opinions. Social scientists concerned with the effect of personality on public opinion and political behavior have utilized one of two approaches, what Bennett (1980) has called the "holistic" and "trait" perspectives. Holistically oriented theorists have focused on trying to understand the primary organizing principle of each personality that motivates all the aspects of a person's thought and behavior. Trait theorists have focused on understanding the importance of a particular trait or personality dimension (such as self-esteem or rigidity of thinking) for a person's political thinking and action.

■ Holistic Approaches

Lasswell's Theory of Personality Development

The development of holistic approaches to the understanding of personality and politics paralleled the emphasis in psychology on broad theories of personality. Harold Lasswell (1960) was one of the first social scientists to attempt to apply psychology to politics. He argued that individuals who focus their lives intensely on politics do so because it is a way of fulfilling some basic personality needs. He proposed a model,

$$p \} d \} r = P$$

that he argued represents the process that takes place. Private dispositions (p) are displaced (d) onto political objects or political issues and rationalized (r) in publicly acceptable motives or standard opinions. Lasswell was particularly interested in people who organize their lives around politics, and he argued that any opinion held very strongly over a long period of time reflects action by the personality to develop a stable, emotionally satisfying environment.

An example of this displacement is provided by Randall Terry, leader of the antiabortion organization, Operation Rescue, that has blockaded abortion clinics all over the United States, attempting to discourage women from having abortions and shut the clinics down. In an interview Susan Faludi (1989) questioned Terry about his past:

> "My wife almost had an abortion a few years ago but I stopped her," Terry says. They had four kids, and she didn't want another. "I fought it. I said, 'No, no, no.'" In the end he followed her into the examination room, where she was lying in a hospital gown. "I came in and snatched her and I said, 'Let's get out of here. Now!' I'm not going to let her be anywhere where I'm not." She had the baby, but then she left him. Tears fill his eyes as he says this. He swats at them and explains, "I'm crying for the unborn babies." (p. 25)

Individuals often carry around with them the pain of previous emotional experiences, sometimes denying that the pain exists or is important, but still needing to present to themselves and to others an explanation for the pain they are feeling. In the situation described above, Terry cries while recalling a difficult experience with his wife who eventually left him (an episode in his life that almost certainly was quite painful), but he explains the pain instead in *political* terms, related to the political issue, abortion, that he is actively involved in. He has externalized the problem so that he doesn't have to blame himself or look within himself for the source of his wife's abandonment.

Another example of passionate political commitment generated by personal experience is provided by Martin Luther King's "Letter from Birmingham Jail":

> Perhaps is it easy for those who have never felt the stinging darts of segregation to say, "Wait." But when you have seen vicious mobs lynch your mothers and fathers at will and drown your sisters and brothers at whim; when you have seen hate-filled policemen curse, kick and even kill your black brothers and sisters; when you see the vast majority of your twenty million Negro brothers smothering in an airtight cage of poverty in the midst of an affluent society; when you suddenly find your tongue twisted and your speech stammering as you seek to explain to your six-year-old daughter why she can't go to the public amusement park that has just been advertised on television, and see tears welling up in her eyes when she is told that Funtown is closed to colored children . . . then you will understand why we find it difficult to wait. (King, 1964, pp. 83–84)

Lasswell also linked his model of political behavior to the Freudian theory of personality development. Freud suggested that an individual's personality evolved through a series of stages of psychosexual development (oral, anal, phallic, and genital). Freud argued that if the normal course of development is disrupted at some point—through some traumatic event, for example—then the individual will grow into adulthood fixed at an earlier stage of development. Thus, individuals who failed to adequately resolve the Oedipal conflict during the phallic stage of development would have an underdeveloped superego (conscience) and would be likely to engage in criminal behavior. Lasswell argued that the way in which we address the political world reflects the needs remaining from personality development. He suggested a series of sociopolitical factors that paralleled the Freudian stages: Individuals in the oral stage would have a focus on security; those at the anal stage would focus on order; persons fixated at the phallic stage would concentrate on authority; and those at the genital stage (normal adult development) would focus on community.

The Authoritarian Personality

An extremely influential theory about the relationship of personality and political attitudes, developed a few years after Lasswell's book, is the theory of the authoritarian personality (Adorno, Frenkel-Brunswick, Levinson, & Sanford, 1950). Following the Holocaust of World War II, Adorno et al. (1950) sought to identify the roots of anti-Semitism. They proposed that a specific personality syndrome, which they dubbed the authoritarian personality, was related to anti-Semitism: a personality associated with a childhood that experienced little affection and harsh punishment, strict authority and discipline, with sex as a taboo subject.

Adorno et al. (1950) suggested that the authoritarian personality was characterized by a distrust of his or her and others' abilities to control their impulses and aggressions; a need for strict hierarchical authority in all situations; an inability to live with uncertainty and a consequential use of rigid black-and-white thinking. Individuals with this personality structure also evidenced a tendency to hold conservative political views and hostility toward deviant groups and ethnic minorities. In terms of the sociopolitical factors Lasswell proposed, an authoritarian personality is dominated by a need for *security*, a desire for *order* and hierarchical *authority*, and a very narrow sense of *community*.

Adorno et al. developed four scales to measure aspects of authoritarianism: anti-Semitism, general ethnocentrism, politico-economic conservatism, and the F scale, which purported to measure incipient fascism. Items from the F scale are included in Table 4-1.

Table 4-1   Items from the F scale of Adorno et al. (1950)

---

1. **Conventionalism.** *Rigid* adherence to and *over*emphasis on middle-class values, and overresponsiveness to contemporary *external* social pressure.
   Sample item: "A person who has bad manners, habits, and breeding can hardly expect to get along with decent people."
   Sample item: "No sane, normal person could ever think of hurting a close friend or relative."

2. **Authoritarian submission.** An exaggerated, emotional need to submit to others; an uncritical acceptance of a strong leader who will make decisions.
   Sample item: "People should have a deep faith in a supernatural force higher than themselves to whom they give total allegiance and whose decisions they obey without question."
   Sample item: "Obedience and respect for authority are the most important virtues children should learn."

3. **Authoritarian aggression.** Favoring condemnation, total rejection, stern discipline, or severe punishment as ways of dealing with people and forms of behavior that deviate from conventional values.
   Sample item: "Sex crimes, such as rape and attacks on children, deserve more than mere imprisonment; such criminals ought to be publicly whipped, or worse."
   Sample item: "No insult to our honor should ever go unpunished."

4. **Anti-intraception.** Disapproval of a free emotional life, of the intellectual or theoretical, and of the impractical. Anti-intraceptive persons maintain a narrow range of conscious-
   (continued)

Table 4-1   *(Continued)*

ness; realization of their genuine feelings or self-awareness might threaten their adjustment. Hence, they reject feelings, fantasies, and other subjective or "tender minded" phenomena.
Sample item: "When a person has a problem or worry, it is best for him or her not to think about it, but to keep busy with more cheerful things."
Sample item: "There are some things too intimate and personal to talk about even with one's closest friends."

5. **Superstition and stereotype.** Superstition implies a tendency to shift responsibility from within the individual onto outside forces beyond one's control, particularly to mystical determinants. Stereotype is the tendency to think in rigid, oversimplified categories, in unambiguous terms of black and white, particularly in the realm of psychological or social matters.
Sample item: "It is entirely possible that this series of wars and conflicts will be ended once and for all by a world-destroying earthquake, flood, or other catastrophe."
Sample item: "Although many people may scoff, it may yet be shown that astrology can explain a lot of things."

6. **Power and toughness.** The aligning of oneself with power figures, thus gratifying both one's need to have power and the need to submit to power. There is a denial of personal weakness.
Sample item: "What this country needs is fewer laws and agencies, and more courageous, tireless, devoted leaders whom the people can put their faith in."
Sample item: "Too many people today are living in an unnatural, soft way; we should return to the fundamentals, to a more red-blooded, active way of life."

7. **Destructiveness and cynicism.** Rationalized aggression; for example, cynicism permits the authoritarian person to be aggressive because "everybody is doing it." The generalized hostility and vilification of the human by highly authoritarian persons permit them to justify their own aggressiveness.
Sample item: "Human nature being what it is, there will always be war and conflict."

8. **Projectivity.** The disposition to believe that wild and dangerous things go on in the world. In the authoritarian personality, the undesirable impulses that cannot be admitted by the conscious ego tend to be projected onto minority groups and other vulnerable objects.
Sample item: "The sexual orgies of the old Greeks and Romans are kid stuff compared to some of the goings-on in this country today, even in circles where people might least expect it."
Sample item: "Nowadays when so many different kinds of people move around so much and mix together so freely, people have to be especially careful to protect themselves against infection and disease."

9. **Sex.** Exaggerated concern with sexual goings-on and punitiveness toward violators of sex mores.
Sample item: "Homosexuality is a particularly rotten form of delinquency and ought to be severely punished."
Sample item: "No matter how they act on the surface, men are interested in women for only one reason."

As indicated above, important studies have noted that individuals who hold extremely conservative political views tend to have significant personality problems. This point of view was carried further by McClosky (1958) in his research on the relationship between personality and ideology. His findings indicated that conservatives generally had low intelligence and education and tended to be hostile, suspicious, rigid, and compulsive. McClosky found them to be quick to condemn others for imperfections and weaknesses and to be very inflexible and unyielding in their perceptions and judgments. He concluded that conservatives were "poorly integrated psychologically, anxious, often perceiving themselves as inadequate and subject to excessive feelings of guilt, inclined to project onto others the traits they fear or dislike in themselves." In contrast, leftists tended to be more intelligent, creative, emotionally stable, and higher in moral development than rightists or average people.

We should note that critics of McClosky's work (such as Schoenberger, 1968) have pointed out that his conservatism measure was not correlated with either liberal/conservative self-ratings or with attitudes on economic issues. His measure of conservatism appears to identify those people who are personally *traditional* and who don't cope with changes very well. Thus, there appear to be two different kinds of conservatism: ego-defensive and issue-ideological conservatism.

■ Authoritarianism of the Left?

Political scientists studying ideology have generally characterized individuals' political beliefs as falling along a liberal/conservative (or left/right) dimension, and the next chapter discusses research on ideology and political thinking in some detail. At this point, we will discuss research arguing that there is an entirely different personality dimension that cuts across the left/right dimension. This position holds that a person's political beliefs do not simply reflect the person's place on a left/right dimension but also reflect whether the person is either tough minded or tender minded. This is a very different position than that pioneered by Adorno et al. (1950).

The theories of personality and politics advocated by Lasswell, by Adorno et al., and by McClosky all reflect what Tetlock (1984) has called the "rigidity of the right" perspective. This position argues that individuals on the right wing of the political spectrum have clear limitations in their thinking and personalities when compared with those on the left wing. An alternative to this position is that authoritarianism is a personality characteristic of individuals with either extreme left or extreme right views. As demonstrated below, evidence indicates that although there are authoritarian leftists, they are clearly far fewer in number than their right-wing counterparts.

Eysenck's Two-Factor Theory of Attitude Structure

A major alternative to the rigidity-of-the-right model is the work of Eysenck (1954; Eysenck & Wilson, 1978). Eysenck proposed that in addition to the left/right continuum, there was a second important dimension with two opposite poles that he labeled "tough-mindedness" and "tender-mindedness." His theory was that, independent of right/left ideological differences, there are also personality differences, reflected in their social attitudes, between individuals of the same ideological orientation. In other words, Eysenck hypothesized that there are strong similarities in psychological approach between individuals on opposite ends of the ideological spectrum: tough-minded leftists and tough-minded right-wingers. Meanwhile, two individuals who are like minded ideologically could differ greatly in personality style: tough-minded leftists and tender-minded leftists.

In a test of personality differences between individuals of different ideological directions, Eysenck and Coutler (1972) studied the attitudes and personalities of several groups of British working-class respondents, including Communists and Fascists. They found that there were no significant differences between these two groups on Eysenck's tough-mindedness factor or on a test of tolerance for ambiguity. In addition, both Communists and Fascists were more rigid in their thinking than a sample of "normal" working-class soldiers.

Rokeach's Value Pluralism Model

Like Eysenck, Rokeach (1954, 1960) argued that the approach taken by many researchers on conservatism and authoritarianism (Adorno et al., 1950) had overlooked the possibility of an "authoritarianism of the left." He proposed an alternative personality dimension called "dogmatism" (varying from close minded to open minded) that he argued was independent of ideology. Close-minded individuals, according to Rokeach, have difficulty assimilating new information and often reject conflicting information outright; open-minded individuals take longer to solve problems when presented with new, conflicting information, and they take the time to analyze it. Open-minded individuals also have a higher tolerance for ambiguity. Individuals high in dogmatism tend to have a more paranoid view of life and lower self-acceptance (Rokeach, 1954). Table 4-2 lists some items from the dogmatism scale.

In addition to the dogmatism scale, Rokeach (1973) has also proposed an alternative to the left/right conception of ideology, his "value pluralism" model. People vary considerably in the values that they hold as most important, what Rokeach called "terminal values." He derived the values in his value pluralism model from the basic elements of political systems. Rokeach argued that in virtually all political systems there are variations in power and economic opportunity between different groups. Thus, one group will have more control over scarce resources, over the means of production, and/or over the means of communication. He argued that the group with greater power (and thus freedom to do what it wants) will seek to maintain or increase that freedom; additionally, other groups with less power (and freedom) will try to gain more equality and freedom.

Rokeach thus argued that different emphases upon these two values, *freedom* and *equality*, underlie different political ideologies. He hypothesized that four different political ideologies—communism, socialism, fascism, and capitalism—differ on two dimensions, rather than vary on a single left/right continuum: high to low equality and high to low freedom. For instance, communism places very high emphasis on equality and little emphasis on freedom; capitalism values freedom

Table 4-2   Items from Rokeach's dogmatism scale

Dogmatism subscale
 1. A man who does not believe in some great cause has not really lived.
 4. It is when a person devotes himself to an ideal or cause that he becomes important.
10. To compromise with our political opponents is dangerous because it usually leads to the betrayal of our own side.
14. It is better to be a dead lion than a live dog.
30. It is by returning to our forgotten and glorious past that real social progress can be achieved.

Self-rejection subscale
35. At times I think I am no good at all.
37. It is only natural for a person to have a guilty conscience.

Paranoia subscale
38. It is generally safer to trust nobody.
40. I have often felt that strangers were looking at me critically.
43. I am sure I am being talked about.

Source: From "A Factorial Study of Dogmatism and Related Concepts" by M. Rokeach and B. Fruchter, *Journal of Abnormal and Social Psychology,* 1956, *53*, 357. Copyright 1956 by the American Psychological Association. Reprinted by permission.

highly but sees equality as much less important; socialism is high on both equality and freedom; fascism is low on both values. To test this model, Rokeach conducted a content analysis of samples of 25,000 words from the writings of individuals representing these four different ideologies: Erich Fromm and T. B. Bottomore for socialism; a sample of the collected works of Lenin for communism; sections of Hitler's *Mein Kampf* as representative of fascism; and a sample from Barry Goldwater's *Conscience of a Conservative* for capitalism. Judges then counted references in each sentence for 17 different terminal values, including freedom and equality, and then rank-ordered the different values according to their frequency of occurrence. The results Rokeach obtained are shown in Table 4-3. As you can see, the rankings of the different values correspond almost exactly to the model hypothesized by Rokeach.

The models that Eysenck and Rokeach have proposed are quite similar. Eysenck's tough-minded/tender-minded dimension closely resembles Rokeach's low-freedom/high-freedom dimension, and Rokeach's low-equality/high-equality dimension parallels the different emphases that conservatives and liberals give to those values, reflected in Eysenck's second dimension, radical/conservative. Both models assert that individuals of extreme-left and -right political orientations may be similar in their personality structures.

Table 4-3   Rank order of 17 terminal values found in writings by socialists, Hitler, Goldwater, and Lenin

Dimension	Socialists	Hitler	Goldwater	Lenin
Equality	2	17	16	1
Freedom	1	16	1	17

To what extent do these similarities actually exist? Smithers and Lobley (1978) studied a group of British university students, administering Rokeach's dogmatism scale and a measure of how radical or conservative they were, using a 16-item scale developed by Eysenck (1954). Their findings are displayed in Figure 4-1. As you can see, there is a U-shaped pattern to their results; individuals with the highest levels of dogmatism are either on the far conservative end of the scale (they answered all or all but one of the 16 questions in a conservative direction) or the far radical end. So you can see that there are similarities on the far ends of the scale.

What is also apparent, however, is that for most of the respondents, as they become more liberal, their level of dogmatism decreases. In fact, dividing the Smithers and Lobley sample as they did into "conservatives" (61 students who scored 1 or 2 on the scale), "neutrals" (408 students who scored between 3 and 8), and "radicals" (72 students who scored 9 or higher), it is very clear from the diagram that the average dogmatism scores of the conservatives are much higher than the dogmatism levels of the radicals.

Presenting the results of a series of national surveys, McClosky and Chong (1985) have argued that there are many similarities between left-wing and right-wing radicals. Both groups show a lack of tolerance to viewpoints opposed to their own, an estrangement from government, and a low tolerance for ambiguity. These findings appear to support the hypothesis of left-wing authoritarianism. There is one

Figure 4-1   The relationship of dogmatism and radicalism/conservatism

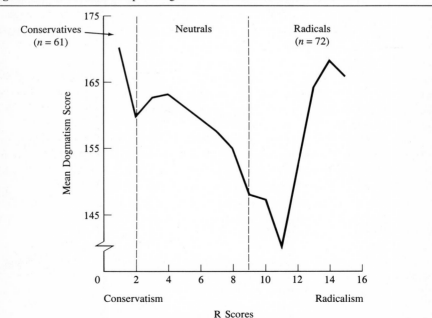

Source: From "Dogmatism, Social Attitudes, and Personality," by A. G. Smithers and M. D. Lobley, *British Journal of Social and Clinical Psychology*, 1978, *17*, 133–142. Reprinted by permission.

aspect of their findings, however, that is quite important to note. Across the national surveys McClosky and Chong (1985) report, the proportion of those on the far right is consistently more than three times as large as those on the far left: 3.7% far left; 83.5% moderate; and 12.7% far right (p. 343). Although some leftists may be characterized as authoritarian personalities, the vast majority of authoritarians are right wing.

These results parallel those of Smithers and Lobley (1978) discussed above, and they point to a synthesis between the rigidity-of-the-right position and of Eysenck's two-factor model. Although it is theoretically possible to have tough-minded or authoritarian individuals with either a far-left or far-right political orientation, one is more likely to find individuals with this particular personality style on the right wing than the left wing, as the results of McClosky and Chong (1985) suggest. Alternatively, if the groups of radicals and conservatives are of equal sizes, as in the Smithers and Lobley (1978) results, then the average rigidity of the right-wing group is higher than that of the left-wing group. When one adds to this the reported shifts of individuals from a radical-left to a radical-right ideology (for example, Ronald Reagan was a liberal union organizer as a young man; he later became the spokesperson for a very conservative political agenda), it is clear that individuals with a more rigid, authoritarian personality structure will more likely be ideologically conservative or right wing in their political beliefs.

The proponents of left-wing authoritarianism imply that authoritarian personalities are as prevalent on the left as they are on the right. Stone (1980, 1988) argues that many social scientists and textbooks persist in entertaining this position, even though the empirical evidence does not support it. It is clear from the research discussed above that although some individuals with extreme-left-wing ideologies have rigid, dogmatic personality structures, they are vastly outnumbered by authoritarians of the right.

Nevertheless, Stone (1983) maintains that it is important to get beyond the good-liberal, bad-conservative stereotype. He cites behavioral evidence such as that from Gaertner (1973), who found that liberals (members of the Liberal party in New York) were more likely than conservatives (the New York Conservative party) to respond to a telephoned request for help from a person with an identifiably Black voice. At the same time, however, liberals tended to hang up more quickly than conservatives before the caller had identified the situation as an emergency. The relationship between personality and ideology is clearly complex.

■ Tomkins's Polarity Theory

Sylvan Tomkins (1964, 1987) has made a major contribution to an understanding of the connection between ideology and personality. Before going further, take a minute to answer the following questions:

Circle one letter for each question corresponding to the answer you agree with most:

1. a. The trouble with democracy is that it too often represents the will of the people.
    b. The trouble with democracy is that it too seldom represents the will of the people.
2. a. Children should be taught to obey what is right even though they may not always feel like it.
    b. Children should be encouraged to express themselves even though parents may not always like it.
3. a. Human beings are basically good.
    b. Human beings are basically evil.
4. a. Life sometimes smells bad.
    b. Life sometimes leaves a bad taste in the mouth.
5. Circle the number corresponding to your position on the following scale:

    1 Extremely conservative   2 Moderately conservative
    3 Slightly conservative   4 Neither liberal nor conservative
    5 Slightly liberal   6 Moderately liberal
    7 Extremely liberal

From "Affect and the Psychology of Knowledge," by S. S. Tomkins. In S. S. Tomkins and C. E. Izard (Eds.), *Affect, Cognition, and Personality*. Copyright © 1965 by Springer Publishing Company, Inc., New York 10012. Used by permission.

Tomkins's Polarity Theory Scale

The items above come from a scale developed by Sylvan Tomkins (1965b) as a measure of his polarity theory. Tomkins proposed that political ideologies can be arranged along a left/right continuum and that different types of personalities (which he called "scripts") are attracted to different ideologies. He differentiated two kinds of scripts (left-wing scripts and right-wing scripts) and suggested that each had characteristic emotional responses reflecting the types of affect emphasized in early childhood socialization. Tomkins argued that individuals with left-wing scripts respond more to positive affects (such as excitement, joy, surprise) as a result of "humanistic" socialization—socialization that values the child as a unique individual. People with right-wing scripts who received "normative" socialization—upbringing that is more concerned with obedience to rules—are more responsive to negative emotions (such as disgust, anger, contempt). Individuals who are politically moderate are people who come from a family background where one parent tended to be normative and the other humanistic.

Using the scale items presented, Tomkins attempted to measure beliefs associated with humanistic or normative socialization. The normative answers are 1a, 2a, 3b, and 4a. Polarity theory would predict that if you chose primarily these normative answers, then you would be likely to describe yourself on the conservative end of the ideological self-rating scale. On the other hand, if you chose the humanistic alternatives, then you would be more likely to characterize yourself as a liberal. Item 4 is interesting in this regard. Tomkins thought that individuals who chose the "taste bad" alternative (he called them "tasters") evidenced a humanistic orientation. This item reflects his belief that liberals let life get closer than conservatives (you must be closer to taste something than to just smell it). How do your answers compare with his prediction?

Left and Right Ways of Seeing

A fascinating aspect of Tomkins's work is his argument that ideology (either a left-wing or a right-wing orientation) is an aspect of all human endeavors. Tomkins suggests that a left-wing orientation focuses more on the independence of individuals, the belief that humans have value in themselves; a right-wing orientation emphasizes more the importance of individuals conforming to some external authority. He sees this polarity (between right and left) in all fields of knowledge, including metaphysics, the philosophy of science, art, education, psychiatry, mathematics, as well as in politics. In mathematics, for example, Tomkins observes that the left-wing position, expounded by the French mathematician Henri Poincaré, argues that mathematics is a construction of the human imagination, the "finest type of play—the most free." On the mathematical right wing, another mathematician, Richard Courant, argues instead that mathematics must serve a greater whole under the "discipline of responsibility" (Tomkins, 1965a, p. 23).

Additionally, Tomkins argues that a person's ideological orientation pervades the way that person looks at life, including what attracts that person to his or her career choice. Left-wing and right-wing individuals may choose the same profession, but, Tomkins (1964, 1965a) argues, they do so for very different reasons. For example, for individuals choosing a career in mathematics, Tomkins found that right-wing mathematicians appear to desire security and were attracted as children by the promise of always being able to have the "right" answer. In contrast, left-wing mathematicians were attracted to this field because of "the promise of excitement, and the 'divine madness' of 'wild, unaccountable spaces'" (Tomkins, 1965a, p. 23).

Roots of Ideological Differences

Tomkins's polarity theory has important implications for the persistent controversy in our culture about child-rearing styles. Tomkins (1965b) notes that the same left/right polarity observed in various fields of knowledge also exists in discussions of child rearing. C. B. Stendler (1950) reviewed 60 years of child-rearing practices in the 18th and early 19th centuries, and she found alternating periods where experts advocated tough treatment and then tender treatment. Tomkins (1965b) has observed that this pattern reflects an alternation between two different emphases in our culture: a humanistic orientation and a normative one. The important point to keep in mind from this discussion is that there are political implications about the way children are raised, not simply what the parents' political attitudes are, as the political socialization literature has studied for years.

This same contrast between styles of child rearing (normative versus humanistic) appears to exist between middle-class and working-class parents in this country.

Mel Kohn's (1977) study of class differences in the values that parents most want to see in their children indicates that working-class mothers put priority on the "behavioral conformity" values of obedience and neatness, but middle-class mothers give a higher priority to values related to "internal dynamics"—such as happiness, consideration, self-control, and curiosity. Kohn suggests that this may be a result of the pressure to obey and conform to employers that working-class parents feel, while middle-class occupations typically require more self-direction.

Although there may have been swings over time in advocated child-rearing patterns, it is unclear that parents' behavior toward children changed very much during these periods. In her history of family violence, Gordon (1988) observes that even individuals in the child protection movement in the 1880s thought relatively harsh beatings were acceptable, drawing the line only at the use of weapons. And although those in the child protection movement of today generally oppose all use of physical punishment for children, Gelles (1979) reported in his study that between 84% and 97% of parents still regularly use physical punishment.

There are parallels between Tomkins' observations about the effects of punitive child rearing on political ideology and the more recent work of Alice Miller (1983). Miller argues that what she calls the "poisonous pedagogy" of raising children has prevailed over the past 200 years. Foremost among the elements of this pedagogy are that parents are the masters of the children and decide in an omnipotent way what is right or wrong for the child. Additionally, the child's "life-affirming feelings" are threatening to the authoritarian parents and the child's will must be crushed while he or she is still young (p. 59). You can see the parallels between the historical German beliefs about child rearing that Miller (1983) identifies and the normative approach to raising children that Tomkins describes, both in terms of the efforts to control the child and the parents' denial of the children's positive emotions.

Tomkins argues that a normative approach to child rearing results in the development of individuals who are attracted to a conservative political ideology. An approach to raising children rooted in the poisonous pedagogy, according to Miller, provided a foundation for the development of the brutal Nazi government in Hitler's Germany. Adolf Hitler's childhood was filled with daily beatings and ridicule from an autocratic father who expected and demanded total obedience from his children. Hitler also learned as a child to deny his feelings of suffering, determined as he was not to show any reaction to his father's beatings. Thus, poisonous pedagogy encouraged this development of an individual filled with unacknowledged rage from his childhood. In addition, Miller (1983) argues, the widespread use of physical punishment, shaming, demands of obedience, and the denial of feelings, pervasive as it was in Germany, resulted in many people's support for Hitler and his policies. Childhood experiences, particularly those in the family environment, provide a basis for individuals' political ideology.

Empirical Support for Tomkins's Polarity Theory

Different studies have reported evidence consistent with predictions made from Tomkins's polarity theory. Tomkins, McCarter, and Peebles (1965) examined individuals' reactions to President Kennedy's assassination, and they found that 38% of "tasters" (those people who chose the alternative that life tastes bad) reported showing their distress by crying; only 10% of individuals who chose the "smell bad" alternative reported crying when they heard the news. This is consistent with Tomkins's suggestion that the punitive socialization received by right-wing individuals minimizes their sympathetic responses. In a different study, Carlson and Levy (1970) showed a series of photographs of individuals' faces to a group of subjects, and they found that the more humanistically oriented "tasters" were more likely to judge the expressions shown as pleasant (consistent with Tomkins's hypothesis that tasters respond more to positive than to negative affect).

Tomkins (1987) has recently argued that humanistic or normative orientations are reflected by different "affect triads," or sets of three emotions. Anger, contempt, and excitement are the normative triad; and distress, shame, and joy constitute the humanistic triad. Carlson and Brincka (1987) applied this ideology/ affect model to individuals' perceptions of the candidates in the 1984 presidential election.

Carlson and Brincka (1987) first formulated four plots of imaginary TV dramas to represent each of the six different emotions (24 plots in all). The researchers then asked respondents to consider each of the four candidates for president and vice president (Ronald Reagan, George Bush, Walter Mondale, and Geraldine Ferraro) and select four of the plots for each person in which they could imagine the candidate playing the leading role. For example, *anger* plots dealt with revenge, punishment, and retribution. The specific story lines they used included fighting invaders in a 14th-century historical drama, a child's encounter with school yard bullies, and prosecuting extortionists. Themes of *joy* included family reunions, old friends meeting again and recalling shared memories of the 1960s, and a godchild's christening.

Quite consistently, the subjects assigned the plots with normative emotions (anger, contempt, excitement) more often to Reagan and Bush; Mondale and Ferraro were seen more often as starring in the plots emphasizing humanistic emotions (joy, distress, shame). This association between the ideological orientation of a candidate and the typical emotion that citizens imagine about that candidate is precisely what Tomkins's polarity model predicts. The typical affect that individuals (such as a candidate) project to the world, either humanistic or normative, is highly related to their ideological position, again either humanistic or normative.

■ Conclusion

We think of an individual's "personality" as an internal structure, unique to that person, though with similarities to other individuals along various dimensions. It is vital to keep in mind, however, that an individual's personality is a result of a variety of social and cultural influences. Patterns of child rearing in a particular culture tend to be consistent for a majority of the population, and as we have seen, the way a person is raised has important implications for that person's political beliefs and actions.

The early arguments of Lasswell and Adorno et al. that a person's political belief structure reflects some unresolved personality issues and emotions from childhood are given a clearer focus in Tomkins's work. Children raised in a punitive, shaming way, in which the children's pain and emotional experiences are not acknowledged and validated, typically are conservative in their personal style and in their political beliefs. When that pain is unacknowledged by an individual in adulthood, evidence indicates that the individual will raise his or her children in a similar way with similar effects on them. On a societal level, this process contributes to the development of individuals who support political actions and movements that are ideologically conservative and potentially fascist.

The Relationship Between Political Thinking and Public Opinion

CHAPTER
FIVE

The Nature
of Political Thought

Depending to a large extent on their level of education, people vary in the level of complexity at which they are able to think about politics. In this chapter, we will examine three alternative approaches to cognitive complexity: Rosenberg (1987), Tetlock (1983), and Georgoudi (1985). An important aspect of all three theories of cognitive complexity is the emphasis on the importance of causal explanations for events. How people will answer the question "Why did this happen?" is a fundamental aspect of the complexity of thinking and of political ideology.

People are not necessarily consistent in the level of complexity with which they think about events. The same person who recognizes various perspectives on housing and development questions (such as balancing the need for affordable housing against the importance of economic incentives for development) may have a completely black-and-white view of another issue, such as support for trade unions or abortion. Different people do vary in terms of the complexity of thinking of which they are capable, and they do not always reason at their top levels. Simpler or more complex thinking may be activated by situational factors such as media coverage of a particular issue or the stated opinion of a trusted public figure.

The first section of this book discussed the nature and sources of public opinion. In the last chapter of that section, we discussed how people "feel" about politics—that is, how unresolved emotional issues from an individual's childhood and the characteristic affects in his or her upbringing influence that individual's political orientation. As a contrast, in this section we turn to an examination of how people "think" about politics. This examination requires first a discussion of the concept of political ideology, a review of research that has examined the ideological consistency of individuals' attitudes, and an analysis of various theoretical perspectives on the cognitive complexity of political thought, all of which are presented in this chapter. In the second chapter of this section, Chapter Six, we examine the relationship of political knowledge structures (schemas) to public opinion.

■ Political Ideology

The concept of *ideology* originated during the French Enlightenment. In 1796 Destutt de Tracy proposed the term to describe a science of ideas with which to analyze the problems of society and to develop solutions to those problems. The original meaning of *ideology* was very positive, focusing on the use of logical thought to understand the causal forces in society. The ideologies that arose from this period (liberalism, socialism, Marxism) tended to be revolutionary and utopian.

The current popular usage of *ideology* now has a pejorative meaning. The term *ideologue* is often used to denote an individual with political views on the right or the left who is particularly narrow in his or her thinking. As Duncan (1987) observes, "To present a political philosophy as an ideology is, however, to diminish it in one way. . . . If we present Hobbes as a liberal ideologist rather than a political philosopher, we challenge his integrity, his separateness and his freedom" (p. 654). In the United States, the contemporary meaning of the terms *liberal* and *conservative* is now opposite to what the originators intended. Classical liberals in the 18th century championed free enterprise, stressed the importance of private property, and sought to limit the power of the state to the enforcement of contracts and the protection of life and property, all positions we associate with conservatives today (Bluhm, 1974).

The Belief Systems Approach to Political Ideology

In the political science literature on voting behavior, the meaning of ideology has generally been taken to mean just the liberal/conservative dimension. In their pioneering study on political attitudes and electoral behavior titled *The American Voter*, Campbell, Converse, Miller, and Stokes (1960) measured what they called an individual's "level of conceptualization" about politics. The authors attempted to ascertain the sophistication with which an individual thinks about politics. They analyzed respondents' answers to a variety of open-ended questions about the political parties and presidential candidates in election year national surveys. They identified four groups: (1) ideologues (and near-ideologues), (2) group benefits, (3) "nature of the times," and (4) no issue content.

Ideologues (and near-ideologues) were those respondents who offered ideological (liberal or conservative) interpretations of political changes or events. Campbell et al. (1960) used *ideologue* in this context in a positive way to denote the highest level of political sophistication. Individuals categorized as "group benefits" viewed politics in terms of how it benefited the respondent or the respondent's immediate social environment. The "nature of the times" label was used to classify people who tended to hold the party in power responsible for current national problems or to reward the party for positive developments; and the "no issue content" category included those individuals whose responses made no reference to political issues and/or those who focused on candidates' personal characteristics.

The most important conclusion Campbell et al. (1960) reached relative to our discussion of political thinking was that only 12% of the total respondents could be placed in the highest levels (ideologue and near-ideologue). They argued that this indicates a very low level of ideological thinking on the part of the American public. This judgment about the nature of U.S. voters' thinking was echoed by additional research of Converse (1964, 1970) on what he called the "nature of belief systems" of the mass public.

Converse (1964) compared the average correlation size between opinions on pairs of political issues for a sample of congressional candidates (political "elites") and a national sample (the "mass public"). He found that the average correlation was much higher for his elite sample than for the mass public and concluded that the constraint (or consistency) of the mass public's attitudes is quite low. Converse (1970) extended this argument with some analyses looking at the stability of attitudes over time, using the 1956–1960 National Election Study panel survey. (A panel study is one in which the same people are interviewed repeatedly.) He found evidence to suggest that the answers to survey questions for a large proportion of the population may, in fact, be what he called "nonattitudes." Such nonattitudes are responses that are generated almost at random and have little or no relationship to other expressed opinions or to the answers to the same questions at a different time.

Support for Converse's conclusions about the lack of consistency in the public's attitudes is found in the results of Free and Cantril (1967). In a large-scale sample of the American public, they identified individuals who were "ideological" liberals or conservatives and individuals who were "operational" liberals or conservatives. For example, individuals who expressed consistent opposition to government programs in general and who agreed with statements like "The federal government is interfering too much in state and local matters" were labeled as ideological conservatives; 50% of Free and Cantril's sample were classified as completely or predominantly conservative on their ideological scale, but only 16% were completely or predominantly liberal.

Free and Cantril (1967) also asked individuals about their support or opposition to various New Deal government programs such as Medicare, federal aid to education, and federal low-rent-housing programs. Using this operational definition of liberal or conservative, they found that 65% of the public could be classified as operationally *liberal*, but only 14% were classified as completely or predominantly conservative on their operational scale. Combining the results of these two scales revealed that 23% of the public could be classified as operationally liberal and ideologically conservative at the same time. Bem (1970) points out that a portion of this 23% may simply be "yea-sayers," individuals who agree with statements that pollsters present to them. Nevertheless, Free and Cantril's (1967) results indicate there is a proportion of the public that does not really care about being ideologically consistent.

Converse's conclusions that the vast majority of the public have nonattitudes have also been challenged by a variety of researchers (Judd, Krosnick, & Milburn, 1981; Judd & Milburn, 1980; Nie & Anderson, 1974; Nie, Verba, & Petrocik, 1976) and remain a subject of considerable debate in the political science literature. In their comprehensive review of the public opinion literature, Kinder and Sears (1985) conclude that although there is considerable evidence of fuzzy thinking on the part of many citizens about political issues, there are times and issues when nonattitudes disappear completely. In the middle 1970s, virtually everyone expressed a stable opinion on busing, equal rights for women, and abortion (Kinder & Rhodebeck, 1982). As Kinder and Sears note, "Whether Americans shrug or become impassioned when confronted with policy alternatives has therefore much to do with the nature of the policy itself" (p. 668).

The Situational Perspective on Ideological Consistency

It is important to keep in mind Bennett's (1980) distinction between the state of consciousness and the situational perspective on public opinion. He argues that a debate on how ideologically consistent the public is reflects a state-of-consciousness fallacy and that there are major situational effects upon the public's opinions. An example is the "rally 'round the flag" syndrome, the observed phenomenon that presidential popularity rises when the president acts decisively, typically by using military force, during an international crisis (Bowen, 1989).

In an analysis of public opinion following several military actions by President Reagan, Bowen (1989) observed a "halo effect." Not only did presidential popularity increase, but support for other, often unrelated presidential policies increased as well. In the aftermath of the air raid on Libya in April 1986, which 76% of the public supported, support for aid to the contras rose to the highest level it ever attained, with 47% of the public saying that it approved of President Reagan's handling of the situation in Nicaragua (*Washington Post*, April 30, 1986, p. 4). This was the only time during the Reagan administration that support for Reagan's policies in Nicaragua exceeded opposition to them, and the support was clearly a result of an external, unrelated event. Similar increases in support for the contras were evident following the invasion of Grenada and during Lt. Col. (ret.) Oliver North's testimony to Congress (Bowen, 1989).

What is particularly interesting in the case of the raid on Libya is the broad range of support the action garnered, particularly among groups that were not generally supportive of Reagan's policies. Fifty-eight percent of blacks, two-thirds of Democrats, and 70% of women supported the air attack of Libya (*Washington Post*, April 30, 1984, p. 4). This finding demonstrates very clearly how specific situational factors such as presidential actions can substantially influence opinion, particularly if the event is remote and the president has control over information about the event (Edelman, 1964), resulting in individuals' expressing attitudes that may not be ideologically consistent with their other opinions.

Ideological Consistency and Political Sophistication

The "belief systems" position on political ideology is that greater political sophistication is associated with higher levels of "ideological consistency"—that is, higher correlations between individuals' policy attitudes (Converse, 1964). Thus, from this perspective, a person with the highest level of political sophistication would be one with no variability in attitudes, being either consistently liberal or consistently conservative. As we will see in the following discussion of political reasoning, this view overlooks the importance of cognitive complexity in political thinking and political sophistication.

■ Political Reasoning

Rosenberg (1987) argued that Converse's belief systems approach, discussed above, tells us how the public does *not* think about politics, but it does not tell us how the public *does* think about politics. Rosenberg (1987, 1988a, 1988b) has proposed what he calls a "structural developmental" approach to political ideology. By this he means that ideology can be understood through an examination of the structure of an individual's thinking about politics. Various components are involved in the structure of an individual's thinking, including the number of perspectives that a person takes on a specific issue and the relationships the person sees among these perspectives.

Rosenberg (1987, 1988a, 1988b) proposed that individuals think about politics in three different ways, which he called sequential, linear, and systematic. Sequential thinkers don't use abstractions or generalizations. They see events that occur close together in time as related to one another. Linear thinkers think in causal terms but do not go beyond models that view one variable causing another. Finally, systematic thinkers go beyond simple causal models and consider that different factors may interact with each other in nonlinear ways and that there may be reciprocal relationships among different variables. This is the most complex political thinking.

Piaget's Model of Cognitive Development

Rosenberg was inspired by Jean Piaget's research on cognitive development. Piaget argued that the human mind is not simply a passive receiver of information but processes information and actively changes and adapts to the world. Following extensive observations and conversations with his children, Piaget proposed that cognitive development progresses through a series of stages. According to Piaget, in the first two stages of cognitive development, an individual is primarily involved in motor behavior: touching, hearing, looking. The child then begins to develop the capacity to utilize symbolic functions such as language and imaginative play and to create internal representations of events (that is, to "think").

Piaget's third and fourth stages are the most important for our discussion of Rosenberg's research on political thinking. He called the third stage the *concrete operations* stage and proposed that between the ages of 7 and 11 a child develops logical thought processes that can be applied to concrete objects or situations but not to abstract or hypothetical ones. The final stage Piaget called *formal operations*. This development occurs between the ages of 11 and 15, following which a child is no longer bound by the concrete or the real and becomes able to apply logical operations to abstract and hypothetical situations.

Piaget assumed that all adults reach this fourth stage. This appears, however, to have been a considerable overestimate of the level of adult cognitive development. Dulit (1975) found that only about 30% to 40% of adults have achieved the formal operations level in their thinking. Other researchers report similar limitations on the extent of adult cognitive development (Commons, Richards, & Kuhn, 1982; Hardy-Brown, 1979; Kuhn, Langer, Kohlberg, & Haan, 1977). Consistent with critics of Piaget, Rosenberg also found that people vary considerably in the level at which they are able to reason about political issues. This may be explained by the fact that political issues generally have both concrete and hypothetical aspects.

Rosenberg's Application of the Piagetian Model

Rosenberg (1988a, 1988b) sought to demonstrate the relationship between an individual's thinking on a Piagetian test of cognitive development (the "chemicals task"; Inhelder & Piaget, 1958) and the person's level of political reasoning. In the chemicals task, the experimenter shows subjects a clear liquid that turns yellow when some drops of another clear liquid are added to it. The experimenter then tells the subjects that the initial liquid comes from one or more of four beakers and gives subjects the opportunity to experiment with the liquids. After observing the way subjects approached this problem, Rosenberg classified them as either sequential, linear, or systematic thinkers. Sequential thinkers did not reason causally. They would try the agent in all four beakers, find that nothing happened, and then give up. If encouraged, they might try some combinations and stumble on the solutions, but they would always attribute the result to one of the liquids as opposed to a combination or interaction. Linear thinkers would think causally. They would try combinations of liquids until they found two that together would turn yellow when the reactive agent was added, but they would be unable to discover the role of the other two liquids. Finally, systematic thinkers would accomplish what linear thinkers did, but they would go beyond to determine that the two other liquids had either a neutralizing or a neutral effect.

Rosenberg (1988b) also presented his subjects with a Piagetian task in which subjects are asked to determine what factors influence a swinging pendulum's rate of oscillation. The experimenter suggests several potential elements to them: the length of the string, the weight of the swinging object, the force with which the object is initially pushed, and the height at which it is started. Rosenberg's subjects' thinking was categorized on this task as well. Rosenberg found that when subjects were presented with a political issue to discuss (for instance, the Iranian hostage crisis), the level of most subjects' thinking paralleled their thinking on the earlier Piagetian tasks. Eighty percent of his sample had exactly the same level of thinking (sequential, linear, or systematic) for the three problems, and no subject's thinking was judged to vary more than one level across the different problems.

Rosenberg's (1987, 1988b) research indicates that individuals differ considerably in the type of thinking they use to solve problems, and that the sophistication of their thinking about politics and political situations is very similar to the way they approach traditional psychological cognitive problem-solving tasks. Rosenberg (1988b) also found that the extremity of a person's ideological (liberal/conservative) self-identification varied according to the complexity of his or her thinking: Systematic thinkers, who were the most complex in their thinking, were also more ideologically extreme than sequential or linear thinkers.

Tetlock's Approach to Cognitive Complexity

Social psychologist Philip Tetlock employs a model that is similar to Rosenberg's, although its origins are quite different. Making use of a coding system originally developed to score open-ended responses to a semiprojective test on the level of cognitive complexity (Schroder, Driver, & Streufert, 1967), Tetlock has evaluated the complexity of various political documents, including letters, diaries, and speeches (Levi & Tetlock, 1980; Suedfeld & Tetlock, 1977; Tetlock, 1979, 1981a, 1981b). This measure of cognitive complexity includes both "differentiation" and "integration." Differentiation relates to the number of different aspects of an issue that an individual recognizes; integration measures whether an individual sees the differentiated characteristics as functioning independently (low integration), in simple patterns (moderate integration), or in complex patterns (high integration). Tetlock (1983) thus makes the same distinctions that Rosenberg (1987) makes: Thinking that takes only a single perspective is judged to have a low level of cognitive complexity; thought that considers the possibility of two perspectives but that focuses on one is considered to be of moderate complexity; and thinking that sees interrelationships between multiple perspectives is judged high in complexity.

Tetlock has examined the cognitive complexity of various political statements by different elites (U.S. senators; British Members of Parliament, or M.P.s; U.S. Supreme Court justices) and determined the relationship of the complexity of thinking to ideological (left/right) position. Figure 5-1 presents the results he obtained from his study of British M.P.s. There is a curvilinear relationship between ideology and complexity; that is, the average complexity of thought is lower for the groups that are more ideologically extreme (extreme socialists and extreme conservatives), and the complexity is higher for those individuals whose political views are more moderate (moderate socialists, moderate conservatives). He interprets this result as consistent with Rokeach's (1973) value pluralism model discussed in Chapter Four. Moderate socialists who value both freedom and equality and who try to balance both in their public policy positions view the world less ideologically and thus evidence more complex thinking about political issues. An important element of Tetlock's work is the different perspective he takes on ideological consistency in relation to that of Converse. The traditional belief systems approach views ideological consistency as evidence of political sophistication; Tetlock's research suggests that such consistency may reflect limitations in the person's ability to think about politics.

Comparing Rosenberg and Tetlock

Rosenberg's and Tetlock's findings about the relationship between ideological extremity and cognitive complexity appear to be substantially different. Rosenberg

Figure 5-1   Results from Tetlock's (1984) study of British Members of Parliament

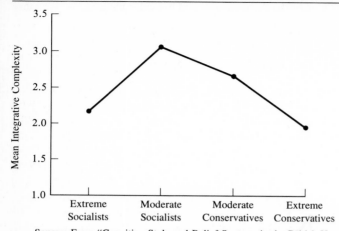

Source: From "Cognitive Style and Belief Systems in the British House of Commons," by P. E. Tetlock, *Journal of Personality and Social Psychology, 1984, 46* (2), 165–175. Copyright 1984 by the American Psychological Association. Reprinted by permission of the author.

(1988b) found that individuals evidencing systematic thinking (the most cognitively complex political thought) were the most ideologically extreme; Tetlock (1983) found that the most ideologically extreme individuals in his study have *lower* complexity than those who were more moderate. What's going on here? How can two studies be in such seeming contradiction and both be right?

A full resolution of this apparent conflict between the results of these two studies has to wait until the next chapter on political schemas, but several observations can be made now about important differences between the two studies. The samples Rosenberg and Tetlock used were quite different. Rosenberg (1988b) studied ordinary people; Tetlock (1983) analyzed the thinking of a political elite, British M.P.s. Additionally, their measures of ideological extremity were also quite different. Rosenberg (1988b) measured subjects' ideological self-identification on a 7-point scale; Tetlock (1983) used each M.P.'s political party membership as an indicator of ideology. You should note also that the "moderates" in Rosenberg's studies were those who rated themselves with a 4 on a 7-point scale, but there was no neutral point in Tetlock's results (Figure 5-1), only "moderate" socialists and "moderate" conservatives, individuals who would be considered fairly radical by U.S. standards. The ideological range of political opinion in the United States is much more limited than in other Western democracies, reflecting the ideological hegemony of liberal capitalism in U.S. political history (Burnham, 1982) that we discussed in Chapter Three. The implications of the differences between Rosenberg and Tetlock are discussed in more detail in Chapter Six, but it should be clear that there are major differences between the two studies that make a direct comparison of dissimilarities in the results not particularly meaningful.

■ Attribution Theory and Dialectical Thinking

Attribution Theory

An important aspect of political ideology, as we noted earlier, is the emphasis on providing causal explanations of events, of providing some way of understanding the political and social events that occur in a society. One approach to the study of the way individuals make explanations for events is "attribution theory," originally proposed by Fritz Heider (1958). Heider suggested that people in general behave like "naive psychologists"; that is, they are concerned and involved in explaining their own and others' behavior. Heider hypothesized that individuals use two primary types of explanations, what he called "internal attributions" and "external attributions." To make an internal attribution for a particular behavior is to attribute the behavior to something internal to the actor—to see the behavior as caused by some aspect of the individual's personality or belief system. An external attribution involves attributing the behavior to some situational cause—such as pressure that someone put on the actor to engage in the behavior.

Georgoudi (1985) utilizes attribution theory to present a different approach to studying the complexity of thought, although she does not apply this perspective to political reasoning. Heider originally suggested that individuals see events as either internally or externally caused. Georgoudi argues that the internal/external distinction is incomplete. She suggested that internal and external influences should be viewed as interrelated, each exerting influence on the other, rather than as discrete and unrelated influences on individuals' thought and behavior. She refers to this perspective on thinking—that events should be viewed as caused by an interaction between internal and external factors—as the "dialectics of attribution theory."

Dialectical Thinking

The term *dialectic* has a long history in philosophy and political thought, only briefly sketched here. In his book *The Republic*, Plato posed the dialectic as a method of thinking that could organize different elements of the world (or "forms") and examine their relationship to each other. In the early part of the 19th century, the philosopher Georg Hegel in his *Encyclopaedia of the Philosophical Sciences* (1832–1840), drawing both from the Greek philosophers and from Immanuel Kant, utilized *dialectic* in its original meaning of "discussion." For example, when two people begin to discuss a topic, they may initially present diametrically opposed positions. Following discussion, each may grow to understand the other's position, and ultimately both may be able to reject their initial positions and accept a broader view that accommodates both of their earlier postures. Hegel viewed thought as unfolding in this dialectical way: An initial *thesis* is proposed, which is subsequently negated by its opposite (called the *antithesis*). Then from a comparison of the two opposing viewpoints, there finally emerges a *synthesis*. Hegel believed that this dialectical process took place in nature and in history as well.

Karl Marx and Friedrich Engels drew heavily from Hegel in specifying their philosophy of "dialectical materialism," the process they argued was inherent in the nature of the material world. They contended that every social system contains its own antithesis, and from the juxtaposition of the system and its opposite will eventually emerge a new form of social organization (a synthesis). Thus, in free-market capitalism there are inevitably greater and greater accumulations of capital until monopolies develop. Marx and Engels concluded that capitalism (the thesis) contains a series of internal contradictions (its antithesis) that would eventually result in the development of a the new social system of communism (a synthesis).

Georgoudi (1985) argues that this dialectical process is important in considering individuals' causal explanations for events. She suggested that different individuals will think about the causes of events in dissimilar ways; some will attribute causes for events to factors internal to the actor or person involved; others will see that external influences play a role; still others will be able to think dialectically and see that internal and external factors are two parts of the same social process that is always unfolding. Thus, according to Georgoudi, a dialectical thinker will see events as caused by an interaction between characteristics of the person involved and elements of the person's past and present situations.

In her experimental study Georgoudi (1985) presented subjects with an event (for example, "A forgot to lock her car. Her stereo was stolen.") and then asked them to rate how important internal causes were, how important external factors were, and how important both factors operating at the same time were. After asking subjects to write two paragraphs to explain the causes of the event and describe why they answered the way they did, she then categorized these written responses into three groups: (1) nondialectical thinking, (2) potentially dialectical thinking, and (3) dialectical thinking. An answer classified as nondialectical included only one cause to the exclusion of others. Events were seen as very simply caused. Answers classified as potentially dialectical thinking might mention more than one cause for a particular event, but one cause was focused on and there was no generation during the written explanation of more novel perspectives to explain the event. Finally, a

Table 5-1   Levels of cognitive complexity

Complexity	Rosenberg	Tetlock	Georgoudi
Low (no explanation or one explanation)	Sequential	Low differentiation/ Low integration	Nondialectical
Moderate (sees potential of two explanations, focuses on one—no interrelationship)	Linear	Moderate differentiation/Low integration	Potentially dialectical
High (sees variety of explanations and relationships among them)	Systematic	High differentiation/ High integration	Dialectical

dialectical-thinking answer entertained two or more possible explanations, with novel and more complex arguments generated from the juxtaposition of the initial causes.

The different approaches to studying cognitive complexity (Rosenberg, Tetlock, Georgoudi) all have some strong similarities, which are summarized in Table 5-1. For a scale of cognitive complexity ranging from low to high, the different levels that each of the theorists suggest are ordered from low to high in the table. There are parallels between each system, although the specific points do not always match directly. Also, there are various intermediate points in Tetlock's approach (such as moderate differentiation/low integration) that are not specifically included in the table, but are nonetheless part of his approach. Figure 5-2 presents an example of political thinking. At what level of complexity would this thinking be judged?

Figure 5-2   An example of political thinking

The following excerpt is from a speech given by Lyndon LaRouche in Manchester, New Hampshire, on January 3, 1988.

"What the President did with Gorbachov was close to treason; that was worse than what Chamberlain did. What Chamberlain did in 1938 with Hitler was bad; it caused World War II. Appeasement of Hitler caused World War II. Reagan's appeasing Gorbachov—and that could cause World War III, or something even worse.

If you don't like war you don't like appeasement! Of course, some people get confused about these things, like the fellow who married a dog, and then found out he didn't have much of a family. The idea would be perfectly fine, but he should have married a wife—not a dog. If you want peace, don't marry appeasement as a way of getting it, you'll get the opposite."

What level of political reasoning (according to Rosenberg, Tetlock, and Georgoudi) does this type of statement reflect?

Source: AP/Wide World Photos

Cognitive Complexity and Explanations for Terrorism

Milburn, Cistuli, and Garr (1988) applied Georgoudi's approach to study the way people think about terrorism. In a survey they presented respondents with descriptions of three acts of political violence (for example, "Ibraham Mohammed Khaled, claiming that he was doing only what any young Palestinian would do, led an attack in the Rome Airport in which thirteen persons died and eighty were wounded, including six Americans"). The authors then asked respondents for their ratings of the importance of internal factors, external factors, and both factors operating at the same time in causing this event; they then asked respondents to explain why they answered the way they did. After categorizing the individuals' responses as nondialectical, potentially dialectical, or dialectical (Table 5-2 provides examples of these types of thinking), they examined the relationship of the type of thinking to the importance ratings that individuals made. Their results are shown in Figure 5-3. As is you can see, when an individual's thinking is more dialectical, he or she sees internal factors as less important and external factors and both internal/external factors at the same time as more important. This is just what Georgoudi (1985) found in her nonpolitical example. In addition, as was expected, the complexity of respondents' thinking about terrorism was significantly related to the respondents' level of education.

While neither Rosenberg nor Tetlock take a specific position on the consistency with which individuals reason at a specific level, their work implies that cognitive complexity is a stable characteristic. In contrast, Georgoudi (1985) argued that the

Table 5-2   Explanations for the Rome Airport massacre

Nondialectical
1. I think he's crazy.
2. He obviously feels that Palestinians were put on the face of this earth to gun down innocent individuals. He doesn't seem to have any motive for his actions.

Potentially dialectical
    When I answered it I thought that it must have an effect on the outcome that he was a Palestinian since the question itself mentioned that he was doing only what any young Palestinian would do. Though now I say that it would take a certain kind of person to commit this act *regardless* of external factors.

Dialectical
    Many persons that act as what they believe to be representative of a "good" citizen of their country, state, whatever, act as a result of not only being brought up to believe such but to have a personality (like an aggressive one) suitable to that action or actions. However, there must exist external factors that spark the whole process to begin with, motivate certain behavior from the individual and strengthen the person's beliefs, no matter how innocent or unrelated the external events seem to an outsider.

Source: Examples from "Survey and experimental studies of the effect of television news on individuals' attributions about terrorism," by M. A. Milburn, B. Cistuli, and M. Garr, p. 10. Paper presented at the 1988 meeting of the International Society of Political Psychology.

Figure 5-3 Results of Milburn, Cistuli, & Garr (1988) study of importance ratings of different factors in explaining perpetrator's actions in the Rome Airport massacre

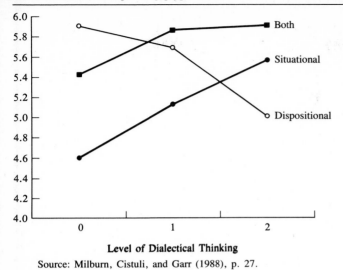

Level of Dialectical Thinking

Source: Milburn, Cistuli, and Garr (1988), p. 27.

level of thinking reflected in individuals' explanations for different events was not consistent; a person might offer a dialectical explanation for one event and a nondialectical explanation for a second event. Georgoudi looked at various chance events (accidents, occurrences, coincidences) and found that different types of events stimulated different amounts of dialectical thinking. There may be specific cues in different situations that either activate or suppress more complex thinking about those specific events. More precisely, complex thinking can be either activated or suppressed, depending upon the presentation and description of events. Evidence from cognitive psychology supports this conclusion.

Pragmatic-Reasoning Schemas

Cheng, Holyoak, Nisbett, and Oliver (1986) studied the effect of training people to reason deductively. Some theorists, including Piaget, have argued that people use general rules of logic that are independent of a particular domain. If this were true, a person would reason at the same level about plumbing and about politics. Others have suggested that individuals develop rules that apply only in the specific domains of their experience (Griggs & Cox, 1982; Manktelow & Evans, 1979; Reich & Ruth, 1982). In contrast to both of these approaches, Cheng and Holyoak (1985) proposed that individuals utilize what they called *pragmatic-reasoning schemas*— rules that are general but are also defined with respect to specific classes of objects and types of relationships. Cheng et al. (1986) found that training a person in the use of a specific deductive rule did not enable the person to solve logical problems any better unless there was some cue that the particular rule was appropriate—that is, unless the particular "reasoning schema" was activated.

This finding parallels Georgoudi's. Individuals will vary in the level of thinking they can bring to different problems, but the same person will also vary in his or her thinking about different problems. Cheng and Holyoak (1985) found that although 60% of their sample solved one problem, only 20% of their sample solved a more abstract but structurally identical problem. Thus, it is not the type of problem per se but specific elements in the description of the problem that activate more or less sophisticated thinking.

The political implications of the activation of pragmatic-reasoning schemas are detailed in the next two chapters. Chapter Six examines the effect of schema activation on cognitive complexity. Chapter Seven provides a concrete example of a political communication that attempts to activate specific types of pragmatic schemas that facilitate attitude change.

■ Conclusion

People vary considerably in the type of reasoning they apply to political issues. Some people reason at only a very low level. They observe events and either are unable to explain them or offer only the simplest or inaccurate kinds of explanations. Others see events as causally related, but the relationships they see involve one factor causing another, without the possibility of interactions or combinations of factors. Finally, there are those individuals, whom Piaget would say have reached the stage of formal operations, who are aware of complex systems of interrelated factors that combine and interact to influence political events.

The same individual does not always utilize the same level of reasoning when considering different issues or problems. This individual variability results from either the presence or the absence of situational cues that stimulate or depress the complexity of individuals' thinking. Rosenberg found considerable consistency in his subjects' reasoning across two different domains, but Cheng et al. found variability. This indicates very strongly that situational cues activate different types of thinking, just as Georgoudi suggested.

As politicians have known for years, the ability to determine the issues is tantamount to victory, and research on the complexity of political reasoning suggests an explanation for this. The way individuals will think about an issue (either as simply or multiply caused) is a function both of the cognitive level at which that person can reason and of the cues the political environment supplies. Politicians most often wish to have citizens think about issues in simple ways (for example, "the issue is communism versus democracy"). Because of the cognitive limitations many individuals have, a simple explanation may be the most effective for persuading them. Also, complex issues are often difficult to communicate in the image-dominated media campaigns that most politicians feel compelled to run. If a simple issue becomes dominant in the minds of a majority of the electorate, it limits the inroads that an opponent's ideas or issues can produce. We will discuss in a later chapter the relationship of the mass media to the complexity of reasoning about political events.

■ ■ ■ ■ ■ ■ ■

CHAPTER
SIX

Political Schemas

The previous chapter began Section Two's consideration of political thinking and public opinion with an analysis of variations in the complexity with which individuals think about politics. We now turn to an examination of cognitive structures and cognitive processes that can influence the complexity level of individuals' political reasoning. We first discuss the cognitive structures that individuals use to organize political and social information. Psychologists call these structures *schemas.* We then examine the effect on individuals' thinking of the activation of these schemas. Research indicates that there is often a reduction of the complexity with which individuals think about politics following activation of political schemas.

The cognitive structures (schemas) individuals possess in relation to politics vary in both the extent of information and the organization of that information. Activation of different schemas has important effects on the complexity with which they think about issues in general and political issues in particular. Psychologists (Tversky & Kahneman, 1974) have identified various "cognitive heuristics"—that is, shortcuts in thinking. The use of these heuristics can result in substantial errors in judgment. I feel that these cognitive heuristics are best understood as a type of pragmatic-reasoning schema, as discussed in the previous chapter. It is thus possible to activate cognitive-information-processing procedures that can either increase the complexity of thinking (Cheng, Holyoak, Nisbett, & Oliver, 1986) or reduce it.

As Fishbein and Ajzen's (1975) model indicates, a person's attitude toward a specific issue is a function of beliefs. These beliefs are structured into that individual's specific knowledge schemas. Which particular schema is activated or accessed thus has important consequences for opinions and for the complexity of thinking.

■ The Schema Concept

Recent work in cognitive psychology has been strongly influenced by Bartlett's (1932) insights into memory processes. Early models of memory—such as those proposed by Ebbinghaus (1885/1964)—suggested that memories were built up through repeated associations of different stimuli. In contrast, Bartlett (1932) proposed that rather than simply operating associatively, memory and cognition are organized in specific thematic structures, which he called *schemas*. This view suggests that when an individual obtains new information, specific cognitive schemas filter, select, encode, and integrate it into new or existing cognitive structures.

Additionally, schemas influence information retrieval. The processing of information from the environment involves selectivity, because we cannot attend to all the information and stimuli to which we are exposed (Broadbent, 1958; Miller, 1956). This selectivity does not occur at random but is influenced by cognitive structures that aid in the perception of social and nonsocial information. These cognitive structures provide criteria for selecting information and guidelines for processing that information. Fiske and Taylor (1984) provide a comprehensive review of recent applications of these cognitive processes to the understanding of social perception and cognition.

Fiske and Taylor (1984) discuss four different types of schemas: person, self, role, and event. Person schemas include information about traits of specific persons or typical people, or goals that influence those individuals' behavior. Self-schemas contain information about a person's own appearance, behavior, and self-concept. Role schemas hold knowledge about general social classifications such as age, race, sex, or occupations; and event schemas include information about different situations such as restaurant visits and social gatherings. Research tends to focus on individual types of schemas, but the ways schemas influence memory and social perception appear very similar for each of the different schemas.

Person Schemas

Person schemas contain knowledge and beliefs about typical people, their characteristics, and their intentions. For example, Zadny and Gerard (1974) investigated the effects of presenting a particular person schema containing goal-related information on individuals' recall. The experimenters showed subjects a film of two people walking through an apartment talking about different objects and aspects of the rooms. When they told subjects that the title of the film was *Drug Bust,* the subjects recalled much more information consistent with a drug bust than they did when they were told the film was titled *Larceny*. An important factor influencing recall was the timing of the schema activation. When the label was applied before the subjects watched the film, the experimenters obtained much larger retrieval differences of schema-consistent information than when the label was presented after viewing the film. An initial presentation can influence both the encoding of information and the retrieval of it, but presentation of the label following the stimulus material can only influence recall of the information. As Anderson and Pichert (1978) also demonstrated, the perspective with which one reads (or views) a story influences significantly the details that one recalls.

These results make understandable one reason for the effectiveness of the Bush campaign in the 1988 presidential election. Members of the Bush campaign began applying the "liberal" label to Dukakis in the very early stages of the campaign.

Their goal was to define Dukakis for the U.S. electorate, and they succeeded very well. Many people—particularly those who are, in Free and Cantril's (1967) terms, ideologically conservative—have schemas of liberals as soft on crime, soft on defense, and big on tax and spend. Bush's campaign succeeded in activating these beliefs about liberals. Dukakis did not really respond to this definition of himself until very late in the campaign (October). Consequently, when he eventually tried to influence the meaning of the label, claiming he was a liberal in the tradition of Roosevelt, Truman, and Kennedy, he was unsuccessful in shifting the negativity associated with the label.

The struggle to invoke a defining image of one's opponents is a constant theme in politics. Sometimes politicians get a little carried away. Consider this observation in September 1989 from John Buckley, the spokesman for the National Republican Committee, when the Democrats had called for an increase in taxes on the wealthiest Americans: "The Democrats are the party that can't help themselves when it comes to taxes. The pathology at work is similar to that of the serial killer's need to keep committing his murders" (Robinson, 1989, p. 21).

In an application of social cognition theory to the domain of politics, Fiske (1982) describes two studies that sought to identify the information in individuals' person schemas of politicians. In an initial study, she chose 50 photographs from the *Almanac of American Politics* and had undergraduates separate them into piles and label them. The most frequent piles used, just looking at the faces and knowing that they were Congress members, were *conservative, crook,* and *Honest Abe.* In a second study Fiske selected four faces and labeled them as either a *person* or a *politician.* She then had subjects evaluate the persons in the photographs on a good/bad scale. Fiske found that when labeled as *politicians* two of the faces had significantly lower evaluative ratings than when labeled as *persons.* For the other two photographs, there was no difference. An examination of the photographs revealed that subjects rated the two people who looked stereotypically like politicians lower when they were introduced as politicians. Fiske concluded that there are clear affective consequences to the use of various political categories or schemas when evaluating political stimuli.

Self-Schemas

Markus (1977) proposed the concept of a *self-schema,* a hierachically organized knowledge and belief structure relevant to the self. She suggested that on a particular dimension an individual might be either "schematic" or "aschematic." On a dimension such as *independence,* individuals who are schematic would see themselves as highly independent or highly dependent; people who are aschematic would see this dimension as irrelevant for their self-description. Research has shown that people recognize information related to their self-schema faster and with more confidence than material unrelated to their self-schema. Researchers have applied the self-schema concept in a variety of domains, particularly to cognitive models of depression (Beck, Rush, & Shaw, 1979; Hammen, Miklowitz, & Dyck, 1986; Ruehlman, West, and Pasahow, 1985; Segal, 1988).

An important part of individuals' political schemas is the extent to which they view themselves in ideological terms. Using Markus's concept of self-schema, Milburn (1987) classified individuals who saw themselves as either highly liberal or highly conservative as "ideologically self-schematic." Those who were not ideological in their self-descriptions he classified as "ideologically aschematic." Schematics were able to recall more information about liberal and conservative issues than were ideological aschematics. These results indicated that there is a relationship between individuals' ideological self-definitions and their ability to access information about liberals and conservatives.

Role Schemas

Schemas influence the way individuals process social information. Bem (1981) has argued that some people are gender schematic; they have extensive beliefs about sex differences, and they pay particular attention to gender-related information. As an example of the effects of role schemas on attention, encoding, and recall, Cohen (1981) presented subjects with videotapes of a woman whose appearance and behavior were balanced for waitress and librarian characteristics. When Cohen told subjects that they were watching a librarian, they recalled significantly more information consistent with the woman being a librarian. The same consistency was found when the woman was introduced as a waitress. Subjects also made recall errors in a systematic way. After they watched the videotape, subjects incorrectly remembered various characteristics that weren't there but that *were* consistent with the stereotype (waitress or librarian) of the woman that Cohen had suggested. In social cognition terms, the subjects recalled characteristics that were consistent with the schema that had been initially activated.

Political Schemas

Various political schemas have been identified as important. Lau (1986) used responses to the University of Michigan's National Election Study (NES) surveys and found he could identify four different political schemas used by respondents: issues, groups, personality, and party. Individual respondents tended to use the same schemas when evaluating different political objects, and these schemas were predictive of respondents' voting behavior. Hamill, Lodge, and Blake (1985) also investigated individuals' use of different political schemas. They identified three different schemas that individuals might use to view the political world: a class schema (rich/poor), a partisan schema (Democrat/Republican), and an ideological schema (liberal/conservative). Hamill et al. found that those individuals who held a particular political schema were more accurate in their analysis of issues relevant to that area. For example, those respondents holding a class schema were more accurate in judging Ronald Reagan's positions on economic policy questions than on noneconomic issues.

■ Schema Accessibility: Expert-Novice Differences

Research on social information processing suggests that the accessibility of constructs (specific categories of information) plays an important role in social perception (Bargh & Pietromonaco, 1982; Bargh & Thein, 1985; Higgins & King, 1981). The accessibility of a construct varies in two ways: (1) between individuals (that is, chronic differences exist) and (2) between situations (that is, accessibility can be manipulated). A number of studies have indicated that the accessibility of social constructs differs among individuals (Dornbusch, Hastorf, Richardson, Muzzy, & Vreeland, 1965; Higgins & King, 1981; Markus, 1977).

Individuals vary in the accessibility of the constructs *liberal* and *conservative*, their ideological schemas. Although these are most appropriately viewed as independent constructs, evidence suggests that individuals have about the same amount of information pertaining to liberals as they do about conservatives. When subjects were asked to "tell me everything that comes into your mind when you think about a liberal," Milburn (1987) found that the number of issue positions the person could recall, the number of personal qualities a person could remember, and the amount of time spent elaborating thoughts about liberals were all significantly correlated with the answers to the same question about conservatives. Thus, subjects tended to spend about the same amount of time trying to recall information about liberals and conservatives, and the number of liberal-issue positions they remembered was very similar to the number of conservative-issue positions they recalled.

Differences between schematics and aschematics (either ideological or partisan) appear to reflect individual differences in political sophistication. In the previous chapter we discussed Converse's (1964) research that found differences in the structure of the belief systems of the mass public and political elites, and we considered research that illustrated important differences in the way different groups of people *reason* about politics (Rosenberg, 1988a, 1988b). Differences in the consistency of individuals' attitudes and the way they think about politics reflect differences in the structure and elaboration of the political schemas individuals have available.

Research indicates that there are substantial differences in the way "experts" and "novices" in a particular area store and process information. Experts tend to have considerably more information in a particular domain than do novices. Somewhat paradoxically, they are able to retrieve it and use it more quickly than novices, despite having more information to search through (Reder & Anderson, 1980; Smith, Adams, & Schoor, 1978). This greater efficiency appears to result from differences in the organization of knowledge, what Chase and Simon (1973) referred to as "chunking" (grouping together related pieces) of information.

Researchers have found differences in the quantity and organization of knowledge content held by experts and novices in physics (Larkin, McDermott, Simon, & Simon, 1980), algebra (Hinsley, Hayes, & Simon, 1977), geometry (Neves & Anderson, 1981), and dinosaurs (Chi & Koeske, 1983). Chase and Simon (1973) demonstrated these kinds of differences between expert and novice chess players. By storing information about different positions in larger chunks, expert players are able to recognize and react to different situations much more quickly. Chase and Simon showed different positions to chess players at three different levels (grand master, class A master, and novice) and asked them to recall the positions. The grand master's recall was two times as accurate as the master's, and both were significantly better than the novice's. Revealingly, when beginning to reconstruct the positions, the grand master put more pieces on the board before stopping than did the other players, suggesting that the information was being accessed in bigger chunks.

Research on political information processing reveals similar differences to those between novice and expert chess players. Fiske, Kinder, and Larter (1983) focused on the processing of consistent and inconsistent political information. Because of the presumably superior information-processing capacity that political experts should have for political information, the authors hypothesized that political novices would be more likely to neglect inconsistent information, since it is more difficult to integrate into an existing schema (Brewer, Dull, & Lui, 1981; Hastie, 1980). Fiske et al. (1983) divided their subjects in expert and novice categories by using a variety of measures of political participation, interest, and media attention. They then presented their subjects with a description of a fictitious country (Mauritius) that was characterized as either a democratic country, a communist country, or neither. This portrayal of the style of government was intended to introduce a particular "set" with which to perceive the additional information.

The description also included statements that were both consistent and inconsistent with the initial portrayal—for instance, "An open and free press keeps Mauritian citizens informed about national events and about what is going on in the government" and "Mauritians generally do not speak out in opposition to the government. Dissenters sometimes end up in jail or get sent to hard labor camps." The first statement would be consistent with an initial characterization of the country as democratic, and the second statement would be inconsistent; for an initial description of the country as communist, the first statement would be inconsistent and the second would be consistent. Fiske et al. then asked their subjects to recall as many facts as they could in 5 minutes. As the authors had predicted, they found that the pattern of recall was very different for different subjects: Novices remembered more consistent than inconsistent information, and the experts showed the opposite pattern, recalling more inconsistent facts. Additionally, Fiske et al. found that the experts organized the information differently than the novices as they processed it.

Lau and Erber (1985) utilized survey data to examine differences between those with high and low political expertise. They found that experts tended to have more stable and consistent attitudes and that experts used a higher number of issues to evaluate presidential candidates (Carter, Reagan, and Kennedy in 1980), again suggesting a higher level of knowledge and a different type of organization. Fiske and Dyer (1985) have found differences in the accessibility of schema-relevant and schema-irrelevant information for experts and novices.

■ Schema Activation

Effects of Schema Activation on Schema Accessibility

There are differences among people in the amount and organization of specific information in such domains as a particular person, a type of person, or an event. In addition, various aspects of a situation will influence the accessibility of different schematically organized information. These include recency of activation (Higgins, Rholes, and Jones, 1977), the motivation of subjects (Cohen & Ebbesen, 1979), subjects' expectations, and the frequency of activation of the specific construct (Higgins, Kuiper, & Olson, 1981). A person's obvious external characteristics such as sex, age, and race are likely to activate observers' schemas and stereotypes related to these attributes (Herman, Zanna, & Higgins, 1986; Jones et al, 1984). Environmental information may also activate relevant schemas. After watching a beauty pageant on TV, a person would be more likely to react to someone in gender or sexual terms than after watching a political debate. Higgins et al. (1977) found that the prior activation of a trait category will increase its accessibility and "prime" (activate) related trait categories.

Milburn (1987) investigated the effect individuals' schemas have upon the consistency of their expressed political attitudes. This study focused on the effects of a specific hypothesized schema: an ideological (liberal/conservative) schema. The primary hypothesis tested in this particular study was that the consistency of individuals' responses to attitude questions (such as "Should the government guarantee each citizen a job, or should people get ahead on their own?") would be increased by first getting them to think in ideological terms (referred to as "schema activation"). This was done by using "cued free recall" (Taylor & Fiske, 1981)— that is, asking them to state everything that came into their mind when they thought of "a liberal" and when they thought of "a conservative." This hypothesis was supported, but only for subjects who were classified as ideologically self-schematic—that is, those who described themselves on the extreme ends of a 7-point liberal/conservative self-rating scale—or who, using an adjective checklist, described themselves with adjectives that other independent raters had judged to be characteristic of liberals or conservatives.

Milburn (1987) found one unexpected result: When schematics were separated from aschematics, using the adjective checklist, the average correlation between attitude items for aschematics was lower in the activation condition than in the nonactivation condition. As predicted, the average correlation between the attitude questions was higher for schematics following activation of the ideological schema than without activation. Thus, after subjects spent time thinking about liberals and conservatives (activating the ideological schema), subjects who tended to define themselves in ideological terms had higher correlations between their opinions than did those who did not go through the schema activation process. Additionally, the nonideological subjects evidenced lower consistency between their attitudes following schema activation. This suggests that when activated, the somewhat idiosyncratic (and non-issue-oriented) information contained in aschematics' schemas of liberals and conservatives influenced expression of less ideologically consistent attitudes.

This finding paralleled the results of Sharp and Lodge (1985). They told one group of subjects to rate how characteristically liberal or conservative a number of political leaders, groups, and policies were. A second group rated the same political referents on how characteristic they were for the Democratic and Republican parties. This liberal/conservative rating closely resembles the schema activation manipulation used by Milburn (1987), but the partisan rating activates a different schema. Sharp and Lodge (1985) then separated their subjects into low and high political sophistication groups similar to Milburn's (1987) schematic/aschematic division. They found that the high sophistication subjects had a higher average correlation among their attitudes after doing the ideological rating than after rating with the partisan categories. This result is comparable to Milburn's (1987) finding that his ideological schematics increased in the consistency of their political attitudes following activation of their ideological schema. Sharp and Lodge's less politically sophisticated subjects showed the opposite pattern. This indicates that the differences between political sophisticates' and novices' information storage and retrieval (the schemas they have available to access) affect the consistency of the attitudes they express. This is particularly true when schemas are activated prior to individuals' attitude reports.

Lodge and Hamill (1986) found important differences in political information processing between individuals with and without what they called a "partisan" schema—for instance, knowledge related to the U.S. Democratic and Republican parties. This included information about prominent politicians belonging to the two parties and about platform positions. Lodge and Hamill differentiated their subjects into three groups on the basis of a series of questions derived from the University of Michigan's NES Surveys that measured interest and knowledge about parties and elections. The authors labeled the third of their sample scoring highest on the interest/knowledge scale as *schematics,* and the bottom third was labeled as *aschematic;* they also included an unlabeled middle group. Lodge and Hamill's (1986) use of *schematic/aschematic* in this case differs from the usual definition.

Lodge and Hamill (1986) then had their subjects read a fictitious biography of a "Congressman Williams," along with a series of statements attributed to him. To half of the subjects, the authors described Williams as a Democrat; to the other half they described him as a Republican. The statements were either consistent or inconsistent with individuals' partisan schemas; for example, "A policy consistent with the Republican party label is 'Congressman Williams calls for major cuts in federal spending on social programs,' whereas an inconsistent Republican policy stand is 'Congressman Williams favors federal government programs to create more jobs'" (p. 510).

After a distraction task, Lodge and Hamill then tested subjects' recall of the policy statements. As you might expect, they found that schematics recalled more of the information overall than did the aschematics. Schematics have some existing knowledge structure with which to integrate new information; aschematics do not. Of more interest, however, are the authors' findings about the types of errors made by the partisan schematics. Schematics were no different than aschematics in recall accuracy for policy statements that were inconsistent with the congressman's party affiliation; actually, their recall was slightly less accurate. Presumably, these statements were inconsistent with the schematics' partisan schemas. Apparently, the politically sophisticated schematics were susceptible to a specific type of cognitive error: While processing information under direction of their partisan schema, they recalled more consistent information than actually was presented.

Schema Activation and Emotion

The activation of a particular schema also has emotional effects. Fiske (1981, 1982) refers to this as a "schema-triggered affect." An individual's schema may have emotional associations with it—for example, the person schema related to a particular ethnic group, Asians. Activation of that schema after meeting a person and categorizing him or her as a member of that social group will activate the person's emotional associations with that ethnic group. This is an important aspect of the process of stereotyping.

Schema Activation and Cognitive Complexity

Consistent with these findings that schemas can result in specific cognitive errors, the results of a recent study (Milburn & Fay-Dumaine, 1988) indicate that the activation of political schemas can also reduce the *complexity* of the thinking that individuals utilize in evaluating political stimuli. Milburn and Fay-Dumaine (1988) used the Milburn (1987) ideological schema activation manipulation and assessed its effect on subjects' cognitive complexity (the integration and differentiation measures employed by Tetlock [1986]). The results are displayed in Figures 6-1 and 6-2) (Milburn & Fay-Dumaine, 1988). As is apparent, in the control (nonactivation) condition, the ideological schematics (those who defined themselves on the extreme ends of a 7-point liberal/conservative self-rating scale *and* who said that the dimension was important for understanding their beliefs) were more complex than the aschematics in their statements explaining their positions on three issues. When the liberal/conservative schema was activated, however, the complexity of the schematics' thinking was significantly reduced ($p < .05$ for differentiation; $p = .06$ for integration). The complexity of the aschematics was lower in both conditions.

This study suggests an explanation for Rosenberg's (1987) and Tetlock's (1984) conflicting findings, discussed in Chapter Five, about the relationship of ideological self-identification and cognitive complexity. Rosenberg found that those who are more complex in their thinking are more extreme in their ideological self-description; Tetlock found the more ideologically extreme members of his elite sample *less* complex in their thinking. When their subjects did not spend time thinking about liberals and conservatives (the nonactivation condition), Milburn and

Figure 6-1 Mean differentiation of subjects' political thinking on three policy questions (Milburn & Fay-Dumaine, 1988)

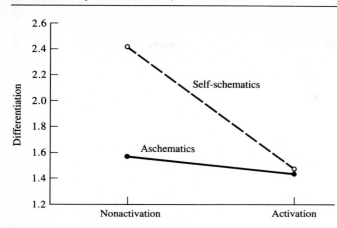
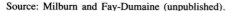

Source: Milburn and Fay-Dumaine (unpublished).

Fay-Dumaine (1988) found that those who were more ideologically extreme (the schematics) were higher in cognitive complexity than those less ideologically extreme. This finding is consistent with Rosenberg's findings. Then what about Tetlock's findings? When the politically sophisticated (schematics) in Milburn and Fay-Dumaine's experiment spent time thinking about liberals and conservatives (the activation condition), the complexity of their thinking decreased. This parallels the lower complexity of Tetlock's extreme groups compared with the moderate socialists. Tetlock's results are from political elites rather than ordinary people, so his

Figure 6-2 Mean integration of subjects' political thinking on three policy questions (Milburn & Fay-Dumaine, 1988)

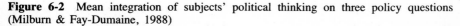
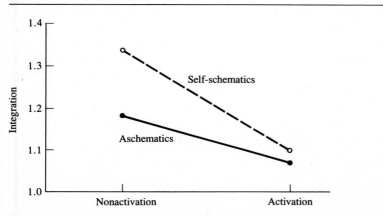

Source: Milburn and Fay-Dumaine (unpublished).

findings can't really predict the complexity of politically unsophisticated individuals. The aschematics in Milburn and Fay-Dumaine's study would almost certainly be less complex in their thinking than the moderate socialist M.P.s that Tetlock studied.

It appears that what Chaiken (1980) called "heuristic processing" takes place following activation of individuals' liberal/conservative schema. The operation of cognitive heuristics is detailed in the next section.

■ Cognitive Heuristics

The simplification in thinking that some schemas appear to produce suggests that they are operating as what Tversky and Kahneman (1974) called "heuristics," or shortcuts for making judgments. Tversky and Kahneman demonstrated that systematic biases and errors in decision-making processes result from use of cognitive heuristics. The authors proposed three different kinds of heuristics: representativeness, the law of small numbers, and availability. These cognitive procedures provide clues to some of the major successes of the Bush campaign for the presidency in 1988. These heuristics can be viewed as types of what Cheng et al. (1986) have called pragmatic reasoning schemas, as discussed in the previous chapter.

Representativeness

Tversky and Kahneman (1974) suggest that individuals use the representativeness heuristic to address the question "What is the probability that object A belongs to class B?" They argue that people make this judgment on the basis of the similarity of A to other objects in class B, regardless of any baseline information. For example, the following description is given: "Steve is very shy and withdrawn, invariably helpful, but with little interest in people, or in the world of reality. A meek and tidy soul, he has a need for order and structure, and a passion for detail." Tversky and Kahneman suggest that if people are asked what the probability is that Steve is either a farmer, salesman, airline pilot, librarian, or physician, they will generally answer that he is a librarian, despite the fact that there are a great many more farmers than librarians in the country. People do this because the description of Steve matches the stereotype that they hold of librarians; that is, his characteristics are *representative* of librarians.

Law of Small Numbers

Tversky and Kahneman's (1974) law of small numbers reflects a similar disregard for probabilistic information. A study of experienced research psychologists found that scientists tended to believe that results based on very small samples were representative of the populations from which they were drawn, despite the considerable possibility of error. The authors suggested that this reflects a human tendency to believe results obtained from small samples.

Availability

A third bias in cognitive processes that Tversky and Kahneman (1974) proposed is the availability heuristic. They argued that individuals make judgments about the likelihood of different events on the basis of how easy it is to bring instances of that event to mind. For example, if people are asked whether there are more words with the letter *r* in the first position (at the start of the word, such as in *ride*) or in the third position (such as in *car*), they generally will estimate that the first-position words are more likely even though words with consonants like *k* or *r* in the third position are much more frequent. Tversky and Kahneman explain this result in terms of the effectiveness of a search set: Words are much more easily recalled by the first letter than by the third letter—that is, they are much more *available*. Hence, people will have easier access to them and believe there are more of them.

Kahneman and Tversky (1984) have found similar context effects on individuals' choices related to decisions involving risks of losses or gains. When an outcome is framed in terms of a *gain*, people are "risk averse"; that is, they will favor sure things to risks. But if the identical outcome is presented as a loss, people will prefer a risky decision. For example, a situation can be presented to subjects with a series of alternatives from which to choose. The situation is that 600 people are expected to die from a new Asian disease. Subjects can then be given a choice between two programs: one that would save 200 lives, or one that had a one-third probability of saving 600 people and a two-thirds chance of not saving anyone. For these alternatives, people will prefer the sure thing. If, however, the same two alternatives are described in terms of losses—a program in which 400 people will die, or one in which there is a one-third chance of no one dying and a two-thirds chance of 600 people dying—people will prefer the riskier choice.

Political Implications of Cognitive Heuristics

These heuristic biases—the tendency to ignore baseline data and rely on representativeness, the belief in the validity of results from very small samples, and the inclination to make judgments on the basis of the ease with which similar events can be recalled—all suggest that in a political campaign one vivid example will be more important than a great number of statistics. The Bush campaign's use of the Willie Horton case in the 1988 presidential election demonstrates this quite well.

Several years before this election, the Corrections Department in Massachusetts had a program that released first-degree murderers from jail on furloughs. Willie Horton was such a prisoner. He had been out on nine weekend furloughs and had returned; on the tenth one, he did not. Several months later in Maryland, he terrorized a young couple, stabbing the husband and raping his wife. Governor Dukakis ended the furlough program after this incident, but it would become an important issue in the later presidential race.

The Bush campaign produced a television ad called the "revolving door" ad. The spot (shot at Utah State Prison) suggested that if Michael Dukakis were elected president, prisons would have revolving doors and murderers and rapists would routinely be released to prey further on society. It was a powerful ad with very vivid, frightening images that millions of voters across the country saw.

What was Dukakis's response? Initially, nothing. He reportedly felt that the electorate would not believe this implication, which he regarded as a complete distortion of his record. After considerable damage to his support—his standing in the polls dropped from 18 points ahead of Bush to ten points behind—he responded to the Willie Horton ad with statistics and verbal explanations. He argued that Massachusetts had one of the lowest murder rates in the nation. He observed that when Ronald Reagan was governor of California, there was a furlough program, and two prisoners released from prison through that program murdered a school-teacher and a policeman. He noted that Vice President Bush had given a presidential award to a halfway house in Houston called New Directions *after* one inmate left the house and raped and murdered a minister's wife (*Boston Globe*, October 10, 1988, p. 10). None of these responses had any effect on Dukakis' declining popularity.

The Bush campaign made extremely effective use of powerful images that served to activate negative emotions (see the earlier discussion of the schema-triggered affect), to simplify voters' thinking, and (from a Democratic perspective) to facilitate cognitive errors. The Willie Horton case was only a single example, but the law of small numbers suggests that people are willing to believe that results from small samples are valid. These images were much more available than dry statistics, so when voters were asked to say who they felt would be more effective in fighting crime, polls indicated that Bush was the overwhelming choice. An ABC poll, conducted on the day of the election (November 8), found that the issue of prison furloughs was the one that voters listed as very important in their choice of candidate George Bush over Michael Dukakis: 83% of Bush voters listed this as very important, compared with 78% for the pledge of allegiance, 74% for the death penalty, and 55% for abortion (*Boston Globe*, November 9, 1988, p. 17).

In addition to the political application of heuristics that Tversky and Kahneman (1974) described, a political application is possible from the Kahneman and Tversky (1984) analysis about decision making under risk. As detailed above, the authors found that when choices were presented as gains, people favored the option with no risk; but when alternatives were phrased in terms of losses, individuals preferred the riskier alternative.

For the 1988 presidential campaign, would it be more appropriate to describe the situation facing voters as a choice between two positive alternatives (gains) or a choice between two negative alternatives (losses)? Given that the media dubbed the two contenders as the "wimp" and the "shrimp," and that there was nearly universal agreement that the contest was one of the most negative presidential campaigns on record, it is fair to say that the public in general perceived the election as a choice between two losses. In the choice between Bush and Dukakis, was one perceived as a sure loss and the other as a risk? As indicated above, Bush's campaign was very effective in suggesting that if Dukakis were to become president, the nation would be overrun with criminals on furlough and patriotism would be absent from the White House. And what was the picture that emerged about what a Bush presidency would be like? A blurred one, at best. Bush's campaign focused very successfully on Dukakis's negatives and presented little or no agenda of Bush's own. Thus, of the two alternatives, one could characterize them as a fairly certain loss (Dukakis) and a sizable risk (Bush). Bush's Iran-Contra involvement, his image as a wimp, and his pronouncement about a "kinder and gentler nation" suggested a risky but potentially better leader to the electorate. Kahneman and Tversky's (1984) model predicts that in the case of a choice between two losses, risk is preferred, and that is just the alternative that a majority of the American people selected.

■ Conclusion

The schema concept provides a conceptual framework for understanding both belief/knowledge structures and problem-solving heuristics. Activation of either type of schema has an important effect on individuals' processing of social and political information. Very often, activation of political schemas results in decreased complexity of political thinking. Just as the advertising industry has learned over the years to activate consumers' schemas about youth, success, excitement, and fear, so now have some political media specialists begun to utilize the same techniques.

As the 1988 campaign so powerfully demonstrated, the mass media can be used to activate political schemas that can either stimulate or depress the complexity of viewers' political thinking, just as Bennett (1980) suggested in his situational perspective on public opinion. In Chapter Nine we will examine the influence of the media's activation of political schemas. In the next two chapters we discuss various theories of attitude change that also prepare us for an examination of mass media effects.

Theories of Persuasion and Opinion Change

CHAPTER
SEVEN

Belief Consistency

In the first section of this book, we examined the effect of background characteristics and personality differences on public opinion. In Section Two, we considered differences between individuals in the cognitive complexity of their thinking about political issues and the cognitive structures (schemas) that individuals use to process political information. In Section Three (the following three chapters), we consider various social psychological theories of attitude change, how they can be applied to an understanding of the process of political opinion change, and the role of the mass media in influencing public opinion.

How do people maintain their support for a president they voted for when the president does something they completely disagree with—for example, trading arms for hostages? In Chapter Two we discussed the Fishbein and Ajzen model of the relationship between beliefs and attitudes. Their model would predict that an individual would perform a belief calculus, summing the negative and positive beliefs about a candidate to obtain a resulting attitude. But what if a person holds both highly positive and highly negative beliefs about a president's performance? How does a person integrate this information? Social psychological models of cognitive consistency provide an approach to this question.

In this chapter, we examine three different and influential approaches to cognitive consistency: Fritz Heider's balance theory, Leon Festinger's theory of cognitive dissonance, and Robert Abelson's modes of resolution of belief dilemmas. These theories vary in the complexity of the process they propose that individuals use to resolve inconsistency among their beliefs. Balance theory and dissonance theory are fairly simple, suggesting that individuals change a single cognition to restore balance or consistency to an individual's cognitive structure. Robert Abelson has been one of the foremost proponents of consistency theory, editing the comprehensive *Theories of Cognitive Consistency: A Sourcebook* (Abelson et al., 1968). Abelson has proposed a variety of different ways that individuals deal with inconsistencies, what he calls "belief dilemmas." In order to demonstrate the usefulness of cognitive consistency models for understanding political communication, we conclude this chapter with an analysis of a specific political speech, utilizing Abelson's proposed modes of belief dilemma resolution. The subject is

President Ronald Reagan's address to the nation following the release of the Tower Board report on the Iran-Contra affair.

■ Balance Theory

Fritz Heider (1958) proposed one of the earliest social psychological models of belief consistency: balance theory. He hypothesized that people prefer a balanced set of relationships among their cognitions about specific objects or individuals. His model involved *triads* of elements and relationships, with each relationship having a *valence*, either a positive or a negative cognition between objects (*valence* being a term borrowed from chemistry denoting the positive or negative charge of a particle). Heider proposed that individuals will prefer that the pattern of relationships be in balance. For example:

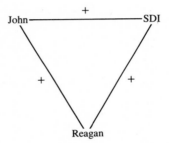

If John likes President Reagan (a + relationship), and John perceives that Reagan feels very positively toward the Strategic Defense Initiative (SDI; also called "Star Wars"), then balance theory would predict that John would also be positively oriented toward SDI.

Relationships between objects can also be negative. For example:

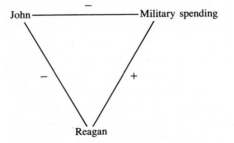

If John is opposed to military spending in general, and he perceives that President Reagan supports large increases in the military budget, then balance theory would predict that John would have a negative attitude toward Reagan. The general rule for determining a balanced triad is that there be an odd number of positive relationships, either one or three.

Although the balance theory approach to the structure of attitudes has some appeal, there are important limitations to its application. When fear or hatred is involved (very strong negative attitudes), individuals' cognitions may persist as imbalanced. For example:

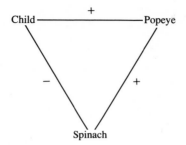

A child may feel very positively toward the cartoon character Popeye, and he or she may also be aware that Popeye likes canned spinach very much, but the child may also be able to tolerate the imbalance and be persistent in his or her own intense dislike of spinach. In fact, when I was a child, I had no trouble maintaining this imbalanced triad myself.

A second situation in which the balance theory prediction may not hold is one where there are two strongly held beliefs that contradict each other. For example:

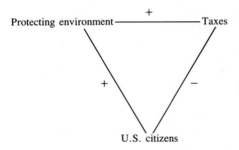

There is generally a high level of support for protecting the environment (Hart & Teeter, 1990): 80% of respondents in a national survey favored strong environmental protection laws, even when those laws resulted in higher prices. At the same time, voters consistently opposed tax increases, even though the costs of environmental cleanup are staggeringly high.

A situation in recent political history suggests additional limitations of the balance theory approach. Prior to the November 1986 revelations about the Reagan administration's policy of selling arms to Iran, most citizens held the following balanced triad:

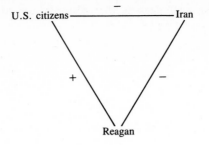

Ever since the Iranian hostage crisis, Iran has been one of the most negatively regarded countries in the world (in a U.S. poll Iran replaced the Soviet Union as the greatest threat to peace in the world). Reagan often made use of this and spoke very negatively about Iran and its leaders. Reagan's popularity was extremely high among U.S. citizens.

Everything changed (or should have, according to balance theory) after November 1988. Reagan's selling arms to Iran made it clear that he was not the implacable foe of Iran that he had claimed to be. Although he was not perceived as a supporter of Iran, he still engaged in behaviors that supported the current regime. This resulted in the following imbalanced triad:

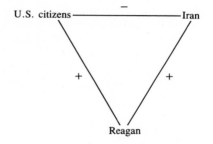

To bring this triad into balance, citizens would either have had to change their attitude toward Iran to a positive one (very unlikely) or change their attitude toward President Reagan to a negative one. A number of them did so (his popularity dropped from 65% to 40%), but a considerable number of people continued to state that they thought he was doing a good job. Balance theory is at a loss to account for this inconsistent pattern of balanced and imbalanced relationships. We shall see in the final section of this chapter how Abelson's modes of resolution of belief dilemmas provide a way of understanding how individuals deal with this type of cognitive inconsistency.

■ Cognitive Dissonance Theory

One of the most influential theories in social psychology during the 1960s and 1970s, stimulating more research than any other attitude change theory, was Leon

Festinger's (1957) theory of cognitive dissonance. Festinger proposed that when a person held two inconsistent cognitions, he or she would experience an uncomfortable state he labeled "cognitive dissonance." Festinger hypothesized that this discomfort motivates the individual to reduce dissonance by altering one of the cognitions.

The Original Demonstration of Dissonance

Festinger originally demonstrated this effect (Festinger & Carlsmith, 1959) by giving subjects a boring task to do. The authors asked subjects to turn repeatedly a series of round pegs set into holes in a board. Then they asked subjects to tell another subject—actually, a confederate (a person who is pretending to be a subject but is actually working for the experimenter)—that it was a fun, interesting experiment. Two conditions existed: The experimenter told subjects either that he could pay them $1 or that he could pay them $20. Virtually all subjects complied with his request to describe the tedious task as if it were interesting (that is, they engaged in counterattitudinal behavior). Festinger and Carlsmith assessed subjects' attitudes toward the task, and they found a significant difference between those who were paid $1 amd those who were paid $20. Consistent with the dissonance theory prediction, but opposite to what most people predict, the subjects who were paid $1 to lie about the experiment reported enjoying the experiment more than did the subjects who were paid $20.

Festinger and Carlsmith (1959) explained this result in the context of cognitive dissonance theory. The subjects in both conditions engaged in a behavior that was inconsistent with their (supposed) attitudes: After participating in a very boring task, they told someone the task was interesting. How could subjects reconcile these two conflicting cognitions? Subjects in the $20 condition had a clear reason: "They paid me $20 to say it was interesting." The participants in the $1 condition had no such justification for their behavior, so consistent with the dissonance theory prediction, subjects in the $1 condition reported liking the task significantly more than did the subjects in the $20 condition.

Additional Aspects of Dissonance

Festinger (1957) proposed that people experience dissonance as an uncomfortable internal mental state. In fact, researchers have demonstrated physiological effects of dissonance. Gerard (1967) found that when subjects experienced dissonance created by having to choose between two attractive alternatives, their blood vessels constricted in the outer part of the body, a typical stress reaction.

People experience dissonance effects in a wide variety of situations. A typical dissonance situation involves a person engaging in a counterattitudinal behavior, so that a potential for dissonance occurs between the person's attitude and his or her inconsistent behavior. Dissonance occurs only when there is no external justification for the behavior (Freedman, 1963). This helps explain the nonintuitive findings generated in the Festinger and Carlsmith (1959) experiment (less positive attitudes toward the task in the $20 condition than in the $1 condition). Linder, Cooper, and Jones (1967) found that this effect exists only if the individual feels free not to comply with the request to engage in the counterattitudinal behavior.

Linder et al. (1967) picked a behavior that they knew the vast majority of students opposed as being a restriction of free speech: to write an essay in favor of banning certain speakers from their campus. The experimenters then told one group of volunteers that they were free to write the essay or not: "The decision to perform the task will be entirely your own." A second group was led to believe that there was no choice: "I want to explain to you what this task that you have volunteered for is all about" (Linder et al., 1967, p. 248). Subjects who were paid 50¢ experienced more attitude change than those paid $2.50 only in the free-choice condition (paralleling the Festinger and Carlsmith results). Subjects who did not perceive that they had a choice changed their attitudes more when they were paid more.

The Importance of Personal Responsibility

An additional key element in the arousal of dissonance in an individual is that the individual feels personal responsibility for some negative consequences that occur as a result of his or her actions (Greenwald & Ronis, 1978; Wicklund & Brehm, 1976). Nel, Helmreich, and Aronson (1969) demonstrated this in an experiment that induced subjects to give a counterattitudinal speech (arguing for the legalization of marijuana). Nel et al. (1969) varied the group to which subjects believed the videotape of their speech would be shown: a group of students that already favored legalization, a group that opposed legalization, or a group that was undecided.

The experimenters reasoned that the potential negative consequences of changing other individuals' attitudes would be greatest when the audience was uncommitted and potentially gullible. Comparatively, giving a speech to people who already favored the proposed legalization should not produce any important change. Finally, presenting arguments to people who were already opposed to legalization was unlikely to change them much.

Nel et al. (1969) found that when they gave subjects an inadequate payment to give the speech (50¢ versus $5), significantly greater attitude change in favor of legalizing marijuana occurred in the group where the potential negative consequences were the greatest: those who thought their speech would be shown to a previously neutral audience.

Dissonance theory has evolved since Festinger's (1957) original proposal. And as Greenwald and Ronis (1978) point out, some of the examples that Festinger (1957) used originally to illustrate his theory would not be considered examples of dissonance theory as it is currently used. For example, Festinger (1957) suggested: "If a person believed that man will reach the moon in the near future and also believed that man will not be able to build a device that can leave the atmosphere of the earth, these two cognitions would be dissonant with one another" (p. 14). Because in this case there is no indication of personal responsibility for not being able to leave the earth's atmosphere, researchers now would not predict dissonance to occur.

Cognitive dissonance provides a powerful model to explain the effect on a person's attitudes of that person's engaging in a counterattitudinal behavior. When there is no clear external, situational reason for having engaged in the behavior, a person is compelled to find some way of dealing with this inconsistency. Cognitive dissonance theory predicts successfully in this case that people will often change their attitudes to be consistent with their behavior. Nevertheless, there are situations in which individuals appear to be maintaining inconsistent beliefs. The next section describes more elaborate cognitive processes whereby individuals can manage this inconsistency.

■ Resolution of Belief Dilemmas

Four Ways of Resolving Belief Dilemmas

Political leaders frequently confront situations in which their supporters are troubled by information (revelations) that seems inconsistent with their existing beliefs about the leader. Politicians then face the task of persuading their constituents that there is nothing to be concerned about. In an inventive perspective on cognitive consistency, Robert Abelson (1959) proposed four ways in which individuals, when confronted with what he termed "belief dilemmas," could resolve the inconsistency. The four modes for resolution of belief dilemmas he suggested were (1) denial, (2) bolstering, (3) differentiation, and (4) transcendence. These modes help us to understand and analyze political communication, and they can be seen as types of pragmatic-reasoning schemas (Cheng, Holyoak, Nisbett, & Oliver, 1986) or cognitive heuristics (Tversky & Kahneman, 1974). I will use Abelson's modes to discuss President Reagan's nationally televised speech on March 4, 1987, that followed the release of the Tower Board Report on the arms-for-hostages deal with Iran.

Abelson proposed that a person's cognitive structure could be either balanced or imbalanced. He focused on consistency or inconsistency between two elements, and he represented this pictorially (Figure 7-1). Cognitive elements could be about either positively or negatively valued objects, and the relationship between the two

Figure 7-1   Abelson's examples of balanced and imbalanced cognitive structures

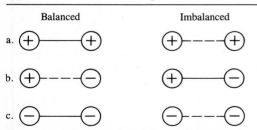

Source: From "Modes of Resolutions of Belief Dilemmas," by R. P. Abelson, *Journal of Conflict Resolution,* 1959, *3* (4), 343–352. Copyright © 1959 by Sage Publications, Inc. Reprinted by permission.

elements could be related either associatively (positively) or dissociatively (negatively). Thus, a positive relationship between two positively valued objects is a balanced cognitive state, while a negative relationship between those two positively valued objects would be imbalanced (Figure 7-1a).

Abelson suggested that when an individual experiences a cognitive imbalance about objects that are particularly salient, a person may attempt one or more of four possible intrapsychic modes of resolving this belief dilemma. A diagram of the application of these four procedures to one kind of dilemma (a negative relationship between two positive elements) is presented in Figure 7-2.

1. *Denial*. This is the simplest way of eliminating inconsistency, just to deny that it exists, either by changing the way one of the objects is valued or by denying the relationship between the two objects (Figure 7-2a). This is also the weakest way to resolve a belief dilemma, and it will fail if it is inconsistent with too much evidence or other existing beliefs.

Recalling our discussion of personality and public opinion in Chapter Four, Miller (1983) argued that denial was an essential element of the poisonous pedago-

Figure 7-2   Abelson's modes of resolution of belief dilemmas

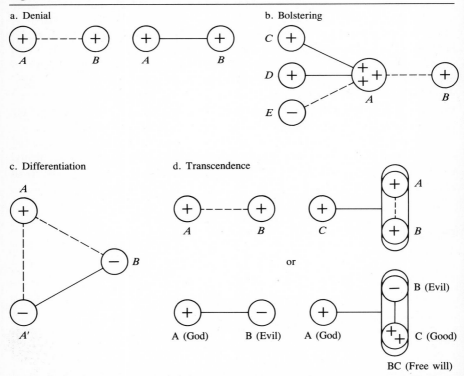

Source: From "Modes of Resolutions of Belief Dilemmas," by R. P. Abelson, *Journal of Conflict Resolution*, 1959, *3* (4), 343–352. Copyright © 1959 by Sage Publications, Inc. Reprinted by permission.

gy, the pattern of child rearing in Western society that she argues has been predominant for the past few hundred years. This would suggest that individuals raised in this way would have learned well the pragmatic schema of denial and would be able to apply it in many situations if that schema was activated.

2. *Bolstering*. This technique involves adding elements to an inconsistent pair of cognitions so that an inconsistent element or relationship is overpowered by other, consistent elements (Figure 7-2b).

3. *Differentiation*. To resolve a belief dilemma through differentiation, a person must divide a particular element into two parts, one inconsistent and the other consistent, thus restoring balance (Figure 7-2c).

4. *Transcendence*. Transcendence involves creating a new cognitive structure using elements of the imbalanced structure. Abelson suggests two ways of accomplishing this process. One way involves embedding one or both of the inconsistent cognitions in a larger structure which itself is consistently related to another cognitive element. Figure 7-2d diagrams two possible transcendent resolutions. The first example shows a belief dilemma, a negative relationship between two positively valued objects (*A* and *B*). This is transformed by grouping *A* and *B* together into a single element and adding a new element *C* that is consistent with this new structure.

Showing a second type of transcendence, Abelson gives the example of an imbalance an individual might experience when recognizing that God allows evil to exist in the world, so that there is a positive relationship between God (positively valued) and evil (negatively valued). A person could utilize transcendence by recognizing that both good *and* evil (associatively related since they both exist in the world) are possible because God gave people free will (Figure 7-2d).

In a more recent statement about belief inconsistency, Abelson (1983) has pointed out that, consistent with our earlier discussion of dissonance theory, important inconsistencies among cognitions are not simply cognitive experiences; they must have personal costs or problems associated with them. People for whom politics is important will likely be motivated to resolve belief dilemmas, but others may not.

An Example of Political Persuasion

The Iran-Contra affair was the most damaging problem to emerge for Reagan during his entire administration. In November 1986 it was revealed that weapons had been sold to Iran in exchange for Iran's influence in releasing U.S. hostages held in Lebanon. The money from the arms sales was subsequently used to aid the Contras fighting against the Sandinista government in Nicaragua. Reagan's popularity was reduced to its lowest level. The Reagan administration had given arms to Iran, after repeatedly saying that it would never deal with countries supporting terrorism. Clearly, many Reagan supporters developed some troubling belief dilemmas upon learning this. Figure 7-3 presents the change from balanced to imbalanced cognitions about Reagan.

Some of the key elements of Reagan's image prior to November 1986 were that

Figure 7-3   Changes in cognitions about President Reagan

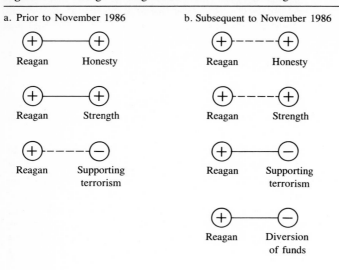

a. Prior to November 1986

b. Subsequent to November 1986

the president was tough, that he was honest, and that he was a leader in the fight against international terrorism and countries that supported it. Following the November press conference, during which Attorney General Edwin Meese announced he had discovered evidence of the Iran-Contra dealings, Reagan appeared to be either dishonest (he was lying about what he knew and when he knew it) or weak (he was a feeble old man who didn't know what was going on in his own administration). Additionally, by selling arms to Iran, he supported a country that the United States had repeatedly denounced as a source of state-sponsored terrorism. Reagan appointed a commission, headed by former senator Tower of Texas, to "find out the facts" about the dealings with Iran. For the next three months he said virtually nothing publicly about the scandal.

We should note that 40% of the public still gave Reagan a positive job rating in February 1987. This suggests that although his supporters may have been troubled by the imbalanced structures outlined in Figure 7-3, many may have simply denied the truth of the various allegations or developed a bolstered structure such as in Figure 7-4. Since the arms-for-hostages deal was only one of the many initiatives the Reagan administration undertook in the first six years of his presidency, all of the other successes may really have outweighed this problem for many people. Clearly, though, for the portion of the public that had previously given him positive ratings, Reagan's past achievements were not enough.

Then, on March 4, 1987, following the release of the Tower Board Report, Reagan gave a nationally televised speech in an attempt to rebuild his sagging popularity (reprinted here in Table 7-1). His speech includes repeated arguments to help his previous supporters resolve their belief dilemmas about him. Let us examine the speech.

At the end of the first paragraph in his speech, Reagan states that the power of

Figure 7-4 Bolstered structured among supporters after November 1986

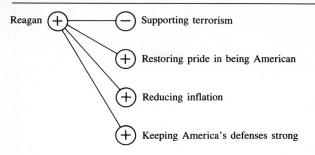

Reagan ⊕———————⊖ Supporting terrorism

⊕ Restoring pride in being American

⊕ Reducing inflation

⊕ Keeping America's defenses strong

Table 7-1 President Reagan's March 4, 1987, speech

1. My fellow Americans. I've spoken to you from this historic office on many occasions about many things. The power of the presidency is often thought to reside within this Oval Office. Yet it doesn't rest here; it rests in you, the American people, and in your trust.

2. Your trust is what gives a president his powers of leadership and his personal strength, and it's what I want to talk to you about this evening.

3. For the past three months, I've been silent on the revelations about Iran. You must have been thinking, "Well, why doesn't he tell us what's happening? Why doesn't he just speak to us as he has in the past when we've faced troubles or tragedies?" Others of you, I guess, were thinking, "What's he doing hiding out in the White House?"

4. I've paid a price for my silence in terms of your trust and confidence. But I have had to wait, as have you, for the complete story. That's why I appointed Ambassador David Abshire as my special counselor to help get out the thousands of documents to the various investigations. And I appointed a special review board, the Tower Board, which took on a chore of pulling the truth together for me and getting to the bottom of things. It has now issued its findings.

5. I'm often accused of being an optimist, and it's true I had to hunt pretty hard to find any good news in the board's report. As you know, it's well-stocked with criticisms, which I'll discuss in a moment, but I was very relieved to read this sentence: "the board is convinced that the president does indeed want the full story to be told." And that will continue to be my pledge to you as the other investigations go forward.

6. I want to thank the members of the panel—former senator John Tower, former secretary of state Edmund Muskie, and former national security adviser Brent Scowcroft. They have done the nation, as well as me personally, a great service by submitting a report of such integrity and depth. They have my genuine and enduring gratitude.

7. I've studied the board's report. Its findings are honest, convincing and highly critical, and I accept them. Tonight I want to share with you my thoughts on these findings and report to you on the actions I'm taking to implement the board's recommendations.

8. First let me say I take full responsibility for my own actions and for those of my administration. As angry as I may be about activities taken without my knowledge, I am still accountable for those activities. As disappointed as I may be in some who served me, I am still the one who must answer to the American people for this behavior. And as personally distasteful as I find secret bank accounts and diverted funds, as the Navy would say, this happened on my watch.

9. Let's start with the part that is the most controversial. A few months ago I told the American people I did not trade arms for hostages. My heart and my best intentions still tell me that is true, but the facts and the evidence tell me it is not.

(continued)

Table 7-1   (*continued*)

---

10. As the Tower Board reported, what began as a strategic opening to Iran deteriorated in its implementation into trading arms for hostages. This runs counter to my own beliefs, to administration policy, and to the original strategy we had in mind. There are reasons why it happened, but not excuses. It was a mistake.

11. I undertook the original Iran initiative in order to develop relations with those who might assume leadership in a post-Khomeini government. It's clear from the board's report, however, that I let my personal concern for the hostages spill over into the geopolitical strategy of reaching out to Iran. I asked so many questions about the hostages' welfare that I didn't ask enough about the specifics of the total Iran plan.

12. Let me say to the hostage families, we have not given up. We never will. And I promise you we'll use every legitimate means to free your loved ones from captivity. But I must also caution that those Americans who freely remain in such dangerous areas must know that they're responsible for their own safety.

13. Now, another major aspect of the board's findings regards the transfer of funds to the Nicaraguan Contras. The Tower Board was not able to find out what happened to this money, so the facts here will be left to the continuing investigation of the court-appointed independent counsel and the two congressional investigating committees. As I told the Tower Board, I didn't know about any diversion of funds to the Contras. But as president, I cannot escape responsibility.

14. Much has been said about my management style, a style that has worked successfully for me during eight years as governor of California and for most of my presidency. The way I work is to identify the problem, find the right individuals to do the job, and then let them go to it. I have found this invariably brings out the best in people. They seem to rise to their full capability and in the long run you get more done.

15. When it came to managing the NSC staff, let's face it, my style didn't match its previous track record. I have already begun correcting this. As a start, yesterday I met with the entire professional staff of the National Security Council. I defined for them the values I want to guide the national security policies of this country. I told them that I wanted a policy that was as justifiable and understandable in public as it was in secret. I wanted a policy that reflected the will of Congress as well as the White House. And I told them that there'll be no more freelancing by individuals when it comes to our national security.

[Lengthy discussion of Tower Board's recommendations]

Conclusion:
You know, by the time you reach my age, you've made plenty of mistakes if you've lived your life properly. So you learn. You put things in perspective. You pull your energies together. You change. You go forward.

My fellow Americans, I have a great deal that I want to accomplish with you and for you over the next two years. And, the Lord willing, that's exactly what I intend to do.

Source: *Boston Globe,* March 3, 1987, p.5.

the presidency resides in the trust of the American people. He uses the phrase "your trust" again in the second paragraph and the fourth paragraph, and he concludes the fifth paragraph with a sentence from the Tower Board that "the board is convinced that the president does indeed want the full story to be told." As we discuss in the next chapter, *source credibility* is one of the primary facilitating factors in determining the effectiveness of a persuasive communication, so it is no surprise that Reagan emphasizes his credibility in the first quarter of his speech. In the second paragraph,

Figure 7-5   Differentiated structure about Reagan

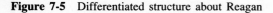
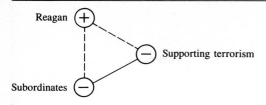

he also refers to the president's "personal strength." For those previous supporters who were only somewhat troubled by the Iran-Contra disclosures, this may have been enough to use denial to resolve the first two dilemmas in Figure 7-3b: to decide that Reagan is honest and strong. In paragraphs 6 and 7 he calls the board's findings "honest" and talks about its "integrity," supporting the board's conclusions about *his* honesty.

But what about the dilemma that those who had supported Reagan previously could *not* deny: supplying Iran with weapons? Resolving this dilemma requires more complex cognitive processes. In paragraph 8, Reagan talks about actions his subordinates took without his knowledge. Here he attempts to facilitate the public's differentiation about the arms-for-hostages actions. Figure 7-5 shows a change from imbalance in Reagan supporters' cognitions to a differentiated (and balanced) structure, in which the subordinates (acting without Reagan's knowledge—this also supports denial of this dilemma) are responsible for the negatively valued support of terrorism (which Reagan has always opposed).

In paragraphs 10 and 11 Reagan's remarks encourage bolstering on the part of his supporters. He says how arms-for-hostages "runs counter to my own beliefs, to administration policy, and to the original strategy we had in mind." Figure 7-6 shows a bolstered structure in which those citizens who still might believe that Reagan knew about the policy and was responsible for it have other factors to outweigh his involvement in selling arms to Iran.

Reagan deals with the fourth imbalanced structure in Figure 7-3b by stating he knew nothing about the diversion of funds. This can obviously support denial of that imbalance, though he does not offer any other remedy for this dilemma.

Starting in paragraph 15, and going to the end of the speech, Reagan outlines

Figure 7-6   Bolstered structure about Reagan

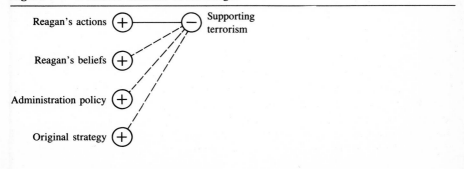

Figure 7-7   Differentiated structure about Reagan

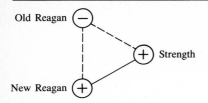

the general values he wants the National Security Council staff to follow in developing policy and the specific policies he will implement to prevent any reoccurrence of the Iran-Contra problem. In paragraph 15 he admits that his old managerial style didn't work well, and he states what he is doing to correct it. This take-charge approach supports differentiation to resolve the second of the four dilemmas concerning Reagan's strength and decisiveness (Figure 7-3b). Figure 7-7 shows the differentiation between the "old Reagan" and the "new Reagan" in relationship to strength and toughness.

Finally, Reagan ends his speech with the statement that "I have a great deal that I want to accomplish with you and for you over the next two years. And, the Lord willing, that's exactly what I intend to do." These comments encourage his listeners to transcend the current concerns about the Iran-Contra affair, and Figure 7-8 shows the operation of transcendence. Although administration goals for freeing hostages led to the Iran-Contra affair, Reagan suggests that he has an agenda for the future; and this is the positive and balanced cognitive structure that he hopes to leave the public with.

Additional Examples of Belief Dilemma Resolution

While Reagan's speech is a very good example of political communication that aims to restructure listeners' cognitions about the political environment, Republicans do not have a monopoly on persuasion attempts of this kind. The problems that Joseph Biden and Gary Hart encountered in their bids for the presidency were responded to in much the same way that Reagan addressed his problems: by encouraging denial, differentiation, bolstering, and transcendence among the public. An analysis of the

Figure 7-8   Transcendent cognitive structure about Reagan

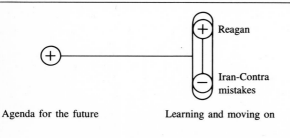

type and the structure of cognitions politicians attempt to create within the minds of voters can aid considerably our understanding of the nature of political communication.

These mechanisms for belief dilemma resolution also influence the attitudes of policy decision makers. Auerbach (1986) documents how differentiation operated in Israeli politicians' changed attitudes toward Germany following World War II. For several years after the end of the war, Israeli politicians referred to Germany as "murderer" and "Nazi." Then in 1952, two Israeli political parties (the Mapai and Mizrachi), responding to the acute shortage of foreign currency and the desperate economic condition of Israel, changed their position and began favoring negotiations with Germany for reparations. Following this change in behavior, members of the Mapai party dropped the pejorative adjectives describing West Germany and began differentiating between "today's Germany" and the "Germany of the past" (although it was only seven years before).

Dissonance versus Belief Dilemma Resolution

When will inconsistencies be resolved through dissonance reduction and attitude change, and in what circumstances will alternative methods, such as those Abelson proposed, be used? Jon Krosnick (1988) has suggested an answer. Using data from a series of public opinion surveys, he found that attitudes important to respondents were much more stable than attitudes described as low in importance. He reasoned that in a situation of attitude inconsistency between an important attitude and one of lesser importance, the less important attitude is most likely to change, in line with Festinger's (1957) initial prediction. Krosnick suggests that when dissonance occurs between two attitudes of equal importance (both of which are likely to be resistant to change), then a person is likely to use one of Abelson's modes of belief dilemma resolution. Krosnick suggested that this may also apply to inconsistencies between important attitudes and their relevant behaviors.

Sherman and Gorkin (1980) conducted an experiment that illustrates the application of Abelson's model to individuals' attempts to resolve the inconsistency of behaving in counterattitudinal ways. Researchers tested the hypothesis that individuals who had some strongly held attitudes (in this case, feminist attitudes) and who behaved in a way inconsistent with these attitudes would subsequently engage in behavior consistent with their initial attitude in order to bolster that attitude. Sherman and Gorkin told subjects they would be participating in two unrelated experiments (they were, in fact, two parts of the same study). In the first part, subjects filled out a questionnaire that assessed their attitudes on feminist issues, and then the researchers gave them a logic problem to solve:

> A father and his son are out driving. They are involved in an accident. The father is killed, and the son is in critical condition. The son is rushed to the hospital and prepared for the operation. The doctor comes in, sees the patient, and exclaims, "I can't operate, it's my son!" (Sherman & Gorkin, p. 391)

An earlier study (Gorkin, 1972) found that most college students fail to come up with the logical solution to this problem, indicating sex role stereotypic thinking (the doctor is the injured man's mother). In this earlier study, subjects who held strongly feminist attitudes were distressed at their apparently unliberated reasoning.

After measuring their subjects' feminist attitudes and giving them the logic problem (which most failed), Sherman and Gorkin (1980) told them that they would now participate in a second, unrelated study, "how people process information to arrive at legal decisions." They were then given an affirmative action case taken from Snyder and Swann (1976) about a woman who had been turned down for a university teaching position because of her gender. After reading the facts of the case, subjects were asked to reach a verdict ranging from finding the university not guilty of sex discrimination to reimbursing and hiring the woman and withholding federal funds from the university for three years.

Sherman and Gorkin (1980) found that subjects who had strong feminist attitudes and who failed to solve the sex role logic problem increased their support for affirmative action. As the authors stated: "When an important part of one's self-image is challenged by one's own behavior, and that behavior can neither be denied nor misperceived, a desire to reestablish that important self-image leads to the adoption of an extreme behavior to counteract or invalidate the implication of the threatening behavior" (p. 397).

■ Conclusion

Abelson (1986) has recently argued that beliefs are like possessions—that people hold on to them, value them, and are often reluctant to let them go. This is an intriguing and useful metaphor that is likely to be influential in theorizing about attitudes and beliefs. It is, in addition, consistent with his earlier model. He suggests that in situations of low involvement, when a person does not "possess" a strong belief, a person may be able to listen to a message and consider whether to adopt a new belief. In contrast, when a person possesses a particular belief, then the processes of maintaining cognitive balance are likely to be activated.

Individuals who confront information that reveals that their beliefs are inconsistent with each other or with their behavior will be motivated to reduce this inconsistency. A variety of different paths are available, depending upon the strength of the beliefs, the person's feelings of responsibility for the behavior, and the freedom the person feels he or she had over the behavior. For strongly held attitudes, people will very often bolster their attitudes with other attitudes or behaviors that are consistent, as Abelson (1959) suggested. When the individual's beliefs are less firmly held, the process of cognitive dissonance or persuasion (discussed in the next chapter) may lead to attitude change.

There are lessons here for persons engaged in the development of political communication. Heider's balance theory research has shown that people prefer balanced to imbalanced situations. Persuasive messages that are not internally consistent are unlikely to be particularly effective. As we saw in the previous chapter, individuals presented with situations that are inconsistent (like the Republican candidate to whom Democratic positions were ascribed) will make errors in recall that restore the consistency of the situation. An understanding of the process of cognitive consistency can aid in the understanding of political rhetoric and the analysis of political communication.

CHAPTER
EIGHT

Persuasive Communications and Attitude Change

A theoretical understanding of the reasons why attitudes do change is fundamental to the application of psychology to politics. Social psychologists have devoted considerable attention to research on persuasive communications—that is, messages designed to change the receivers' attitudes concerning a particular issue. We consider several different approaches to this topic in this chapter. First, we review an area of research originated by the Yale Communication and Attitude Change Program. Carl Hovland and his colleagues (Hovland, Janis, & Kelley, 1953) framed the basic research questions in this area with a systematic set of studies on the factors that determine how effective a particular persuasive communication will be in changing an individual's attitudes. These researchers identified a variety of important factors, including characteristics of the source of the communication, aspects of the message itself, and attributes of the audience to which the message is directed.

We then consider a second approach to attitude change that adds to the analysis of communication effects: a consideration of how discrepant the position of the message is from the position of the audience. Sherif and Hovland's (1961) social judgment theory describes the procedure by which individuals' existing attitudes influence both the way they perceive a particular message and the likelihood that the message will change the receivers' attitudes. After discussing this theory, we consider Fishbein and Ajzen's (1975) model of persuasive communications that makes the variables included in the Yale studies of persuasion and social judgment theory mathematically explicit.

Finally, we consider Petty and Cacioppo's (1981) conceptual model that presents a unified way of looking at persuasive communication situations. Their elaboration likelihood model focuses on the extent to which individuals elaborate their thoughts or think in detail about the arguments presented in a persuasive message. Additionally, their model specifies that there are two different routes to persuasion, "central" and "peripheral," and the different variables identified in the earlier theories of persuasion have different effects depending on the particular route. Petty and Cacioppo's model provides a way of understanding the results of the vast array of studies done on persuasive communications. The four approaches to attitude change discussed in this chapter should be seen as complementary and building sequentially upon each other.

■ The Yale Model of Persuasion

"Who said what to whom with what effect?" Thus asked Harold Lasswell regarding communication research. This question embodies the central elements of the research program that Hovland et al. (1953) undertook. These researchers argued that the important factors determining whether a persuasive message would be effective in changing the listeners' attitudes depended on characteristics of the source (who), aspects of the message (what), and features of the audience (to whom). This framework for examining the effect of persuasive communications set the pattern for research in this area.

Source Characteristics

A variety of different aspects of the person giving a speech influences whether that person's speech will be effective in persuading the audience. Foremost among these aspects is source credibility. If a person is not considered to be an expert on a particular topic, or if trustworthiness comes into question, then that person is likely to be ineffective in changing people's attitudes. Other factors can be important too, including the attractiveness of the speaker and various aspects of the style that the speaker uses to present the speech.

Experiments on the effect of different source characteristics have generally presented a message to two different groups of subjects and attributed it to two different sources to determine the consequence of that variation. An early study on source credibility (Hovland & Weiss, 1951) presented subjects with a communication arguing for the feasibility of building a nuclear powered submarine. For half of the subjects, the message was attributed to a high-credibility source (Robert J. Oppenheimer, a U.S. physicist); and for the other half of the subjects, a low-credibility source was used (the official newspaper of the Soviet Communist party, *Pravda*). As you can imagine, the high-credibility source in this case was much more persuasive.

Expertise and Trustworthiness

The expertise of the source is a particularly important aspect of communicator credibility. Bochner and Insko (1966) presented a message to their subjects about the number of hours of sleep a person needs, and the researchers attributed the message either to a high-expertise source (a Nobel Prize–winning physiologist) or a low-expertise source (a YMCA director). The more extreme the high-expertise source's position was (down to arguing that as little as 1 hour per night was needed), the more the subjects' attitudes changed. When the low-expertise source's message became extreme, however, the amount of attitude change began to decrease. A highly expert source, then, can be much more persuasive than a person who is low in expertise.

The perception of a source's trustworthiness is a second important aspect of credibility that affects the persuasiveness of the message that a source presents. How honest a communicator is perceived to be is influenced by whether the person is speaking for or against his or her own self-interest. Walster, Aronson, and Abrahams (1966) found that a high-prestige prosecuting attorney was much more persuasive than a low-prestige criminal in arguing that the courts should be less powerful. But when they presented a message arguing for increased power for the courts (obviously against the self-interest of the criminal), the criminal was more persuasive than the prosecutor. This effect operates politically as well. In the 1976 presidential campaign, Jimmy Carter presented his proposal to give amnesty to Vietnam War draft evaders to the American Legion convention (obviously not a situation with a sympathetic audience that would cheer and applaud his proposal). He didn't change many of his listeners' attitudes, but it was a clear demonstration to the American people of his sincerity.

The Intent to Persuade

If a person is perceived as *not* trying to persuade someone, that person is seen as honest and trustworthy and, consequently, as persuasive. Walster and Festinger (1962) had undergraduate students listen to a conversation between graduate students, although what they heard was actually a tape recording. When the subjects believed that the graduate students were unaware of being overheard and were thus not trying to persuade anyone, the information in the conversation was much more persuasive than if subjects believed that the speakers were aware of being overheard. The experimenters obtained this effect when the issue was of relevance to the subjects (campus regulations). The persuasive effectiveness of communications when there is presumably no persuasive intent clearly contributes to the power of television news to influence its audience's attitudes, particularly when the news is seen as objective ("just the facts"). The effect of television news on individuals' attitudes is discussed in more detail in the next chapter.

One final point about communicator credibility: When the issue involved in the communication is of high personal relevance to the audience and the audience gives the message a lot of thought, then the impact of source credibility decreases (Petty & Cacioppo, 1981; Sigall & Helmreich, 1969). Petty and Cacioppo's elaboration likelihood model of attitude change (discussed at the end of this chapter) accounts for this result.

Physical Attractiveness and Style of Presentation

A communicator's physical attractiveness and style of presentation also affect how influential he or she will be. The better looking an individual is, the more persuasive that person will be (Chaiken, 1979). John F. Kennedy's victory in the close election of 1960 has been attributed in part to his superior appearance in the televised debates between him and Richard Nixon (McGinniss, 1969). The style a person uses to present a message also influences how persuasive the message is. Helmsley and Doob (1978) found that when a videotape of a witness showed the person looking directly into the eyes of the questioner, the witness was perceived as more believable. This effect may also have been important in the Kennedy/Nixon debates in 1960. Kennedy looked straight into the camera, appearing to face the American people directly, while Nixon tended to face Kennedy. The speed with which a person speaks is also important. Miller, Maruyama, Beaber, and Valone (1976) found that with two speakers giving the same message, the faster speaker was seen as more intelligent, knowledgeable, and objective. John F. Kennedy was viewed as a very effective speaker and occasionally spoke as fast as 300 words a minute (140–150 words a minute is normal).

Since the early 1950s, studies have identified a variety of different characteristics of the person presenting a message that influence how persuasive the message will be. The credibility of the source (expertise and trustworthiness) is most important, but attractiveness and style of delivery can also be influential. All of these characteristics can be important in a political context. We next give consideration to characteristics of the message and of the audience to which the communication is directed.

Message and Audience Characteristics

Hovland et al. (1953) argued that different features of the message (that is, how the message is presented) and various aspects of the recipients of the message will also influence how persuasive the message will be.

Message Characteristics

Consider two people, each giving a speech arguing for the legalization of drugs as one approach to the drug problem. The first person (who prides himself on his erudition and extensive education) uses many big words to show off his vocabulary, and he goes into various meandering digressions from the arguments he is presenting. The second person expresses the same arguments but in everyday language and in a straightforward and organized way. Which speaker do you think is more likely to be persuasive? Since the comprehensibility of the message has been found to be an important factor in persuasion (Eagly, 1974), we would expect the second speaker to be more effective. Simpler messages are more persuasive.

A related issue that researchers have addressed is: Are communicators more likely to persuade an audience on a particular issue if they present both sides of an issue or just one side, the one they are arguing for? The answer is, it depends. Hovland, Lumsdaine, and Sheffield (1949) tested this question in a study conducted for the U.S. War Department. The War Department wanted to find an effective way to persuade soldiers that the war in the Pacific might go on for a long time. Hovland et al. (1949) considered two alternative approaches: a one-sided message about Japan's strengths and resources, and a two-sided message that included the arguments in the first message but also first considered and then refuted arguments about Japan's potential weaknesses. They found that the two-sided message was most persuasive for those soldiers who were knowledgeable about the issue and who had initially believed that the war in the Pacific would be protracted. For those relatively uninformed subjects who initially disagreed with the message, the simpler one-sided communication was more effective. Thus, the effect of the structure and content of the message (one-sided versus two-sided) was different for different types of recipients of the message (in terms of their knowledgeability and initial position).

Having roots in the one-sided/two-sided message debate, McGuire (1964) proposed his "inoculation" theory of resistance to persuasion. McGuire used the analogy of biological inoculation in which people are given a weakened or killed virus with the expectation that the individuals will develop antibodies to the virus and be able to resist infection when the live virus is encountered. In an attitude change context, McGuire (1964) reasoned that a person could be inoculated to a persuasive message. If an individual is given some counterarguments and refutations for a message that he or she has not yet heard, then when the person is subsequently exposed to the persuasive communication, the person will be able to effectively counterargue and thus resist being persuaded. There is empirical support for this theory (McGuire & Papageorgis, 1961), and this model is the basis for the elaboration likelihood model (Petty & Cacioppo, 1986a, 1986b) discussed in detail later in the chapter. Inoculation is also important when one considers the impact of negative political advertising, which is discussed in the next chapter on the mass media.

Audience Characteristics

Intelligence and education determine a person's general knowledge. How do these factors relate to persuasion? Most studies show that individuals who are higher in intelligence tend to be less easily persuaded (McGuire, 1969). A similar argument can be made for education.

Political Implications of Persuasive Communication Research

Successful politicians must know which messages are effective and how to present them. It is clear that simple messages are more comprehensible through the media and also more persuasive to the general public. Some politicians also know that less intelligent and less educated people respond to simple, one-sided messages. Therefore, many have tended to rely on such arguments. Studies of the content of political advertisements have reached exactly this conclusion (Joslyn, 1980). An important consequence of this emphasis on simple messages is a decrease in the complexity of individuals' thinking about political issues. We will return to this question in Chapter Nine when we discuss the mass media in detail. In addition to the various external characteristics of source, message, and audience that we have considered, how a message is perceived greatly affects how persuasive it will be. This is the issue that social judgment theory addresses.

■ Social Judgment Theory

Sherif and Hovland (1961) proposed a theory of attitude change called "social judgment theory." As the name implies, this theory explains the process of attitude change in terms of how persuasive communications are perceived (or judged) by the receiver. Sherif and Hovland's model was grounded in the considerable literature on perception of physical stimuli, notably the adaptation level theory proposed by Helson (1948, 1959).

The Physiological Basis of the Social Judgment Effect

Helson was initially intrigued with the perception of colors, and he discovered that the same color reflected light very differently if it had a white background rather than a gray or black background (Helson, 1948). Thus, the context in which a stimulus was presented affected how individuals perceived it. He subsequently changed the type of stimuli he used and had subjects lift small objects. Nash (1952), reported in Helson (1959), gave subjects weights to lift that varied from 100 grams to 600 grams, and asked them to judge their relative weight (for instance, very heavy, light, very light). As an analog to the background color in his color experiments, he had one group of subjects handle a 900-gram weight before lifting the lighter weights. After handling the 900-gram weight, subjects judged the 100- to 600-gram weights as *lighter* than if they had had no experience with the heavy weight.

This effect is comparable to another demonstration that you have probably seen: Hold one of your hands in a bowl of hot water and the other hand in a bowl of cold water. Then place both hands into a bowl of lukewarm water; the hand that was in the hot water will experience the new water as cool, while the other hand will perceive the water as warm, because the two hands have different comparison points (or anchors).

These physiological experiments have important political implications in that the anchoring process influences the perception of persuasive communications. Sherif and Hovland (1961) applied Helson's research in the development of their social judgment theory.

Cognitive Anchoring

Sherif and Hovland (1961) hypothesized that a person's attitude serves as a cognitive anchor that will influence his or her perception of the extremity of different persuasive communications, and they proposed that the amount of attitude change will be a function of the perceived discrepancy between the person's existing position and the communication. Messages that are very similar to a person's existing position will be seen as the same, and little or no change will take place; that is, the message will be assimilated. Communications that are very different from the person's position will be seen as even further away (the message will be contrasted) and little or no change will take place. Thus, the greatest potential for change comes from messages that are moderately discrepant.

Sherif and Hovland (1961) hypothesized that for each person, messages of different discrepancies from the person's own position would fall into different regions, which they called "latitudes." They posited that messages similar to the person's existing position could be described as falling into the person's latitude of acceptance; messages that are very discrepant fall into the person's latitude of rejection; and messages that are in between fall into the latitude of noncommitment. Figure 8-1 displays an example of these latitudes for a person's existing attitude. As you can see, the various latitudes extend outward from the anchor point of the person's existing attitude.

This anchoring phenomenon can contribute to various cognitive errors. In an experimental study, Tversky and Kahneman (1974) asked their subjects to estimate the percentage of African countries in the United Nations; but before estimating, they were asked to spin a wheel to produce a random number. The number that was produced, however, was not random; it was manipulated to be either 65 or 10. Tversky and Kahneman then asked their subjects to say whether the random number was larger or smaller than their African estimate and then to say by how much. Even though the subjects knew that the random number was irrelevant to their estimation task, it nevertheless served as an anchor and significantly influenced their estimate. When the random number was 65, the average estimate was 45%; when the random number was 10, the average estimate was 25%. Thus, even apparently unconnected external stimuli that provide anchors can result in individuals making cognitive errors. We talked earlier in this chapter about simple messages in political advertising campaigns. Cognitive errors produced by this anchoring phenomenon provide an additional tool for manipulative messages in the media.

Attitude Intensity and Importance

A particularly significant aspect of attitudes is the intensity with which the individual holds them. This characteristic of attitudes has been conceptualized in various ways: ego involvement (Krech & Crutchfield, 1948; Sherif & Cantril, 1947); centrality (Converse, 1970; Katz, 1960); and salience (Lemon, 1973; Smith, Brun-

Figure 8-1   Sherif and Hovland's (1961) proposed latitudes of acceptance, rejection, and noncommitment

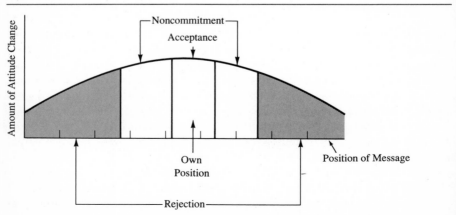

er, & White, 1956). When a person's involvement in an issue is very high, then the latitude of noncommitment decreases, and the latitude of rejection becomes larger (Sherif & Sherif, 1967). Thus, when individuals hold an attitude very strongly, they are much less tolerant of opinions differing from their own.

Krosnick (1988) has demonstrated the function of attitude importance in individuals' voting preferences. In the National Election Study (NES) surveys in 1968, 1980, and 1984, respondents were asked a variety of opinion questions, and they were also asked how important those issues were to them personally. Krosnick examined the effect of holding each specific attitude on the respondents' candidate preference. He found that for attitudes of low importance (1 on a 4-point scale), only two of the 13 items over three surveys significantly predicted respondents' choice between the political candidates in each specific election. In contrast, for attitudes stated as high in importance, 11 of the 13 items were significant predictors of candidate choice. Virtually all the respondents' highly valued attitudes predicted respondents' candidate choices.

We can see that Krosnick's (1988) findings fit Fishbein and Ajzen's (1975) theory of reasoned action quite nicely (see Chapter Two). They hypothesized that a person's attitude toward an action would be a combination of the person's beliefs about the results of such an action and the evaluation that the person attaches to each of the beliefs. An important attitude would be analogous to the highly positive or negative evaluations associated with beliefs in the Fishbein and Ajzen model. Just as strongly positive or negative evaluations paired with beliefs contributed disproportionately to the person's attitude about a particular action, the attitudes rated as important in Krosnick's study predicted the respondents' candidate preferences.

Thus, a person might consider the action of voting for or against candidate X. If the person believed that voting for candidate X would contribute to outlawing abortion, and if the person also felt that outlawing abortion would be extremely bad, then the person would be likely to vote against candidate X. This is equivalent in Krosnick's terms to the person holding the attitude "I favor abortion rights and this attitude is very important to me."

Krosnick (1988) also found evidence to indicate that the highly important attitudes were more cognitively accessible; that is, they were mentioned spontaneously at the start of the interview as reasons to vote for or against a particular candidate. Krosnick observed that these attitudes thus served as stronger anchors for the respondents' perceptions in the election campaign. Additionally, the respondents who rated their attitudes of high importance were also more likely to perceive a larger difference in the candidates' positions on that attitude. Thus, Krosnick found evidence of stronger contrast effects when the individuals were highly involved in a particular issue.

An Experimental Demonstration of the Social Judgment Effect for Attitude Change

The social judgment process was first demonstrated in an experiment conducted by Hovland, Harvey, and Sherif (1957). The researchers at that time held positions at the University of Oklahoma, and they used prohibition of alcohol as an issue, conducting their experiment shortly after a prohibition referendum passed by a small margin in Oklahoma. Hovland et al. were intrigued by findings in the literature that some subjects, when presented with a persuasive communication, changed their attitudes in the opposite direction to that intended. They called this a "boomerang effect." The authors reasoned that this might be a contrast effect similar to that observed in the psychophysical literature produced by a different perceptual anchor.

Hovland et al. (1957) collected statements made during the referendum campaign from newspapers and also from 500 people in several towns. To determine the actual position of these statements on a wet-to-dry scale, 20 judges sorted them and the researchers chose nine statements as representative of the range of major positions in the campaign. For example:

> *Extremely dry:* Since alcohol is the curse of mankind, the sale and use of alcohol, including light beer, should be completely abolished.
> *Moderately dry:* Alcohol should not be sold or used except as a remedy for snake bites, cramps, colds, fainting, and other aches and pains.
> *Neutral:* The arguments in favor and against the sale and use of alcohol are nearly equal.
> *Moderately wet:* The sale of alcohol should be so regulated that it is available in limited quantities for special occasions.
> *Extremely wet:* It has become evident that man cannot get along without alcohol; therefore, there should be no restriction whatsoever on its sale and use. (Hovland et al., 1957, p. 246)

Before subjects were exposed to a persuasive communication, Hovland et al. (1957) asked them to indicate the statement on the 9-point scale that came closest to their own position; the statement or statements they found objectionable; and the statement or statements that were not objectionable to them. This permitted the researchers to determine each subject's cognitive anchor, latitude of rejection, and latitude of acceptance.

Some weeks after this first session, subjects heard one of three persuasive communications, either extremely dry, extremely wet, or moderately wet (as indicated above). After hearing the communication, subjects again rated their own position, the statements they could accept, and the statements they found objectionable. Hovland et al. (1957) wanted to examine the effects of these persuasive communications on subjects who were fairly ego involved in this issue, so they recruited subjects with a known strongly dry position (members of the Women's Christian Temperance Union), individuals with a strongly wet position (25 friends and acquaintances of the experimenters), and a group of students as a moderate control group.

The results they obtained are displayed in Figure 8-2. Subjects' favorable judgments of the three different persuasive communications (wet, moderately wet, and dry) are shown as a function of their existing opinion toward prohibition. For example, in the leftmost graph, subjects who strongly supported the availability of alcohol (positions F and G) are quite favorable to the very wet message. For subjects whose initial positions were less favorable to easy access to alcoholic

Figure 8-2 Evaluation of message by individuals with different existing attitudes

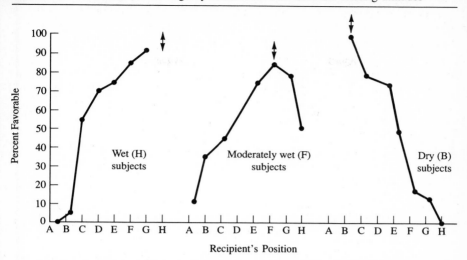

Source: "Assimilation and contrast effects in reactions to communications and attitude change," by C. I. Hovland, O. J. Harvey, and M. Sherif, *Journal of Abnormal and Social Psychology,* 1957, *55,* p. 247.

beverages, the level of agreement with the wet communication decreases, until there is a precipitous drop in favorable evaluations among those who strongly support prohibition (positions A and B). The inverse pattern occurred for the very dry communication; the moderately wet message had the lowest amount of support among those at the extremes.

The predicted pattern of assimilation and contrast is shown most clearly in Figure 8-3. Hovland et al. (1957) asked their subjects to evaluate how wet or dry they perceived the moderately wet communication to be (position F on their scale as determined previously by 20 judges), obtaining the subjects' perception of the message. Subjects whose initial position was extremely dry (position A) saw the message as very wet (between G and H). Those subjects who were less extreme (position B) did not judge the message to be quite as extreme (position G). The inverse pattern again emerges for subjects whose initial positions were extremely wet (positions G and H). Thus, individuals with extreme positions, either dry or wet, contrasted the message—that is, saw the moderate message as more opposed to their own position than it actually was.

Applications of the Social Judgment Effect

Individuals' judgments of public opinion and government policies demonstrate these assimilation and contrast effects. Using data from the 1976 NES survey Granberg, Jefferson, Brent, and King (1981) found that individuals' estimates of

Figure 8-3   Perception of communication as a function of existing position

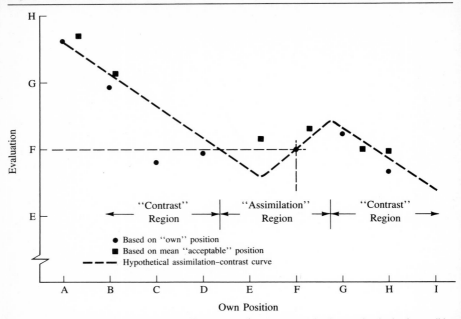

Source: "Assimilation and contrast effects in reactions to communications and attitude change," by C. I. Hovland, O. J. Harvey, and M. Sherif, *Journal of Abnormal and Social Psychology*, 1957, *55*, p. 248.

how different groups (for instance, Blacks, Whites, young, old) feel about specific policy issues appeared to reflect assimilation. Individuals tended to attribute the same attitude to the group that they themselves held. Thus, liberals tended to think that both Blacks and Whites were liberal; conservatives tended to believe that both Blacks and Whites were conservative.

The opposite effect occurred when researchers asked individuals to evaluate the policies of the federal government. Granberg and Robertson (1982) examined national survey data on respondents' judgments of governmental policy on defense spending, aid to minority groups, and spending on social services. Individuals perceived that the policy was ideologically opposed to their own position. Figure 8-4 displays the results they obtained. Conservatives on the average viewed governmental policy as liberal, and liberals saw the policy as conservative. This may reflect the general level of distrust and cynicism directed toward the federal government that has increased over the past 30 years (Nie, Verba, & Petrocik, 1976).

Social judgment theory is very useful for understanding events in the current political environment. Over the past several years there has been a continuing struggle to define (or redefine) the meaning of *political moderate*. Since most people consider themselves in the center politically, this self-identification serves as an anchor for many individuals' perceptions of political issues. In recent years, conservative politicians have for the large part succeeded in changing the term

Figure 8-4 Contrast effects in individuals perception of government policy on three different issues

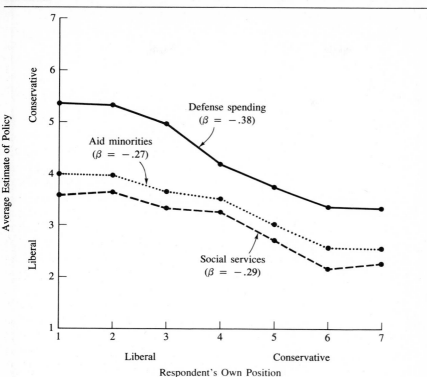

Source: From "Contrast Effects in Estimating Policies of the Federal Government," by D. Granberg and C. Robertson, *Public Opinion Quarterly*, 1982, *46*, p. 47. Copyright © 1982 by The University of Chicago Press. Reprinted by permission.

liberal to mean "radical" to most people. They have thus succeeded in making liberal issues unacceptable. The avoidance of a self-description of *liberal* by democratic politicians is widespread. Michael Dukakis's statement in the 1988 campaign, "This election is not about ideology, it's about competence," was a deliberate attempt to get voters to forget his liberal record. As we noted earlier in the discussion of Tetlock's work on ideology and cognitive complexity, the ideological range in the United States, particularly on the left, is much more limited than in most other Western democracies. Of course, this is not to say that politicians have all studied social judgment theory. Politicians often have an intuitive feeling for processes that social scientists study systematically.

Comparing Dissonance Theory and Social Judgment Theory

It is interesting to compare the predictions that two different theories make in the same situation, particularly when the predictions are different. An example that

Aronson (1988) presents is the effect that the size of the discrepancy between a person's attitudes and a persuasive communication has upon attitude change following exposure to that message. Dissonance theory would argue that since we like to be correct on issues, when someone disagrees with us and presents arguments and evidence that are inconsistent with our beliefs, this will arouse dissonance. The larger the discrepancy, the greater the dissonance—and thus the greater the attitude change. This was the result that Zimbardo (1960) obtained. In contrast, social judgment theory would predict that the greatest amount of attitude change would occur for a communication that is only moderately discrepant.

Zimbardo (1960) recruited female college students to participate in an experiment on how friends analyze social problems, and in this context he asked each subject to come to the experiment with a girlfriend. Zimbardo first used a manipulation to increase the subjects' belief in the credibility of their friend's judgments compared with their own. Each subject was asked separately to judge a series of photographs, attempting to identify delinquents. Zimbardo told each subject that her own score was "good" and her friend's score was "expert." Following this manipulation, each subject read a fictitious case study about a crime committed by Johnny Rodriguez and assessed where the blame for the crime should be on a scale from 1 ("There is no question that the blame for Johnny's crime must be placed *entirely* on his shoulders") to 9 ("There is no question that the blame for Johnny's crime must be placed *entirely* upon his background").

After each subject made her judgment, she was told either that her friend disagreed with her *slightly* or that her friend's judgment was *very different* from her own. Several minutes after providing this false information, the experimenter asked each subject to make another rating of the case study "to make new evaluations after they had considered the problem and materials in more detail" (Zimbardo, 1960, p. 89). Zimbardo found that the subjects who believed that their friend expressed a highly discrepant opinion changed their attitude toward the cause of the crime significantly more, and in the direction of their friend, than did subjects in the low-discrepancy condition. Thus, the dissonance prediction that high discrepancy produces high attitude change was supported.

In contrast, social judgment theory predicts that as message discrepancy increases, attitude change will increase, but only while the message falls into the individual's latitude of noncommitment. As the message becomes very discrepant (that is, falls into the latitude of rejection), the amount of attitude change decreases. As the discussion above shows, there is considerable evidence to support this prediction.

So which theory is right? What would be your prediction for the following experiment conducted by Aronson, Turner, and Carlsmith (1963)? Female college students were paid to participate in "an experiment in esthetics." Subjects first rank-ordered nine stanzas from different, little-known, modern poems according to "the way the poet uses form to aid in expressing his meaning," and then they read a two-page essay discussing the use of alliteration in poetry. Included in the essay was a discussion of a specific stanza, and for each subject the stanza discussed was always the one ranked eighth-best by that subject. For about a third of the subjects, there was a small discrepancy between their own rating of the stanza and the evaluation of it in the essay; for another third there was a moderate discrepancy; and for the remaining third there was a large discrepancy. The essay that the subjects read was attributed either to a high-credibility source (T. S. Eliot) or a mildly credible source (Miss Agnes Stearns, a student at Mississippi State Teachers College). After reading this essay, they were asked again to rank the poems by using the same criterion.

Before reading further, you should apply both dissonance theory and social judgment theory to generate predictions of the outcome of this experiment. As discussed above, dissonance theory predicted greater attitude change from greater discrepancy, but social judgment theory predicted a curvilinear relationship. The actual results of this experiment are disclosed in the following section.

■ Fishbein and Ajzen's Model of Persuasive Communication Effects

The conflicting predictions made by dissonance theory and social judgment theory are integrated in Fishbein and Ajzen's (1975) general algebraic model of the effect of persuasive communications. Fishbein and Ajzen make mathematically explicit the effect of various source, message, and audience characteristics identified as important in the persuasive communication literature. Additionally, they quantitatively specify the effect of message discrepancy on acceptance of the message that social judgment theory identified as fundamental.

Message Discrepancy and the Probability of Message Acceptance

Fishbein and Ajzen (1975) argued that a prerequisite for attitude change is *acceptance* of a message. Unless a person accepts a message, the message cannot produce any change in the receiver's attitudes. Fishbein and Ajzen's model states that the likelihood of a person accepting a particular message [they call this $p(a)$, the probability of acceptance] depends on the existing attitude and how different it is from the message (Fishbein and Ajzen call this the discrepancy D of the message). The probability of acceptance of a message, $p(a)$, is inversely related to the discrepancy D of the message from the attitude held by the person receiving the message. This simply means that the further away a message is from what the person who is hearing it feels, the less likely the person is to believe the message. In mathematical terms:

$$p(a) = 1 - D \qquad (1)$$

Thus, if there is no discrepancy (that is, $D = 0$) between an individual's attitudes and the message the person is exposed to, then the probability of an individual's accepting the message is 1 (absolutely certain). If, however, the message is very discrepant (for example, .9 on a scale of 0 to 1), then the probability of accepting the message is very low [$p(a)$ = .1]. Figure 8-5 displays a graph of this simple relationship.

Facilitating Factors

Of course, there are many different factors in addition to discrepancy that influence whether a message will be accepted. Earlier, we discussed various determinants such as source expertise and credibility, number of arguments, and so on. Fishbein and Ajzen (1975) call these "facilitating factors" and denote their value as f. They suggest that the expression $(1 - D)$ be raised to the power of the reciprocal of f. The equation for the probability of acceptance of a message (equation 1) thus becomes

$$p(a) = (1 - D)^{1/f} \tag{2}$$

The effect of this modification is displayed in Figure 8-6. As you can see, there is now a family of relationships depending upon the size of f. Thus, when facilitating factors are high, the probability of a person's accepting a message is high even when it is fairly discrepant, as in line (a). In this case, assuming $f = 5$, a fairly discrepant message ($D = .8$) still has a high probability of acceptance [$p(a) = .72$]. (To arrive at this number without doing numerical calculation, simply find .8 on the

Figure 8-5   Probability of message acceptance as a function of message discrepancy

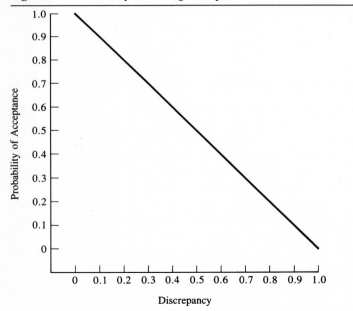

Source: From *Belief, Attitude, Intention, and Behavior: An Introduction to Theory and Research,* by M. Fishbein and I. Ajzen, p. 462. Copyright © 1975 by Addison-Wesley Publishing Company. Reprinted by permission.

Figure 8-6 Family of message acceptance gradients as a function of message discrepancy, and facilitating factors

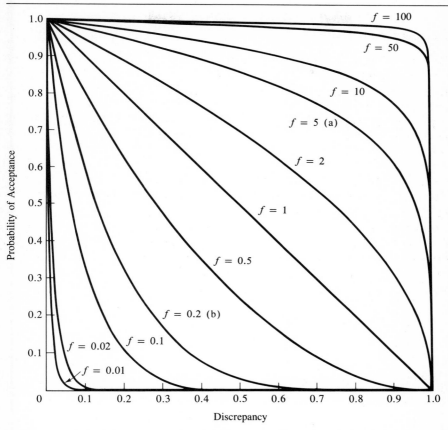

Source: From *Belief, Attitude, Intention, and Behavior: An Introduction to Theory and Research,* by M. Fishbein and I. Ajzen, p. 465. Copyright © 1975 by Addison-Wesley Publishing Company. Reprinted by permission.

horizontal x axis, go straight up to intersect with the curve labeled $f = 5$, and then go horizontally to the left to the vertical y axis.) On the other hand, a message with low facilitating factors (such as one attributed to an untrustworthy source) will not be likely to be accepted, even if it is only moderately discrepant, such as in line (b). Assuming $f = .2$, a message with $D = .2$ produces a *p(a)* of .33.

Attitude Change

So far, we have focused on message acceptance. Fishbein and Ajzen (1975) proposed that the amount of attitude change is a function of both the probability of acceptance of a message and its discrepancy. Mathematically, Fishbein and Ajzen represent this relationship as the product of acceptance and discrepancy:

$$C = p(a) \cdot D \tag{3}$$

Figure 8-7 displays the predictions for attitude change derived from equation (3). This model obviously implies that if there is no discrepancy between a person's attitudes and the position of the message, there will be no attitude change, even though the message was certain to be accepted (1 times 0 equals 0).

What experimental evidence supports this model? It is a fairly complex model, so an overall test is somewhat difficult. Two recent studies (Fishbein & Lange, in press; Lange & Fishbein, 1983) both found, consistent with social judgment theory and the Fishbein and Ajzen (1975) model, that increased message discrepancy resulted in increased attitude change.

Figure 8-7   Attitude change as a function of message discrepancy, message acceptance, and facilitating factors

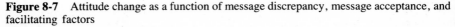

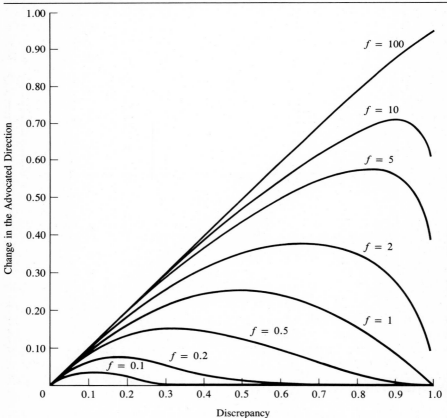

Source: From *Belief, Attitude, Intention, and Behavior: An Introduction to Theory and Research*, by M. Fishbein and I. Ajzen, p. 469. Copyright © 1975 by Addison-Wesley Publishing Company. Reprinted by permission.

Using the Fishbein and Ajzen Model to Predict the Outcome of Aronson et al. (1963)

What does the model predict for the outcome of the experiment described in the beginning of this section? There are two different source conditions, high credibility and mild credibility. These would correspond to two different values of f; we might assume a high-credibility source in this situation has $f = 3$ and a low-credibility source has $f = 1$ (a facilitating factor of less than 1 would be appropriate if there were some reason not to trust the communicator). In addition to the two levels of communicator expertise, there are also three different levels of message discrepancy (low, moderate, and high). We could assume that the discrepancy D levels would be .2, .5, and .8, respectively. We can obtain our predictions from Figures 8-5 and 8-6 or compute it mathematically.

Using the Fishbein and Ajzen (1975) model, we would predict that for the high-credibility model, the amount of change C for the low, moderate, and high-discrepancy conditions should be .19, .39, and .46, respectively. For the mildly credible communicator the corresponding change would be .16, .25, and .16 for low, moderate, and high discrepancy, respectively. How do these predictions compare with the actual amount of change in the Aronson et al. (1963) experiment? Figure 8-8 displays the theoretical predictions from the Fishbein and Ajzen model and the empirical findings from Aronson et al. As you can see, the fit between the predictions and the actual findings is extremely close. The scales used in the model and the experiment are different, but the fit is so close that it strongly suggests that working with a particular scale would allow a researcher to determine the appropriate transformation between that scale and the theoretical model.

■ The Elaboration Likelihood Model

The approaches to attitude change discussed so far have emphasized the importance of source, message, and audience characteristics related to persuasive communications and the impact of message discrepancy on attitude change. The model considered in this section integrates the findings of the previous sections and extends the analysis of persuasive communication effects with the argument that persuasion is not a singular process.

Two Routes to Persuasion

Petty and Cacioppo (1981, 1986a, 1986b) have argued that persuasion may occur in two very different ways, by a "central" route or a "peripheral" route. They maintain that the method of persuasion influences the amount and persistence of any attitude change. Petty and Cacioppo developed their model to organize and explain the disparate set of persuasive communication research findings.

Figure 8-9 diagrams the two routes of persuasion and the outcomes predicted by the elaboration likelihood model (ELM). This model reflects a set of underlying assumptions about the nature of attitudes and attitude change. Petty and Cacioppo

Figure 8-8 Predictions from Fishbein and Ajzen's (1975) model of attitude change compared with the results of Aronson et al. (1963)

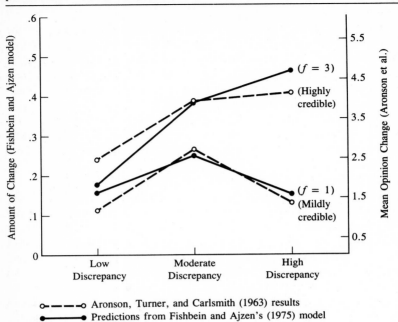

o— — —o Aronson, Turner, and Carlsmith (1963) results
•————• Predictions from Fishbein and Ajzen's (1975) model

(1981, 1986a, 1986b) argue first that individuals are motivated to hold "correct" attitudes, but they vary in their ability and willingness to think about different issues and evaluate political or social messages. In addition, the authors suggest that situational factors will influence whether people can or will take the time to think about a particular issue. These postulates are certainly consistent with the theory and research on cognitive complexity that we discussed earlier in Chapter Five. Thus, from Figure 8-9, after exposure to a persuasive communication, the route of persuasion depends first on the person's motivation to process the message and then on the person's ability to evaluate the message.

Thus, if a person is not interested in thinking about an issue or is unable to (for instance, the person doesn't know anything about the topic or is distracted), then the only possibility of change is a peripheral one. Petty and Cacioppo (1981, 1986a, 1986b) suggest at this point that if a peripheral cue is present (for example, an expert source, a well-liked source, pleasant music playing while the communication is presented), then attitude change will occur, but it will be temporary and not predictive of subsequent behavior. If such peripheral cues are not present, little or no attitude change will occur.

The Cognitive Response to a Persuasive Message

If the person exposed to some persuasive communication is motivated to process the information and also has the ability to do so, then the nature of the person's cog-

Figure 8-9 Schematic display of Petty and Cacioppo's two proposed routes of persuasion

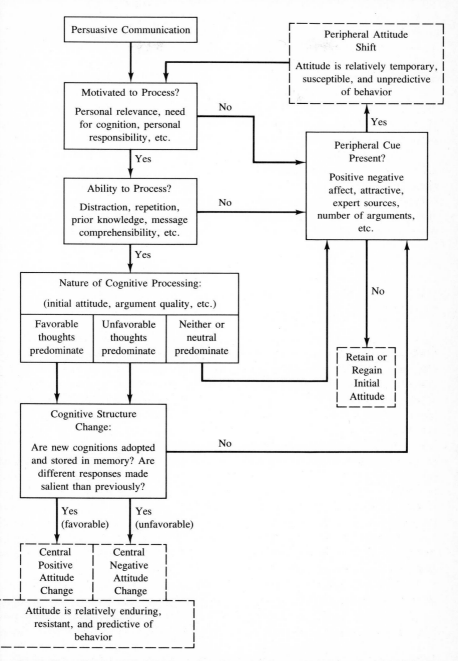

Source: From *Communication and Persuasion,* by R. Petty and J. Cacioppo, p. 4. Copyright © by Springer-Verlag. Reprinted by permission.

nitive responses to the message determines whether the central or peripheral route of attitude change will occur. If the person thinks about the message in a neutral way (neither positive nor negative), then the peripheral route is taken, and attitude change will occur if peripheral cues are present. Instead, if either favorable or unfavorable thoughts predominate, then enduring attitude change will take place if these thoughts are incorporated into the person's memory. If the person primarily rehearsed negative reactions to the message, then a boomerang effect will occur, and significant attitude change in the opposite direction of the message will result. If the person's thoughts are predominately positive, then the person's attitudes will change toward greater agreement with the message. If there is no change in the person's cognitive structure, then the peripheral route is again activated.

Why is this model called the "elaboration likelihood model" of attitude change? As you can see from our above discussion and Figure 8-9, the extent to which a person actively engages in detailed deliberation about a message that he or she has been exposed to is a critical juncture in the two routes. For enduring changes in attitudes to take place—changes that are predictive of later behavior—the person must devote time and energy to thinking about the message. Without this elaboration, the most that can occur is temporary attitude change in reaction to superficial cues in the situation.

Differences Between Individuals in Their Interest in Thinking about Issues

As was detailed in Chapter Five, there are differences between individuals in their apparent ability to think about various topics, including political issues. Petty and Cacioppo have determined that people vary in their intrinsic motivation or need to deliberate. They developed a scale called the Need for Cognition Scale (NCS) (Cacioppo & Petty, 1982; Cacioppo, Petty, & Kao, 1984). Their scale includes items such as "I would prefer complex to simple problems"; "The notion of thinking abstractly is appealing to me"; and "Thinking is not my idea of fun." As you would expect, scores on this scale are negatively correlated ($r = -.27$, $p < .05$) with close-mindedness (Petty & Cacioppo, 1986a). Individuals whose thinking is fairly rigid generally do not enjoy considering different perspectives on various issues or problems.

These findings are consistent with the body of research reviewed in Chapter Four and would suggest that individuals whose thinking is more rigid (for example, authoritarians) are more likely to be influenced by peripheral cues in persuasion situations. These rigid thinkers are thus less likely to experience enduring attitude change through the central route.

Individuals' interest in obtaining political information is influenced, then, by a desire to think carefully. In a study conducted during the 1984 election Cacioppo, Petty, Kao, and Rodriguez (1986) found that individuals measured as "high in need for cognition" thought more about the election and the candidates than did individuals measured "low in need for cognition." Furthermore, those high on the NCS were also able to relate more facts about the two presidential candidates than could those low on the scale. Petty and Cacioppo (1986a) argue that this individual difference plays an important role in the process of persuasion. Thus, individuals high in need for cognition generally will engage in more thoughtful consideration of a specific communication, thus utilizing the central route; those low in need for cognition will be more likely to utilize peripheral cues. This will occur unless strong situational factors alter the typical processing of information. Situational activation of different schemas may have this effect (Milburn, 1987), as we noted in Chapter Six.

Affect and Persuasion

To what extent does a person's emotional reactions to a set of arguments or to some object influence how persuasive a message is? Petty, Cacioppo, Sedikides, and Strathman (1988) explain that affect can play a variety of roles in the overall ELM model. When a person is actively involved in processing the arguments of a message—that is, engaged in the elaboration process—the affect itself may serve as a persuasive argument. When individuals lack the necessary skills or interest to actively think about the message, then the affect associated with a particular message will probably serve as a peripheral cue.

Self-Schemas and Message Perception

In Chapter Six we discussed in some detail the differences between experts and novices in their processing of information. Individuals with different schemas (for instance, political experts compared with political novices) perceived and recalled information in very different ways. These types of individual differences can influence the way individuals respond to persuasive communications. Cacioppo, Petty, and Sidera (1982) examined the effects of the activation of different self-schemas on reactions to a persuasive message. They identified a number of self-descriptive terms that discriminated between a "legalistic" characterization of a person and a "religious" description. For example, someone who is legalistic describes himself or herself as *shrewd;* a religious person is more likely to use terms such as *honest.* Cacioppo et al. (1982) classified their subjects as religious or legalistic depending on how quickly the individuals described themselves with the respective adjectives (assuming that a legalistic person would more quickly identify with the legalistic adjectives than would a religious person.)

Cacioppo et al. (1982) were interested in how the two groups of subjects, each with a schematically different way of looking at the world, would respond to messages that were compatible with their attitudes but that used different approaches; they presented either religious or legalistic arguments for the same position. Pretesting of the subjects' attitudes had determined that both the legalistic and religious subjects were opposed to government support of abortion and capital punishment. Cacioppo et al. (1982) then developed two different sets of arguments consistent with subjects' attitudes on these topics: one with primarily legalistic arguments (for example, "The right to life is one that is constitutionally safeguarded") and a second message filled mainly with religious arguments (for example, "There is a sacramental quality to the nature of life that demands that we show the utmost reverence for it"). Before showing these messages to their two groups of subjects, Cacioppo et al. had the arguments evaluated by a different group of judges, who rated the arguments as relatively weak and unpersuasive.

After presenting either the legalistic or the religious set of arguments against abortion and capital punishment to the two different groups of subjects, the researchers asked them to rate how persuasive the message they read was and to list all the favorable thoughts the subjects had while reading the message. Figure 8-10 displays the results they obtained. As you can see, there is a statistical interaction; that is, the legalistic and religious subjects reacted to the two different messages very differently. The subjects classified as religious felt that the message with the religious arguments was more persuasive than the legalistic message, and they had more positive thoughts about the communication while reading it, even though the messages supported the *same* position. The reverse was true for the legalistic subjects. This means that the activation of a schema that is particularly relevant for a person (for example, using religious arguments with a person who sees himself or herself as religious) will significantly increase how positive the person's reaction is to the message. The reaction to a relevant schema will be more positive than to a message that supports the same position but does not activate the relevant schema.

The Personal Relevance of the Persuasive Communication

A major component of the ELM is that the route of processing a persuasive communication will depend on a person's motivation to process the message. The personal relevance of the message for members of the audience is a key factor that influences whether individuals will think about the message in some detail. As we

Figure 8-10   Results from Cacioppo et al. (1982)

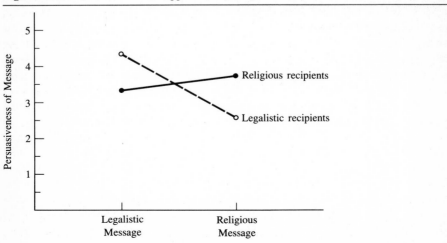

saw earlier in the discussion of social judgment theory, personal relevance (ego involvement) has a considerable impact on the effectiveness of a particular communication to change individuals' attitudes. Petty and Cacioppo (1986a) extend this earlier research to argue that high personal relevance will stimulate increased thinking about issues raised in the communication, thus activating the central route. Alternatively, the ELM model predicts that low relevance will result in peripheral attitude change, if any change occurs at all.

The Political Implications of the ELM Model

What are the political implications of this aspect of the ELM model? Interest in politics has declined over the past two decades. Voter turnout in presidential elections has decreased steadily since 1960 (Brody, 1978; Kinder & Sears, 1985). Krosnick and Milburn (1990) found that levels of opinionation—the extent to which people express opinions on issues (as measured in national surveys)—has also declined consistently over the past 30 years. Given the decreasing interest in politics—that is, the low personal relevance that politics has for most people—the ELM model would predict that most people would give relatively little thought to political messages they are exposed to through the mass media. Thus, attitude change in election campaigns will most likely be produced by peripheral cues (for example, attractiveness of the source) rather than by a careful consideration of the issues. This tendency on the part of voters to pay little attention is probably enhanced by the costs to individuals (in time and money) of obtaining political information (Bennett, 1980). Thus, in short-term situations such as election campaigns, attitudes will be susceptible to change, and large swings in opinion (as happened in the 1988 election) will be fairly likely. Consistent with the argument that only peripheral change was responsible for the electoral outcome, Kurkjian (1989) has observed that one year after the presidential campaign, the major issues in the campaign (the pledge of allegiance, Willie Horton) had virtually vanished.

As a contrast to this somewhat despairing picture, the ELM would predict more positive results for our election campaigns if more people tended to be higher in "need for cognition" and were less likely to be influenced by peripheral cues. An educational system that encourages critical thinking rather than simply factual memorization would be more likely to produce citizens with the capacity to think about political issues with greater complexity. As we saw in Chapter Five, complexity in thinking and communication appears to be associated with a greater likelihood of conflict resolution. Individuals who think in more complex terms are probably more likely to resist simple messages and peripheral persuasion cues.

■ Conclusion

There are a variety of factors that influence the effectiveness of persuasive communications. Characteristics of the source of the communication, attributes of the message itself, and qualities of the audience all contribute to the persuasiveness of a particular communication. Additionally, social judgment theory underscores how the perception of a message is influenced by the discrepancy between the position taken in the message and the position held by the audience.

The ELM model incorporates these observations and adds to them the idea that persuasion may occur by one of two different routes, the central route producing more long-lasting effects and occurring perhaps less frequently. An important implication of this model is that individuals who are dogmatic and rigid in their thinking and personality structure will be more likely to be influenced by peripheral cues such as communicator attractiveness and will be less likely to think about messages or experience lasting attitude change. The primary source of persuasive communications in politics is the mass media. The structure and effects of the mass media are the subject of Chapter Nine.

CHAPTER
NINE

The Mass Media
and Public Opinion

In this chapter we consider the impact of the mass media on public opinion, using our awareness of the various social and cognitive processes discussed in earlier chapters. The mass media, particularly television, have the capacity to communicate powerful images. In earlier chapters of this book we examined research that will help to facilitate our analysis of the effects of these images. In Chapter Five we discussed the cognitive complexity of political thought, and in Chapter Six we discussed the impact of schema activation on the complexity of individuals' political reasoning. In Chapter Seven, the first chapter of Section Three, we used Abelson's model of cognitive consistency to analyze the persuasive elements of a political communication. In this chapter we will consider evidence of how images and themes in the mass media activate political schemas and influence individuals' thinking and opinions.

Are the messages in the mass media politically biased? If so, what is the direction of the bias and what is the source of the bias? To what extent does the societal and economic context in which the mass media operate influence the coverage of political events, and what effect does this coverage have on individuals' political thinking and attitudes? These questions are important for an understanding of the operation of our political system and citizens' political behavior within that system.

Research evidence indicates that the structure and content of television news has a considerable effect on the political issues that individuals regard as important and on the complexity with which individuals reason politically about these issues. These findings suggest that U.S. television coverage of political events has a damaging effect on the level of citizen political interest and participation. The findings do not imply that there is an intentional conspiracy on the part of the media. Rather, these media effects are a result of broad political, economic, and cultural forces operating in the United States.

■ The Structure and Content of the Mass Media

A. J. Liebling once noted that freedom of the press is limited to the people who have the money to buy one. The mass media in the United States are owned and operated by large corporations. Increasingly, the sources of news in the United States and the world are concentrated in fewer and fewer hands (Bagdikian, 1989).

Some studies estimate that over 97% of U.S. cities have only one daily paper (Graber, 1980). A vast majority of papers have no reporters outside that city's metropolitan area. They depend, therefore, on news wire services for national and international news. The primary services used are the Associated Press (AP), United Press International (UPI), and Reuters (a European service). For a number of years there were only three television network national news programs at the evening dinner hour. Now there are two more: *The MacNeil/Lehrer Hour* on the Public Broadcasting Service (with a much lower audience rating) and the Cable News Network (CNN). The clear implication of this monopolistic trend is a limitation on the diversity of opinion available in society. One can also argue that the First Amendment's guarantee of free speech is compromised by such concentration of ownership of the means to express and exercise this right.

But whether the number of news sources remains fairly small or increases over time, the primary issue is the diversity of perspectives—or lack of it—found in news coverage of political events. There is considerable evidence to indicate that the news we receive is very homogeneous. As W. Lance Bennett (1988) argues in his book *News: The Politics of Illusion*:

> The seemingly broad range of information in the news is really a wide assortment of packaging for much the same information. The point is, that the news we are given is not fit for a democracy. It is superficial, narrow, stereotypical, propaganda-laden, of little explanatory value and not geared for critical debate or citizen action. (p. 9)

This narrowness of perspective in the news we receive is a function of a variety of factors. The definition of what constitutes *news* is a major contributing factor to this problem.

The Definition of *News*

As W. Lance Bennett (1988) points out, news producers orient coverage toward *events* instead of ongoing social problems. This is predictable from what reporters and producers define as *news*. Epstein (1973) interviewed a variety of news reporters and correspondents, all of whom defined *news* in terms of change: "News is what is new in the world since our last broadcast," "News is what has happened today," and "News is change."

The values underlying news coverage selection are relevant for a discussion of public opinion. In the mid-1970s sociologist Herbert Gans spent several months observing the process of news production at CBS, *Newsweek*, and the *New York Times*. In his book *Deciding What's News* (1979), he discussed a number of values or themes that he saw underlying television and print coverage of the news. The most important of these were "ethnocentrism," "altruistic democracy," and "responsible capitalism." By *ethnocentrism*, Gans meant that media consider the United States superior to all other countries and that other nations are judged by the extent to which they measure up to U.S. standards.

Gans (1979) used the term *altruistic democracy* to describe the media's tendency to assume that the basic form of government in the United States is good, and when politics and politicians deviate from a course based on public service in the public interest, that this is news. Thus, corruption, nepotism, and deals deserve media attention. The considerable news coverage of the Iran-Contra affair during the last two years of the Reagan administration illustrates this principle very well. The news media focused on the individuals involved (Colonel Oliver North, Admiral Poindexter, and so on) but never questioned the system that permitted them to operate as they did.

The value of responsible capitalism is similar to that of altruistic democracy and refers to an optimistic belief that in the U.S. economic system businesspeople will honestly compete in order to create prosperity for all, avoiding exploitation of workers and excess profits. Gans (1979) suggests that corruption and waste is looked down on but is tolerated in business much more so than in government. The values in the news media of altruistic democracy and responsible capitalism that Gans identified are the current manifestation of the uncontested hegemony of liberal capitalism that Burnham (1982) argues has been a unique aspect of U.S. political history.

Consistent with the value of responsible capitalism, Gans (1979) observes that the media criticize Communist and Social Democratic economies. I will always remember a news story I saw in 1975 when a coalition government in Portugal was formed in which the Communist party was to play a role. Garrick Utley was the reporting correspondent, and he concluded his story by saying, "But the question remains, can you ever trust a Communist?" Incidentally, 13 years later, the government of Portugal remains a democracy.

Ideology and the Mass Media

Do the mass media have a liberal bias? Are they very conservative, or just supportive of the status quo? Because the mass media exert considerable control over the content of political communication in the United States and in other countries, an important struggle among ideologically oriented groups is to attempt to label the media as ideologically extreme (for example, conservatives complain about the liberal bias in the media). Such labeling serves two purposes: (1) to put pressure on the media to present their coverage of events in the ideological direction of the complaining group and to select stories that reflect that ideological perspective, and (2) to attempt to shift the definition of the anchor points of ideological extremity in society in one direction or another. Thus, the question of the ideological orientation of the media is not just an academic question but one central to the continuing struggle taking place over the political and ideological direction of the country.

But the media must have some ideological orientation, mustn't they? Before we attempt to answer that question, you should answer two questions yourself:

1. In general, how would you characterize the ideological content of the news?

*if you're lib → T V Conser
vice versa*

That is, does TV present news with predominantly a liberal or a conservative perspective?

1	2	3	4	5	6	7
Extremely Liberal						Extremely Conservative

2. How would you characterize yourself politically?

1	2	3	4	5	6	7
Extremely Liberal						Extremely Conservative

If you answered the way that over 90% of the students have in all the classes in which I have asked these questions, then you saw the media as moderate (3, 4, or 5) and yourself as moderate (3, 4, or 5); or you saw the media as conservative (6 or 7) and yourself as liberal (1 or 2); or you ranked the media as liberal (1 or 2) and yourself as conservative (6 or 7). This is the pattern of results that is predictable from a study of perceptions of the mass media done by Vallone, Ross, and Lepper (1985).

Vallone et al. (1985) collected news stories about the Israeli invasion of Lebanon in 1982, including coverage of the massacres of Palestinian civilians in several refugee camps. They then showed these excerpts to students who were either pro-Israeli or pro-Arab. Each side viewed the media as supporting the other side in the conflict. Pro-Israeli students rated the news as being pro-Arab, and pro-Arab students made just the opposite rating. Vallone et al. dubbed this finding the "hostile media phenomenon."

This result is clearly understandable through the social judgment theory perspective. Students who are strongly pro-Israeli or pro-Arab would tend to have narrow latitudes of acceptance and wide latitudes of rejection when it came to messages about the Arab/Israeli conflict. Thus, the same news story could easily fall into the latitudes of rejection for both the groups and thus be seen as supportive of the other side.

From this perspective we can also consider the way people view the ideological orientation of the mass media. Ideologically committed liberals or conservatives (those with high involvement) will tend to have fairly narrow latitudes of acceptance and noncommitment and fairly wide latitudes of rejection. Thus, the same messages (in this case, news stories) that many might call moderate may fall into both groups' latitudes of rejection, be contracted, and be seen as more discrepant than they actually are. So liberals may see the story as conservative, and conservatives may see it as liberal.

A Liberal Bias?

About 20 years ago, Vice President Spiro Agnew argued that the media was composed of "effete" intellectuals and that they were "nattering nabobs of negativism." Conservative politicians and analysts have remained critical of the media since then. Lichter, Rothman, and Lichter (1986) authored a book *The Media Elite* in which they argue that the media are dominated by a liberal perspective that shapes the way news is presented. They suggest that reporters' backgrounds, the sources they use, and their underlying motivations all influence the news in a liberal way.

Lichter et al. (1986) point out that reporters have tended historically to be liberal and Democratic. A survey by Rosten in 1936 of the Washington Press corps found that 64% favored Roosevelt and 6% favored Communist or Socialist candidates, despite the fact that most papers were controlled by Republican publishers. In Lichter et al.'s survey of 238 journalists and reporters from the major television networks and elite newspapers such as the *Washington Post* and the *New York Times*, they found that 54% identified themselves as liberal. In comparison, in a 1986 survey of Columbia University journalism students (future journalists), Lichter et al. (1986) found that an even higher percentage (85%) considered themselves liberal. The current journalists expressed a variety of liberal social attitudes (for instance, 97% said the government should not regulate sex; 90% said a woman has the right to decide on abortion; 80% favored strong affirmative action for Blacks; and only 15% thought homosexuals shouldn't teach in public schools).

The reporters also expressed a series of somewhat conservative economic positions: only 13% thought big corporations should be publicly owned; 86% said that people with more ability should earn more; 70% thought that private enterprise is fair to workers; and 63% agreed that less regulation of business is good for the United States. Despite these conservative economic positions, Lichter et al. (1986) suggested that there is an antibusiness bias among media professionals. When the researchers asked the journalists what sources they regarded as reliable, Lichter et al. found that "the paucity of business-oriented sources is also notable. . . . Only 22 percent cite some business-related source of information" (p. 58). While these data suggest that the media are dominated by liberals, past studies have shown that the social characteristics of media personnel are comparable to individuals employed in other professions in the United States (Johnstone, Slawski, & Bowman, 1976).

Lichter et al. (1986) also present some data from content analyses of news coverage of the nuclear power issue and of the energy crisis. They conclude that the accident at the Three Mile Island nuclear power plant was a turning point in media coverage of nuclear power. In Lichter et al.'s view, before the accident newsmagazines and the *New York Times* were evenhanded; afterward, the coverage was overwhelmingly antinuclear. Lichter et al. suggested that this change in coverage reflected a liberal bias because the nuclear energy specialists they interviewed after the accident were not as critical of the nuclear industry as the mass media were. One could argue, of course, that interviewing a group of people whose professional life is heavily invested in nuclear power will inevitably bring out some pronuclear bias. Nevertheless, Lichter et al. are probably correct in concluding that the media were not pronuclear.

The authors also discuss the media's coverage of energy issues, particularly the role the U.S. oil companies played in the energy crisis. They found repeated stories about high profits, lack of competition, and manipulation of oil supplies. According to Lichter et al. (1986), the media tended to blame the oil companies ("big oil") and were more critical of the oil industry than were various academic experts. Although many (such as Barry Commoner) have argued that the oil companies did, in fact, play a role in the energy crisis and reap immense profits, it certainly appears that the media presented a somewhat liberal picture on this issue.

Finally, Lichter et al. (1986) discuss the media's coverage of court-ordered desegregation to achieve racial balance (busing) and conclude that the media acted as "enlightened liberals" (p. 252). The media agreed with this policy and presented stories that supported change. Their data indicated that the media adopted a fairly liberal position on this issue as well. Lichter et al. (1986) concluded:

> Our impression is that they (the media) attempted to act as responsible citizens in helping their country adapt to reforms that were, in their view, necessary and long overdue, despite the short-term conflict and disruption. Thus, their coverage may reflect not mass opinion but the enlightened opinion of liberal intellectuals in universities, think tanks, and federal courtrooms. (p.252)

Another Perspective

Do we conclude, then, that the media are controlled by a bunch of liberals who consistently slants the news in a liberal direction? Well, no. There is considerable evidence to indicate that the media often present a fairly conservative perspective. Michael Parenti, in his 1986 book *Inventing Reality: The Politics of the Mass Media*, cites numerous examples of the ways the mass media continually reinforce the existing capitalist economic system and denigrate opposing systems (especially those in Communist countries), just as Gans (1979) observed.

Parenti (1986) notes that commercial television is supported by advertising revenues from corporations who strive to promote a "consumer ideology." This ideology encourages the public to find meaning in buying consumer goods and suggests that real human needs for love, companionship, and escape from boredom can be satisfied through the purchase of specific products and services. AT & T's "Reach out and touch someone" campaign is a clear example. Moreover, in the 1970s corporations began to spend millions of dollars on enhancing their corporate images. Even public service announcements are dominated by business interests represented by the Advertising Council. As Parenti (1986) concludes:

> Those who wish to make monopoly profits, occupational safety, unemployment, and environmental protection the central themes of popular debate have no way of reaching mass audiences. The public service air time that could be used by conservationists, labor, consumer, and other public interest groups has been pre-empted by a business-dominated Advertising Council that passes off its one-sided, ideological ads as noncontroversial, nonpolitical, and in the public interest. (p. 74)

Ideological Bias in Newspapers' Coverage of Foreign Events

Parenti's (1986) analysis of the coverage in the *New York Times* of the Allende regime in Chile and its overthrow in a military coup in September 1973 illustrates the way news outlets portray leftist governments. Allende was elected president of Chile in 1970 with a plurality of 37% of the vote. The U.S. press repeatedly mentioned the fact that he was a "minority" president, even though Allende's conservative predecessor was also elected by a plurality—and various U.S. presidents from Abraham Lincoln to Richard Nixon were also elected with less than half of the popular vote. Allende was a Socialist and while in office pursued a policy of land reform, nationalization of the U.S. copper mines, and food for the poor. The economic benefits to most of the Chilean population were rarely, if at all, mentioned in the U.S. press. These reforms challenged the power and profits of the wealthy in Chile, as well as of some U.S. multinational corporations, and they generated fierce political opposition. There was freedom of the press (unremarked on in the U.S. media) during Allende's regime, and most of the newspapers and television stations were owned by his opponents, who were vociferously critical of the government. Economic sabotage was widespread, and although the U.S. government maintained that it had no involvement, it was later revealed that the CIA had been funding a trucking strike (by providing funds to striking drivers) that had crippled the economy. The *New York Times* routinely attributed Chile's economic problems to Allende's mismanagement and overambitious reforms.

When the Allende government was overthrown in a military coup in September 1973, the *Times* blamed Allende in one of its editorials, and subsequent coverage portrayed General Augusto Pinochet, the leader of the coup, in a favorable light as "energetic" and "tough." In the years of the Pinochet regime, the widespread and systematic use of torture of political prisoners was generally unremarked on by the U.S. government and the press. It was not until the son of an American citizen was burned to death by a Chilean policeman in 1987 that the press began its currently somewhat negative coverage of the Chilean government. In 1989, in the first free election in Chile since 1973, Pinochet lost his bid for the presidency.

Parenti (1986) also analyzes the U.S. media's acquiescence in the U.S. government's misrepresentations about Vietnam, Cuba, Nicaragua, El Salvador, the Soviet Union, and the invasion of Grenada. It is interesting to note that in Lichter et al.'s (1986) indictment of the media as controlled and influenced by liberals, there are no examples of biased foreign policy presented.

The Ideological Orientation of Television News

The network news coverage in April 1988 of President Reagan's veto of the Trade Bill illustrates the media position on economic issues. The president vetoed the bill primarily because of his opposition to an amendment that required plant owners to give 60 days notification if they planned to close a plant. Both ABC and CBS began their coverage of this story as a personal conflict between the president and Congress (as Peter Jennings said, "There was a showdown today on the trade issue, and Congress blinked"). This is precisely the kind of dramatic conflict that Henry (1981) noted is characteristic of the media's presentation of the news. It also represents the kind of personalization of the news that Bennett (1988) observed. Both networks went on to interview workers who had lost their jobs and who said that some notification would have been a big help to them. CBS even talked about the "golden parachutes" that various executives get when they are fired or leave an organization and the huge salaries that some corporate executives receive (for example, Jim Manzi of Lotus received $26 million in 1987).

This is clearly not a perspective that business interests would favor. Does this mean that the media are liberal? Consider what the networks did not discuss. The networks did not present any analysis of the cost to individual communities and the nation of employers' closing plants and utilizing cheaper labor in Third World countries. Nor did they discuss proposals to fund a Cooperative Investment Bank that would finance worker organizations that wanted to buy a plant that management wanted to close down.

The veto of the Trade Bill was a specific event that occurred in an overall context of economic and political conditions; the media reported only on that specific event in a fairly personalized and dramatic way. Sixty-days notification is a fairly modest proposal to give workers a modicum of control over their lives. The media's support of this proposal is just another example of what Gans (1979) called their belief in the virtues of responsible capitalism.

The Critical Media Studies Approach to the Mass Media

Burnham's (1982) hypothesis of the uncontested hegemony of liberal capitalism in this country clearly has important implications for the study of the mass media. In this context, Stewart Hall (1982) reviews the development of what is called the critical paradigm for media studies. A fundamental observation from this perspective is that the mass media play a crucial role in the maintenance of support for the current economic and political system and are involved in the "production of consent." As Hall (1982) observes, a society with considerable inequalities in the distribution of wealth and power would wish to generate consent among the population for the values that underlie that society and support its continued existence. Thus, it is particularly important to analyze the values implicit in the news media.

To understand why the media may be conservative on some issues and somewhat liberal on others, we need some background discussion. Several social scientists have argued that there is a "ruling class" in the United States (Mills, 1956). If this were the case, given that the media are controlled by large and powerful corporations (clearly part of this ruling class), one might expect that the media would be consistently conservative. Some authors (Lichter et al., 1986) use this absence of a consistently conservative message to argue against the hypothesis of a conservative elite controlling the messages that the media broadcast. Conservative authors (Lichter et al., 1986), in fact, generally go further and argue that the media are controlled by a liberal elite.

The problem is mainly conceptual: A ruling class, made up as it is of many different individuals, does not have to be in total agreement about all issues to still be a ruling class. Domhoff (1967) suggested the term *governing class* instead of *ruling class,* and he has argued that there is ideological conflict and division within the governing class, though its members are all heavily invested in the current economic system. Thus, it is possible for the media to reflect conservative positions on some issues (particularly foreign policy questions), to be liberal on other social issues (such as busing), but to remain consistently supportive of the current economic system—that is, to support the uncontested hegemony of liberal capitalism.

The media may still present news on economically related questions such as energy issues (nuclear power, big oil) that could be labeled *liberal* (Lichter et al., 1986). This is consistent with two other factors we have discussed that influence content in the TV news: Gans's (1979) observation of the media's belief in responsible capitalism, and Henry's (1981) observation of the media's search for dramatic unity in its coverage of news. The issue of nuclear power, particularly after the Three Mile Island power plant accident, raised the question for many people of how responsible the nuclear industry was. Its claims that a nuclear accident was almost inconceivably unlikely were clearly falsified (in fact, recent reports have indicated that the TMI accident was much closer to the very serious Chernobyl accident than was originally thought). As Gans (1979) points out, the media can be very hard on individuals or companies that deviate from the expectation that those with capital will work in the public interest.

In this context, the depiction by the media of oil companies as "big oil" and the nuclear industry as "bad guys" is also consistent with the dramatic requirements for TV news stories—that there be dramatic tension with identifiable protagonists. We should note that although the negative press that the oil industry received might have contributed to the passage in Congress of the Windfall Profits Tax, there was never a movement to nationalize the oil industry. Some have advocated nationalization, arguing that oil is a national resource that belongs to all the people, not just to those few who own the ground under which the oil lies. In fact, corporate profits of the petroleum and coal industry have risen substantially more than other industries that had similar profits in 1972. The petroleum and coal industry went from $3.5 billion in 1973 to a high of $36.5 billion in 1981. In comparison, the food industry earned $3.2 billion in 1970 and only $8.7 billion in 1981; chemicals and allied products went from $3.9 billion in 1970 to only $8.2 in 1981 (*Statistical Abstract of the United States: 1988*, p. 514).

There are many forces at work shaping the content of the mass media. Foremost among them is the uncontested hegemony of liberal capitalism in this country that influences the underlying values inherent in the presentation of the news. Additionally, the news media, particularly television, operate as part of a system of commercial entertainment. Consequently, there are considerable demands for the dramatic unity of news stories that may result in reports that are not overtly conservative, as in the coverage of the energy crisis, but that nevertheless support the system in which the protagonists (such as "big oil") operate.

■ Effects of the Mass Media

Researchers have speculated that the mass media, particularly television, may have a wide range of important effects, some very detrimental. Of particular concern to social scientists and policymakers has been the relationship between viewing television violence and subsequently engaging in aggressive behavior. The study of the effects of television violence on aggressive behavior parallels research on the political effects of the mass media.

As indicated in the next section on the political effects of the mass media, many researchers maintained for years that the media had little or no effect on individuals' attitudes. Similarly, various researchers, particularly those who supported the "catharsis hypothesis" of television violence (Feshbach & Singer, 1971), argued that the violence on television has no negative effects and may have positive effects by providing a release for viewers' aggressive impulses, thereby reducing violence in society.

Television producers have consistently expressed their belief in the validity of the catharsis hypothesis. Since television producers and networks make a great deal of money by providing violent television shows, it is in their economic interest to maintain that there are no negative effects of such programming. Unfortunately, the weight of evidence has consistently failed to support the catharsis hypothesis of positive effects of watching television with violent content. Additionally, many studies have indicated increased aggression associated with viewing violent television shows, although the history of the surgeon general's report on the effects of television violence reveals the attempts of the television networks to influence the content of the report by excluding prominent social scientists who they considered biased against the networks (Liebert & Sprafkin, 1988).

Recently, Jonathan Freedman (1984, 1986) generated controversy with his review of research on this relationship and his argument that evidence does not support the conclusion that watching television violence causes aggression. A major reply to Freedman was offered by Friedrich-Cofer and Huston (1986), and in their book *The Early Window*, Liebert and Sprafkin (1988) document the 20-year history of research on television violence and aggression. Liebert and Sprafkin (1988) conclude from this research that watching televised violence can teach aggressive and antisocial behavior and may, depending on characteristics of the viewers and the situation, increase the likelihood of aggressive behavior.

Documentation of the effect of viewing television violence is provided by Huesmann and his colleagues (Huesmann, 1986; Huesmann, Eron, Lefkowitz, & Walder, 1984). These researchers found in a 22-year longitudinal study that the extent of exposure to violence on television for children at age 8 was significantly related to the seriousness of criminal acts performed by the same individuals at the age of 30. The data Huesman et al. (1984) collected were correlational; nevertheless, the longitudinal nature of their data permit a stronger causal conclusion to be drawn than would typically be the case with correlations. At the same time, it is important to note that the effects of watching television violence are not the same on everyone. Wendy Josephson (1987) found that exposing second- and third-grade boys to a violent TV program resulted in increased aggressive behavior primarily in the boys who already tended to be aggressive. Violent shows on television are obviously not the only cause of aggressive behavior, but research evidence indicates that they contribute to the increasing level of violence in our society.

Political Effects of the Mass Media

For a number of years, researchers of the effects of the mass media on political attitudes have argued that the media exert only minimal effects on viewers' opinions (Hovland, Lumsdaine, & Sheffield, 1949; Klapper, 1960; Lazarsfeld, Berelson, & Gaudet, 1944). In his book *Effects of Mass Media*, Klapper (1960) argued that the media would have very little effect because of several psychological processes operating—particularly, selective exposure. People will generally expose themselves to information that is consistent with their existing views. Therefore, Klapper suggested, the mass media will primarily reinforce existing attitudes. It is only fairly recently that clear evidence for mass media effects has emerged. We should note that the television networks looked very favorably on Klapper's opinions; later in his career he became research director for CBS and played a major role in defending the television industry against the negative findings contained in the report of the Surgeon General's Scientific Advisory Committee on Television and Social Behavior (*Television and Growing Up: The Impact of Televised Violence*).

Evidence suggests that the process of selective exposure may operate in the short term but that long-term media campaigns can overcome its effects. Lord, Ross, and Lepper (1979) showed two supposedly new research studies on capital punishment to Stanford University students, half of whom favored the death penalty and half of whom opposed it. The two studies reached opposing conclusions; one reported evidence that the death penalty deterred crime, and the other reported just the opposite conclusion, that the death penalty had no deterrent effect. With students reading these conflicting results, one might expect that their attitudes toward capital punishment might become more moderate. In fact, just the opposite occurred: The difference between the attitudes of the two groups became greater as students became more extreme in their support of or opposition to the death penalty. This certainly suggests a selective-exposure effect: Individuals accepted the findings that supported their position, and they were very critical of the opposing study.

This effect also appears to have operated on the attitude of individuals watching the American presidential debates. In 1960, 1976, and 1980, those viewers who already supported one of the nominees felt that their candidate won by nearly a 10-to-1 margin (Kinder & Sears, 1985). Thus in many situations, ambiguous information can increase disagreements between individuals rather than help them see their opponents' viewpoint.

The selective-exposure effect appears to operate in the short term, suggesting that the media should have little effect. Evidence indicates, however, that media campaigns over a long period of time can overcome this effect. In a longitudinal test of the selective-exposure hypothesis (Milburn, 1979), I found that exposure to the Stanford Heart Disease Prevention Program's three-year media campaign significantly increased health knowledge, and there was no evidence of a selective-exposure effect. Over the long term, we can expect that the mass media will exert a considerable influence on individuals' knowledge and opinions. Let us examine various ways the media exerts its effects.

The Mass Media and Agenda Setting

Bernard Cohen (1963) wrote that the press "may not be successful much of the time in telling people what to think, but it is stunningly successful in telling readers what to think *about*" (p. 13). Maxwell McCombs and Donald Shaw (1972) called this the "agenda setting" capacity of the mass media, and a variety of subsequent studies have found evidence to support this effect. Funkhouser (1973) examined the attention that the national press paid to various issues in the 1960s and found that its coverage paralleled the problems that the public felt were important. Other studies found similar correlational evidence between coverage of issues in the media and the public's ratings of importance of those issues, although the effects were often not very strong (for a review, see McCombs, 1981).

Interpreting these correlational studies poses potential problems. One argument suggests that if the media are just reporting what happens in the real world, then it would make sense that the public finds the same issues important. The media are thus serving as a conduit, reporting important real-world events. It is the real-world events, not the media, that are creating the public agenda. Some argue that correlational results are subject to some alternative explanations. It may be that the direction of causality is different than the one assumed by the agenda-setting model; the media may simply be covering the issues that the public sees as important, rather than the other way around. Finally, the agenda-setting model in its simple form assumes that the effect of the media is the same for all viewers. It may be that different members of the newspaper and television audiences—because of their education, personal experiences, motivation, and interest in the news—are affected differently. Shanto Iyengar and Donald Kinder (1987) conducted a very comprehensive set of studies on the issue of agenda setting that clarifies many questions.

The Real World

To what extent does media attention to specific problems simply reflect actual real-world events? Behr and Iyengar (1985) attempted to assess this question by using time-series data on public opinion about the most important problem, in addition to indicators of current conditions in three areas. Time-series data are measurements on the same variable(s) at regular intervals over time. For example, the public's approval rating of the president every month over a 4-year period is a time series. For *inflation* they obtained measures of economic health such as the consumer price index; for *unemployment* they used the unemployment index; and for *energy* they used a variety of measures, such as heating oil and gasoline prices. They also included the number of presidential speeches on each of the three topics in their prediction equations.

Behr and Iyengar (1985) concluded that television news reporting on these three issues was "at least partially determined by real-world conditions and events" (p. 47). Actual changes in economic conditions influenced the level of television coverage of these issues, although there was still a good deal of unexplained variance in the amount of news coverage. Consistent with the arguments discussed earlier about the impact of government pronouncements on news coverage, presidential speeches on a particular issue also significantly influenced the level of news attention to that issue. And what effect does this have on the public's agenda? They found consequential effects of media coverage (though only when the stories were in the lead position) on the public's importance ratings for two of the three issues (energy and inflation). The media does not set the public's agenda completely independent of real-world events, but there remains strong evidence of media effects.

The Direction of Causality

As noted above, correlational evidence of a relationship between the media coverage of particular issues and the public's concern about those issues does not provide unambiguous evidence of media effects. It may be that media attention to national problems simply reflects concern in the public about those problems. Two ways to obtain less equivocal evidence of causal direction are to use longitudinal or time-series data and to do experiments. In their time-series study discussed above, Behr and Iyengar (1985) found the causal influence between the media and the public to be unidirectional; there was little or no influence of public concern upon the issues the media chose to cover. Experiments are also an important source of information about the direction of causal inference.

Shanto Iyengar, Mark Peters, and Donald Kinder (1982) reported a clever experimental test of the effects of news coverage on the perceived importance of various national issues, what is called the agenda-setting function of the mass media. They had subjects come to their laboratory every night for a week and watch the news, supposedly as it was broadcast. In fact, each night they showed the news from the night before with various stories added or deleted; for example, in the defense condition subjects watched five stories on defense preparedness covering 17 minutes. They found for three out of four issues that they presented, subjects' ratings of the importance of the particular issue that they saw many stories about significantly increased. Thus, Iyengar et al. demonstrated that the news items the television networks select as important result in corresponding increases in viewers' ratings of the importance of those problems.

Iyengar and Kinder (1987) report the results of over a dozen experiments on different aspects of the agenda-setting effect of the news media. Their results provide strong evidence for media influences, particularly for lead stories. Iyengar and Kinder placed the same news stories either first in a news broadcast that their subjects watched or in the middle, embedded with other stories. They found that the same stories had a greater impact on the subjects' importance ratings of that problem when that story was in the lead position rather than in the middle, replicating the earlier time-series result that Behr and Iyengar (1985) obtained.

Personal Characteristics

In their experimental studies, Iyengar and Kinder (1987) tried to identify the characteristics of those in whom the agenda-setting effects were most pronounced. They found that the impact was highest for those with low levels of education (high school or less), low levels of party identification (independents), and low political involvement (people who follow politics rarely and who are politically inactive).

Personal experience with the particular problem reported on television is also an important mediating variable for agenda-setting effects. In their investigation of agenda-setting effects, Erbring, Goldenberg, and Miller (1980) found evidence of what they called "audience-contingent" influences. They utilized survey data, augmented with a content analysis of the issues covered in the newspaper that each respondent reported reading. In looking at the impact of stories about unemployment, for example, they discovered that for people for whom unemployment was salient (whether there was a union member in the family or unemployment in the family), the number of front-page news stories about unemployment greatly increased the importance attributed to that issue.

Also using the issue of unemployment, Iyengar and Kinder (1987) examined the importance of personal experiences in mediating the agenda-setting effects of television experimentally. In two different experiments they obtained opposite results. In the first experiment they found that the subjects who were unemployed responded to media stories about unemployment (in their assessment of the importance of the problem of unemployment) much more than did subjects who were employed. In the second experiment the opposite was true: The employed had higher importance ratings after seeing media stories about unemployment. Their explanation for these conflicting results reiterates the importance of the real-world context in which these studies took place. They conducted the first experiment at a time when unemployment was relatively low; the second experiment occurred at a time when unemployment was much higher. This suggests that when a problem is not widely perceived as important, media attention to the issue will increase concern about it primarily in those directly affected. When the problem has received attention for some time, however, additional media coverage will exert greater influence on those who are not directly impacted.

The agenda-setting effect of television news can best be understood as an example of priming (see Chapter Six). The more attention the media gives to a particular event, the more the schema related to that event is primed, and the more important that issue becomes for the public's evaluation of how well a president is doing. Krosnick and Kinder (1990) found that following the extensive media coverage of the Iran-Contra affair (after Edwin Meese's disclosure that there had been weapons sales to Iran and a diversion of the proceeds to aid the Contras), individuals' attitudes toward U.S. policy in Central America became significantly more important in their evaluations of President Reagan's performance.

The Effect of Negative Political Campaign Advertisements

Use of the mass media is critical in a political campaign, and increasingly, political campaign ads have become negative (Joslyn, 1986; Sabato, 1981). Is "going negative," as the pundits and pollsters would say, an effective strategy? Under what circumstances does it work? Must a candidate always respond to a negative campaign ad? A series of recent studies have investigated the effectiveness of political commercials that overtly attack a political opponent. These studies indicate that negative ads can be very effective, but the research indicates some potential limitations on their persuasiveness. Additionally, the application of inoculation theory (McGuire, 1964; see Chapter Eight) to the area of political advertising suggests important strategic approaches for candidates in political campaigns.

Roddy and Garramone (1988) experimentally tested the effect of attacking political commercials on viewers' impressions of the commercials and viewers' impressions and preferences of the candidates attacked or supported in the commercials. Roddy and Garramone (1988) developed two different types of negative commercials, one ad based on issues and one based on image. Their results indicated that the negative-issue ad was more effective in decreasing viewers' intention to vote for the attacked candidate.

Garramone (1985) found experimentally that a negative ad attributed to a source independent of the attacking candidate was more effective in decreasing support for his opponent than one presented by the candidate himself. This is consistent with the research on source credibility reviewed in the previous chapter. Additionally, however, Garramone (1985) found that when viewers also saw a rebuttal of the negative ad, their support decreased for the candidate originally producing the negative ad, thus underscoring the importance of responding to negative political commercials.

Studying the effect of negative campaign advertising in a state assembly general election in California, Merritt (1984) found that negative advertising appeared to have a boomerang effect (see Chapter Eight). The negative ads that attacked a Democrat appeared to activate counterargument among voters who identified with the Democratic party, reinforcing their initial dispositions. Thus, Merritt (1984) concluded that negative advertising is a risky strategy for a candidate whose party is in a minority. The advertising must instead give voters a positive reason to switch, rather than simply attack the opponent, which may reinforce voters' initial predispositions. These results imply that negative campaign advertising may be most effective in districts with large numbers of independents or weak party identifiers.

Despite Merritt's (1984) findings and the results of other studies (Stewart, 1975) suggesting limitations on the effectiveness of negative advertising, most political professionals are convinced of its effectiveness (Sabato, 1981). Professionals tend to rely on three types of political advertisements: positive ads that stress the qualities of the supported candidate, negative ads that attack the opponent, and rebuttal ads that respond to negative ads from a candidate's opponent. Pfau and Burgoon (1988) propose using a fourth type of campaign ad based on inoculation theory (McGuire, 1964; see Chapter Eight).

In the context of an ongoing U.S. Senate election, Pfau and Burgoon (1988) presented voters with information that refuted attacks on candidates to which the voters were later exposed. Pfau and Burgoon consistently found that exposure to inoculation information increased voters' resistance to later attacks, and this effect was strongest for strong party identifiers as one would expect. Although the effects were statistically significant, they were not large; nevertheless, even small effects may make the difference in a close election.

Research indicates that negative campaign tactics have a demonstrable negative effect on voters' perceptions of the targeted candidate. But research also indicates that responding to the attack from an opponent can counteract that negative effect. Thus, Dukakis's decision to "take the high road" during the 1988 election campaign and not respond to Bush's negative campaign ads about Willie Horton did substantial damage to his campaign. This damage might have been greatly reduced if the Dukakis campaign had employed one of the three strategies described above: inoculation—by preempting the attack; by responding directly to the charges in a nonstatistical, emotionally accessible way; or by using negative tactics himself.

Mass Media Effects on Policy Attitudes, Affective Responses, and the Complexity of Thinking

News Effects on Individuals' Policy Attitudes

As indicated above, considerable evidence supports the agenda-setting hypothesis—that the news media influence what people think about. Suggesting even stronger effects, research also indicates that the media sway individuals' policy attitudes and affect how people think and feel about political events and actors. Page, Shapiro, and Dempsey (1987) identified 80 different pairs of policy attitudes over the past 15 years (each pair consisted of the same question asked about three months apart) and compared this data with a content analysis of the news coverage from two months preceding the first question until after the second question had been asked. They found that "news commentary" (that is, pro or con statements regarding specific issues presented by network anchors, reporters in the field, or special commentators) had a striking effect on policy opinions: "a single 'probably pro' commentary is associated with more than four percentage points of opinion change" (p. 31). They found that "experts" (labeled by the networks) also had an impact upon citizen's attitudes, as did popular presidents. Presidents whose popularity was low, however, were unable to use the media effectively to change viewer's attitudes on particular policy questions.

Given this fact that unpopular presidents are not effective in using the media to change citizens' attitudes, it is important to note that the media also has an impact on the way people feel about political actors, the foremost of whom is the president. In a series of experimental tests of media effects, Iyengar et al. (1984) found that enhanced coverage of specific issues increased the importance of specific ratings of how well the president was coping with those problems on the overall ratings of the president's performance. For example, subjects' ratings of President Carter's performance on the energy crisis had a greater impact on their overall evaluation of Carter's competency for subjects who saw several news stories about energy than for subjects who did not see the energy stories.

The power of the media has been an important issue in presidential election campaigns, particularly when presidential debates have been televised. Newton,

Masters, McHugo, and Sullivan (1987) showed their subjects the 1976 debates between Jimmy Carter and Gerald Ford and obtained a measure of the subjects' emotional reaction to the candidates (how warm or cold they felt toward the candidates) after watching the debates alone, watching the debates and the instant analysis that the networks conducted immediately after the debates, or watching the news coverage on the next day. Newton et al. found that after watching either type of news coverage following the debates (the instant analysis or the next-day coverage), their subjects had significantly less positive affect toward both of the candidates. As is consistent with the research we discussed in Chapter Six about the differences between experts and novices, those subjects who were more politically sophisticated (those who had three regular sources of political information, who always or almost always voted, and who had participated in some federal election campaign) were less likely to show an impact from the media coverage.

The Impact of News Structure on Cognitive Complexity

An important element of the news that we discussed earlier in this chapter is the focus on events rather than ongoing social processes or problems. What is the effect of this type of coverage on the complexity of the explanations for events offered and on the way viewers think about events? Evidence suggests that this kind of coverage results in fairly simple explanations, and watching TV news in turn results in simple thinking about events.

David Altheide (1987) compared U.S. and British coverage of an IRA bombing in London and found that the coverage, particularly in Britain, tended to be what he called of the *event type* rather than of the *topic type*. That is, the coverage relied on visuals (which are more entertaining) rather than on discussion and analysis of the events. It was only in the United States (not the subject of the attack in this case) that there were interviews with individuals who "rejected a simplistic and unambiguous view of the situation" (p. 171). He concludes that the way terrorism is generally covered "will be to retard understanding of the complexities of international affairs in the mass audience" (p. 174).

Recent work on the effects of the mass media coverage of terrorism on individuals' attributions about terrorism (Milburn, Bowley, Fay-Dumaine, & Kennedy, 1987; Milburn, Cistuli, and Garr, 1988) suggests that the media does influence the complexity of political reasoning. Milburn et al. (1987) used content analysis to study the way the television news offered explanations for terrorism and political violence. They found that 40% of the stories offered no explanation at all; in Rosenberg's (1987) framework this would be called sequential thinking, the lowest level of political reasoning. Seen in the context of the Georgoudi (1985) research on attribution theory discussed earlier, this indicates a tendency on the media's part to present simple explanations.

Milburn et al. (1988) followed up this research with two studies. First, they conducted a small survey (a probability sample of 78 people in the Boston area) and asked respondents for their explanations for terrorism in general, the amount of television watched, and various background characteristics. Milburn et al. (1988) also obtained respondents' explanations for three specific acts of political violence (for example, "Ibraham Mohammed Khaled, claiming that he was doing only what any young Palestinian would do, led an attack in the Rome Airport in which thirteen persons died and eighty were wounded, including six Americans"). These open-ended responses were coded for dialectical thinking (Georgoudi, 1985) and summed.

A multiple regression analysis indicated statistically significant positive effects of education, sex, and age on the complexity of individuals' attributions about terrorism, consistent with the effects of social factors on public opinion discussed in Chapter Three. Individuals with more education, respondents who were older, and women were more complex in their explanations for terrorism. More important, however, was that even after controlling for the effects of these variables, there was a significant negative effect of television watching on the complexity of the attributions offered for terrorism. Individuals who reported watching a great deal of television were more likely to offer no explanation for terrorism or an internal explanation (such as "terrorists are insane"); those who watched less television were more likely to offer an external explanation or to offer a combination of internal and external explanations. These results were consistent with the earlier content analysis results (Milburn et al., 1987), but since the analysis was correlational, the direction of causal influence was ambiguous.

In a second study, Milburn et al. (1988) experimentally manipulated exposure to television news stories about political violence with a small sample ($n = 45$). In the political violence condition, three television reports (a story about the lone surviving attacker in the Rome Airport massacre; a story about a Tamil separatist group in Sri Lanka killing 150 civilians; and a story about the one-year anniversary of the U.S. bombing of Libya) were edited together with other news stories about Vanna White and Jimmy Swaggart. In the control condition, the White and Swaggart stories were edited together with three other nonpolitical violence stories. A significant interaction ($p < .05$) emerged between exposure to the political violence stories and belief in the accuracy of the news. Individuals exposed to the political violence stories and who believed that the television news was accurate most of the time rated internal factors as more important than external factors in explaining the behavior of Ibraham Mohammed Khaled in the Rome Airport massacre. The opposite effect was obtained for those with low beliefs in the accuracy of the media. These results are displayed in Figure 9-1.

Differences among individuals in the complexity of their thinking on political issues appear to be related to the individuals' general cognitive sophistication (Rosenberg, 1987). In addition to these individual differences, situational cues also appear to exert an influence on the complexity of their thinking (Georgoudi, 1985), with schematic processes indicated as a major factor (Milburn & Fay-Dumaine, 1988). The Milburn et al. (1988) findings indicate that the mass media—in particular, television news—are a major source of the schematic influences that simplify individuals' complexity of thinking about political events.

The Effect of the Dramatic Coverage of News Events

In producing TV news, networks have a limited amount of airtime during which to relay the events the network deems important. The stories tend, therefore, to be

Figure 9-1   Relative importance ratings for internal and external causes of the Rome Airport massacre

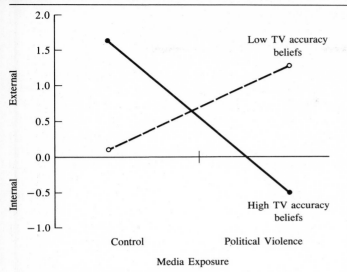

Media Exposure

Source: From *Survey and experimental studies of the effect of television news on individuals' attributions about terrorism*, 1988, by M. A. Milburn, B. Cistuli, and M. Garr. Paper presented at the International Society of Political Psychology annual meeting.

formatted in the most efficient way possible, without losing audience attention or appeal. Reuven Frank, former executive producer of the *NBC Evening News,* proposed a formula in 1963 by which to accomplish this:

> Every news story should, without any sacrifice of probity or responsibility, display the attributes of fiction, of drama. It should have structure and conflict, problem and denouement, rising action and falling action, a beginning, middle and an end. These are not only the essentials of drama; they are the essentials of narrative. (Epstein, 1973, pp. 4–5)

What is the effect of such dramatic coverage of news events? Milburn and McGrail (1990) reasoned that television stories formatted in a dramatic way, evoking emotional responses and relating the events to a more general story or myth, would activate simplifying schemas (see Chapter Six) for the viewers and reduce the cognitive complexity with which they thought about the political events in the stories.

To test this hypothesis, Milburn and McGrail (1990) selected a series of highly dramatic news stories and edited from them the dramatic scenes. Subjects watched either the dramatic stories or the nondramatic stories and then tried to recall as much information from the news stories as they could. Additionally, subjects wrote out in several paragraphs their opinions of what the United States should do in two situations raised in the news stories: the trade imbalance with South Korea and the upcoming election in Chile. After controlling for various background variables such as parents' education and the person's political ideology, Milburn and McGrail found that the individuals who watched the dramatic stories recalled significantly less of the information in the stories and the cognitive complexity of their political thinking was significantly lower.

Additional Negative Effects of Television

The above findings are consistent with research from studies conducted in Canada that compared the reading proficiency and creative abilities of children in towns with no television and children in towns with one channel or multiple channels. The reading skills of second-graders in the town with no television were substantially higher than those of similar children in towns with television; after the introduction of television, the differences in reading disappeared (Corteen & Williams, 1986). Similarly, the children in the town with no television scored significantly higher, on the average, on a test of creativity; following the availability of television, their creativity levels dropped and were no different from those of the children in the other towns (Harrison & Williams, 1986). Singer (1982) found similar results. Exposure to commercial television appears to reduce the imaginative abilities of children, comparable to the effects of television news on adults.

Media Credibility

Since Milburn et al. (1988) found that news shows had a considerable influence on the complexity of viewers' political thinking when individuals believed in the accuracy of the media, the extent to which citizens accept the media's portrayal of reality as accurate is a key question. Historically, there have been some interesting inconsistencies in the public's attitudes toward the media. Erskine (1970) reviewed surveys from the 1930s to the 1960s and found that although the public often recognized some potential for bias in the news, the majority found the news accurate. In 1938 and 1939, the Gallup and Roper organizations asked questions about a series of potential sources of bias. Between 48% and 57% of those interviewed thought that advertisers in the newspapers influenced the treatment of the news; 66% of those interviewed by Roper felt that newspapers soft-pedaled news that was unfavorable to friendly politicians or friends of the publisher; and almost 60% felt that newspapers softened news unfavorable to big business. Nevertheless, 59% believed that newspaper headlines "usually give you an accurate idea of what really happened" (Erskine, 1970, p. 640), and around 68% of those who listened to radio news felt that the news was reported truthfully. Having some awareness of potential sources of bias in the news does not always lead to disbelief.

This finding is replicated in recent poll results. Gaziano (1988) reported that a majority of the people surveyed by Times-Mirror, Gannett, and ASNE (the American Society of Newspaper Editors) believed that newspaper editors are well trained and try to be objective. *Credibility* and *believability* appear to be two different concepts for many people. Times-Mirror wrote that "there is no credibility crisis for the news media. If credibility is defined as believability, then credibility is, in fact, one of the media's strongest suits" (Gaziano, 1988, p. 271). Although the public may believe the news stories, they don't always have great confidence in the media's desire to serve the public's best interests. Robinson and Kohut (1988) reach a similar conclusion: When *credibility* is narrowed to *believability,* the evidence indicates that the public generally believes the media.

■ Conclusion

Given that the effects of the media on the complexity of individuals' attributions about political events are highest among those who believe that the media are credible, the above findings that the public generally believes the stories in the media are disturbing. A variety of studies indicate that watching television— particularly, television news—lowers the cognitive complexity with which individuals think about political events. Given these findings, it is not surprising that the public rarely questions the uncontested hegemony of liberal capitalism in the United States, supported as it is by the underlying values of responsible capitalism and altruistic democracy in the mass media coverage of news events.

■ ■ ■ ■ ■ ■ ■

CHAPTER
TEN

Conclusion

■ The Political Psychology of Public Opinion— a Summary

We begin this final chapter with a summary of ideas about the ongoing interaction between personal and situational factors that is a major aspect of the social psychology of public opinion. We then move to a consideration of how the various concepts presented in this book help us to understand the current crisis in American political participation. Research in political psychology provides an essential perspective on politics and public opinion.

Understanding political attitudes requires keeping in focus simultaneously a variety of causal factors and processes. Researchers trying to understand public opinion are confronted with a sometimes bewildering array of social and personal forces that influence the way individuals feel about political issues. In this book I have tried to demonstrate a social psychological perspective on public opinion, one that explores the interaction between an individual's personal characteristics (personality, intellectual capacity, need for thinking about issues) and the various situational influences (attitude change messages structured in various ways, political information provided in the mass media) that an individual in American society normally encounters. This extension of the situational approach to the understanding of political attitudes (Bennett, 1980) provides an important way of discerning the complex patterns in the fabric of public opinion.

At the outset of our discussion of public opinion we considered the importance of various social background factors in an individual's life and how they appear to influence significantly the type of opinions that this individual holds. The effects of social factors on opinions reflect both the process of socialization and the result of group membership or identification. While looking individually at the variety of social factors that shape an individual's attitudes (such as age, race, sex, religion, education, income), we encountered an initial problem in disentangling their effects: The same factors tend to have different effects for different types of political attitudes. For example, people with high incomes may be more liberal on social issues but more conservative on economic issues than people with low incomes.

We then confronted an additional problem facing social scientists: the interrelationships between different social variables. Individuals who are higher in education are more conservative on some issues than those lower in education. The same pattern holds for income. But since education and income are highly correlated (people with more education tend to have more income), are their attitudes shaped by their higher education or their higher income? The statistical procedure of multiple regression allows us to address questions such as these.

Additionally, research on political socialization pointed strongly to the effect of the social context in which a person is raised. Young Whites in rural Appalachia did not show the same attachment to important U.S. political symbols (for instance, the presidency) as did middle-class White youths—nor did Blacks. We also noted, however, that social factors alone failed to explain a great deal of variation in individuals' attitudes, suggesting that other factors are at work.

Following the analysis of social factors and public opinion, we turned to research on personality and public opinion, not to argue that personality explains more or less about people's political attitudes than do social factors, but to observe the interrelationship among social background, personality structure, and attitudes. We considered the controversy between the rigidity-of-the-right perspective, embodied in the research on the authoritarian personality, and the assumption of authoritarianism of the left, contained in Eysenck and Rokeach's two-factor models of ideology and personality. It became clear that although some left-wing individuals may exhibit the rigidity of thinking typically associated with the authoritarian personality, the vast majority of authoritarians are politically conservative.

After an analysis of personality and politics, we discussed various approaches to the way that individuals understand the political world and the causal forces that influence events. Different approaches by Tetlock, Rosenberg, and Georgoudi paralleled each other in their conceptions of the complexity with which individuals think about events. Clear differences among individuals emerged in the complexity with which they were able to think, and these differences were linked to education, an important social background variable: People higher in education generally reason with greater complexity. In addition, situational influences appeared also to affect the sophistication of individuals' thinking through the activation of pragmatic schemas, which either stimulated or reduced complexity. Thus, the complexity with which individuals think about politics is a function of both personal characteristics and situational influences.

After examining the nature of cognitive complexity, we next discussed the way schemas influence the complexity of political thought. As my colleagues and I found in several different studies, the activation of political schemas may result in more ideologically consistent political attitudes, but this schema activation is associated with more simplified political thought. Again, we found that characteristics of individuals—for example, whether they were experts or novices in a particular domain—interacted with situational factors (such as the activation of specific schemas) to influence the complexity of political thought.

Subsequent to our analysis of political thought and the situational factors that influence it, we considered the cognitive processes through which individuals maintain consistency among their beliefs. Balance theory and dissonance theory were both discussed, and then we considered Abelson's more elaborate model of various modes of resolution of belief dilemmas. When we used Abelson's model to analyze Reagan's speech following the release of the Tower Board Report on the Iran-Contra affair, it became quite clear that the speech could stimulate specific modes of belief dilemma resolution in the public. By viewing denial, bolstering, differentiation, and transcendence as pragmatic schemas that a communicator may activate, we are able to integrate the process of persuasion into a broader social cognition framework.

After this analysis of a specific political communication, we considered social psychological research on attitude change that has identified important factors influencing the effectiveness of political communication. We considered elements such as the perceived expertise and trustworthiness of the source, the distance from the position advocated in the persuasive communication to the target individual's existing attitudes, and how Fishbein and Ajzen's model represented these relationships mathematically. Thus, how much attitude change a message produced was a function of situational influences (for instance, source credibility) and of the elements an individual would bring into the influence situation (for instance, the person's existing attitude).

The elaboration likelihood model was then presented as an integration of the previous research on persuasive communication. Petty and Cacioppo proposed that persuasion may occur through either the central (elaborate) or peripheral (limited) route, depending primarily on the amount of thinking or cognition an individual directs toward the persuasive message. They developed a need-for-cognition scale to measure how individuals differ in the amount of thinking they typically do when exposed to a persuasive message. Petty and Cacioppo found that an individual's need for cognition correlated negatively with dogmatism: The more rigid an individual was in his or her thinking, the less the individual would be interested in thinking about issues raised in a message. Thus, the personality dimension discussed in Chapter Three plays an important role in the process of persuasion, and the interaction between personal characteristics and situational factors is again evident.

Finally, we discussed the most important source of political communications, the mass media. We observed that the ideological position of the viewer will influence his or her perception of the ideological position of the media. We then examined the ideological content of the national news and found an interesting pattern of somewhat liberal content on social issues and more conservative views on economic and foreign policy issues. This parallels the pattern of opinions that we discussed earlier—that higher income is associated with liberal social views and more conservative economic views. This pattern of news presentation reflects quite clearly the uncontested hegemony of liberal/capitalist ideology in this country.

Evidence indicates that the mass media can have a significant impact on the complexity of thinking that viewers will use to consider political events, both in general and in reaction to specific news stories. The simple explanations for terrorism presented in the news (such as the explanations offered about the Rome

Airport massacre) appear to produce more simple, internal explanations for political events. Additionally, the dramatic structure utilized in many television news stories appears also to be associated with reduced complexity of political thinking among viewers. The more television people watch, the more they are exposed to simple explanations for political events; and the more simplifying schemas that are activated, the simpler their thinking is about such events.

■ Political Psychology and Political Analysis

How do all the different psychological processes reviewed in this volume help us to understand what is taking place politically in this country? Let us consider their joint application to the presidential election in 1988, remembering the current crisis in U.S. political participation.

George Bush ran a particularly aggressive and negative campaign. Michael Dukakis did not respond immediately, as the research on negative campaign advertising discussed in Chapter Nine indicates is necessary, so considerable damage was done to Dukakis's campaign. What was the content of the negative campaign that Bush conducted? As we discussed in Chapter Six, Bush was able to activate various schemas with strong affective components. The Willie Horton ad activated citizens' fear of crime; and since all the prisoners portrayed in the ad were Black, this ad also activated any racist attitudes and emotions toward Blacks that viewers held. Additionally, Bush's use of the American flag and the pledge of allegiance controversy served to activate individuals' emotions of patriotism, which are ultimately one way in which individuals who feel alienated can experience feelings of belonging.

As we saw in our discussion of child rearing in this country, there is a pervasive use of what Sylvan Tomkins called normative patterns of child rearing that emphasize the importance of obedience. Since the characteristic affects of fear and disgust are strongly associated with this type of socialization, in most individuals these emotions are readily available for activation. As we also saw in Chapter Four, Tomkins's polarity theory suggested that these affects are most likely to be associated with a conservative political ideology. Bush's campaign was able to successfully tap into these right-wing scripts and the associated negative affect.

What was the likely effect of the emotional activation that Bush was able to accomplish in his campaign? As we saw in our discussion of Petty and Cacioppo's elaboration likelihood model in Chapter Eight, emotion can play an important role in the overall process of persuasion. When individuals have little interest in processing a message—as is the case in the United States today, with people showing increased levels of political alienation and decreased political participation—affect becomes an important persuasive cue. Michael Dukakis was unable to develop any powerful emotional messages in his campaign that could have offset those employed in Bush's campaign. Dukakis tried to respond with statistics; and as we saw in Chapter Six, statistics are no match for powerful emotional images.

And what was the overall political context in which the election occurred? As we saw in Chapter Nine, the media as well as other political elites in this country continue to promote the uncontested hegemony of liberal capitalism. This is reflected in a conservative and nonanalytical news media that discourages complexity of political thinking. Little in the way of causal explanations for events is offered, and the format of the news, oriented as it is to the dramatic presentation of news events, additionally discourages analytical thinking. Consequently, with the decline of the electorate's capacity for critical thinking, peripheral cues such as emotional responses to negative campaign messages become extremely influential.

Psychological processes influence the way individuals develop political attitudes and think about political events. It is extremely important to keep in mind these various psychological processes when one is trying to understand the effect of political communications, both from politicians and from the news media. Unless there are substantial changes in the current content of the political environment, the "governability crisis" (Burnham, 1982) developing in this country is likely to continue to worsen.

In the Harris Poll survey of alienation among U.S. citizens, recent results show an increase in alienation from 1988 to 1989 (*The Harris Poll*, October 29, 1989). Particularly striking among the results are that Blacks, Hispanics, people earning less than $7500, and women are all groups that have higher-than-average alienation levels. These alienation levels coincide generally with lower political participation levels among these groups.

How can this alienation and lack of participation be remedied? The research in this book suggests a variety of changes for both individuals and the system. At the core of individuals' responses to political events is the training in unquestioning obedience that many individuals receive in childhood, generally reinforced in schools and in the workplace. There is also widespread use of physical punishment in families, with some individuals calling for the reintroduction of corporal punishment in schools. This type of socialization helps explain many current political opinions—for example, the tremendously high rate of support for presidential use of military intervention in international crises. Our patterns of child rearing must change so that respect for individual dignity is foremost and individual expressions of creativity are reinforced; at the same time the pervasive use of shame and physical punishment must be curtailed.

These changes must also carry over into our educational system. Education is foremost in developing the capacity of individuals to understand political events. Yet for the most part the educational system in this country today emphasizes rote memorization over the development of a capacity for critical thinking. This is not to say that students should not be required to learn facts; perceiving events without understanding the context in which they occur prevents individuals from adequately comprehending what has happened. However, memorizing places and dates without an awareness of historical processes results primarily in information forgotten after the next exam.

The family and the educational system create the context in which individuals perceive political events. Individuals working in the news media must provide some historical and political context for the events they report and consider the underlying assumptions that pervade their reports. Research shows that the dramatic coverage of news events decreases the complexity with which individuals think about political events. Possibly, historical and contextual information can be integrated with dramatic information in television news stories in a way that does not hinder individuals' thinking about political issues. Further research should investigate this issue; and the mass media, as part of their public mission to inform the public, should assume responsibility for funding it. Until the media (particularly television) change the way news is covered, viewers must seek out alternative sources of information.

The nature of political campaigns needs to change as well. Although research shows that negative campaigning is effective, there is also evidence demonstrating that people do not like it and recognize that it does not contribute to the health of our political system. Politicians must find some way to present powerful emotional images that are positive and at the same time not a denial of important social problems in this country. In order to do this, politicians must have the courage to deal with substantive issues that look beyond their next election. They must do more than Reagan's "Morning in America" campaign, which took place in the context of an increasing national debt, continuing environmental degradation from toxic wastes, a growing drug crisis, and a declining educational system.

The promise of democracy in this country is not being fulfilled. The educational system and the mass media do not contribute adequately to citizens' understanding of the political processes that operate in this country. Political psychology can contribute to the nation's political health by identifying the role that psychological processes play in the political system and by describing how changes should be made.

References

Abelson, R. P. (1959). Modes of resolution of belief dilemmas. *Journal of Conflict Resolution, 3,* 343–352.

Abelson, R. P. (1983). Whatever became of consistency theory? *Personality and Social Psychology Bulletin, 9,* 37–54.

Abelson, R. P. (1986). Beliefs are like possessions. *Journal for the Theory of Social Behaviour, 16,* 223–250.

Abelson, R. P, Aronson, E., McGuire, W. J., Newcomb, T. M., Rosenberg, M. J., & Tannenbaum, P. H. (Eds.). (1968). *Theories of cognitive consistency: A sourcebook.* Chicago: Rand McNally.

Adorno, T. W., Frenkel-Brunswick, E., Levinson, D. J., & Sanford, R. N. (1950). *The authoritarian personality.* New York: Harper & Row.

Ajzen, I., & Fishbein, M. (1980). *Understanding attitudes and predicting social behavior.* Englewood Cliffs, N.J.: Prentice-Hall.

Allport, G. W. (1954). *The nature of prejudice.* Reading, Mass.: Addison-Wesley.

Allport, G. W. (1985). The historical background of social psychology. In G. Lindzey & E. Aronson (Eds.), *Handbook of social psychology* (Vol. 1). New York: Random House.

Altheide, D. L. (1987). Format and symbols in TV coverage of terrorism in the United States and Great Britain. *International Studies Quarterly, 31,* 161–176.

Anderson, R. C., & Pichert, J. W. (1978). Recall of previously unrecallable information following a shift in perspective. *Journal of Verbal Learning and Verbal Behavior, 17,* 1–12.

Aronson, E. (1988). *The social animal* (5th ed.). New York: W. H. Freeman.

Aronson, E., Turner, J. A., & Carlsmith, J. M. (1963). Communicator credibility and communication discrepancy as determinants of opinion change. *Journal of Abnormal and Social Psychology, 67,* 31–36.

Auerbach, Y. (1986). Turning-point decisions: A cognitive-dissonance analysis of conflict reduction in Israel–West German relations. *Political Psychology, 7,* 533–550.

Bagdikian, B. H. (1989, June 12). The lords of the global village. *The Nation,* pp. 805–818.

Bainbridge, W. S. (1989). *Survey research: A computer-assisted introduction.* Belmont, Calif.: Wadsworth.

Bargh, J. A., & Pietromonaco, P. (1982). Automatic information processing and social perception: The influence of trait information presented outside of conscious awareness on impression formation. *Journal of Personality and Social Psychology, 43,* 437–449.

Bargh, J. A., & Thein, R. D. (1985). Individual construct accessibility, person memory, and the recall-judgment link: The case of information overload. *Journal of Personality and Social Psychology, 49,* 1125–1146.

Bartlett, F. C. (1932). *Remembering: A study in experimental and social psychology.* London: Cambridge University Press.

Beck, A. T., Rush, A. J., & Shaw, B. F. (1979). *Cognitive therapy of depression.* New York: Guilford.

Behr, R. L., and Iyengar, S. (1985). Television news, real–world cues, and changes in the public agenda. *Public Opinion Quarterly, 49,* 38–57.

Bem, D. J. (1970). *Beliefs, attitudes, and human affairs.* Pacific Grove, Calif.: Brooks-Cole.

Bem, S. L. (1981). Gender schema theory: A cognitive account of sex typing. *Psychological Review, 88,* 354–364.

Bennett, W. L. (1980). *Public opinion in American politics.* New York: Harcourt Brace Jovanovich.

Bennett, W. L. (1988). *News: The politics of illusion* (2nd ed.). New York: Longman.

Bluhm, W. T. (1974). *Ideologies and attitudes: Modern political culture.* Englewood Cliffs, N.J.: Prentice-Hall.

Bochner, S., & Insko, C. A. (1966). Communicator discrepancy, source credibility, and opinion change. *Journal of Personality and Social Psychology, 4,* 614–621.

Bowen, G. L. (1989). Presidential action and public opinion about U.S. Nicaraguan policy: Limits to the "Rally 'Round the Flag" syndrome. *PS: Political Science & Politics, 22,* 793–800.

Bowles, S., & Gintis, H. (1976). *Schooling in capitalist America: Educational reform and the contradictions of economic life.* New York: Basic Books.

Bradburn, N. M., & Sudman, S. (1988). *Polls and surveys: Understanding what they tell us.* San Francisco: Jossey-Bass.

Bradshaw, J. (1988). *Bradshaw on: Healing the shame that binds you.* Deerfield Beach, Fla.: Health Communications.

Breckler, S. J. (1984). Empirical validation of affect, behavior, and cognition as distinct components of attitude. *Journal of Personality and Social Psychology, 47,* 1191–1205.

Brewer, M. B., Dull, V., & Lui, L. (1981). Perceptions of the elderly: Stereotypes as prototypes. *Journal of Personality and Social Psychology, 41,* 656–670.

Broadbent, D. (1958). *Perception and communication.* Oxford, England: Pergamon Press.

Brody, R. A. (1978). The puzzle of political participation in America. In A. King (Ed.), *The new American political system*. Washington, D.C.: American Enterprise Institute.

Burnham, W. D. (1982). *The current crisis in American politics*. Oxford, England: Oxford University Press.

Cacioppo, J. T., & Petty, R. E. (1982). The need for cognition. *Journal of Personality and Social Psychology, 42,* 116–131.

Cacioppo, J. T., Petty, R. E., & Kao, C. (1984). The efficient assessment of need for cognition. *Journal of Personality Assessment, 48,* 306–307.

Cacioppo, J. T., Petty, R. E., Kao, C., & Rodriguez, R. (1986). Central and peripheral routes to persuasion: An individual difference perspective. *Journal of Personality and Social Psychology, 51,* 1032–1043.

Cacioppo, J. T., Petty, R. E., & Sidera, J. (1982). The effects of a salient self-schema on the evaluation of proattitudinal editorials: Top-down versus bottom-up message processing. *Journal of Experimental Social Psychology, 18,* 324–338.

Calatone, R. J., & Washaw, P. R. (1985). Negating the effects of fear appeals in election campaigns. *Journal of Applied Psychology, 70,* 627–633.

Campbell, A., Converse, P. E., Miller, W. E., & Stokes, D. E. (1960). *The American voter*. New York: Wiley.

Campbell, B. A. (1980). A theoretical approach to peer influence in adolescent socialization. *American Journal of Political Science, 24,* 324–344.

Carlson, R., & Brincka, J. (1987). Studies in script theory: III. Ideology and political imagination. *Political Psychology, 8,* 563–574.

Carlson, R., & Levy, N. (1970). Self, values and affects: Derivations from Tomkins' polarity theory. *Journal of Personality and Social Psychology, 16,* 338–345.

Chaiken, S. (1979). Communicator physical attractiveness and persuasion. *Journal of Personality and Social Psychology, 3,* 1387–1397.

Chaiken, S. (1980). Heuristic versus systematic information processing and the use of source versus message cues in persuasion. *Journal of Personality and Social Psychology, 39,* 752–766.

Charters, W. W., Jr., & Newcomb, T. M. (1958). Some attitudinal effects of experimentally increased salience of group membership. In G. E. Swanson, T. M. Newcomb, & E. L. Hartley (Eds.), *Readings in social psychology* (pp. 415–420). New York: Holt, Rinehart & Winston.

Chase, W. G., & Simon, H. A. (1973). The mind's eye in chess. In W. G. Chase (Ed.), *Visual information processing*. New York: Academic Press.

Cheng, P. W., & Holyoak, K. J. (1985). Pragmatic reasoning schemas. *Cognitive Psychology, 17,* 391–416.

Cheng, P. W., Holyoak, K. J., Nisbett, R. E., & Oliver, L. M. (1986). Pragmatic versus syntactic approaches to training deductive reasoning. *Cognitive Psychology, 18,* 293–328.

Chi, M. T. H., & Koeske, R. (1983). Network representation of a child's dinosaur knowledge. *Developmental Psychology, 19,* 29–39.

Cohen, B. C. (1963). *The press and foreign policy*. Princeton: Princeton University Press.

Cohen, C. E. (1981). Person categories and social perception: Testing some boundaries of the processing effects of prior knowledge. *Journal of Personality and Social Psychology, 40,* 441–452.

Cohen, C. E., & Ebbesen, E. B. (1979). Observational goals and schema activation: A theoretical framework for behavior perception. *Journal of Experimental Social Psychology, 15,* 305–329.

Commons, B., Richards, A., and Kuhn, D. (1982). Systematic and metasystematic reasoning: A case for levels of reasoning beyond Piaget's stage of formal operations. *Child Development, 53,* 1058–1069.

Converse, P. E. (1964). The nature of belief systems in mass publics. In D. Apter (Ed.), *Ideology and discontent*. New York: Free Press.

Converse, P. E. (1970). Attitudes and non-attitudes: The continuation of a dialogue. In E. Tufte (Ed.), *The quantitative analysis of social problems*. Reading, Mass.: Addison-Wesley.

Corbett, M. (1982). *Political tolerance in America: Freedom and equality in public attitudes*. New York: Longman.

Corteen, R. S., & Williams, T. (1986). Television and reading skills. In T. Williams (Ed.), *The impact of television: A natural experiment in three communities* (pp. 39–84). Orlando, Fla.: Academic Press.

Crotty, W. (1970). *Public opinion and politics: A reader*. New York: Holt, Rinehart & Winston.

Cumming, E., & Henry, W. E. (1961). *Growing old*. New York: Basic Books.

Dawson, R. W., Prewitt, K., & Dawson, K. S. (1977). *Political socialization* (2nd ed.). Boston: Little, Brown.

Domhoff, G. W. (1967). *Who rules America?* Englewood Cliffs, N.J.: Prentice-Hall.

Dornbusch, S., Hastorf, A., Richardson, S. A., Muzzy, R., & Vreeland, R. S. (1965). The perceiver and the perceived: Their relative influence on the categories of interpersonal perception. *Journal of Personality and Social Psychology, 1,* 434–440.

Dowse, R. E., & Hughes, J. A. (1971). Girls, boys and politics. *British Journal of Sociology, 22,* 53–67.

Dulit, E. (1975). Adolescent thinking à la Piaget: The formal stage. In R. E. Grinder (Ed.), *Studies in adolescence* (3rd ed.) (pp. 536–556). New York: Macmillan.

Duncan, G. (1987). Understanding ideology. *Political Studies, 35,* 649–659.

Eagly, A. H. (1974). Comprehensibility of persuasive arguments as a determinant of opinion change. *Journal of Personality and Social Psychology, 29,* 758–773.

Easton, D., & Dennis, J. (1969). *Children in the political system*. New York: McGraw-Hill.

Easton, D., & Hess, R. D. (1962). The child's political world. *Midwest Journal of Political Science, 6,* 229–246.

Ebbinghaus, H. (1885/1964). *Memory: A contribution to experimental psychology* (H. A. Ruger & C. E. Bussenius, Trans.). New York: Dover. (Original work published 1885.)

Edelman, M. (1964). *Symbolic uses of politics.* Urbana: University of Illinois Press.

Epstein, E. J. (1973). *News from nowhere.* New York: Random House.

Erbring, L., Goldenberg, E., & Miller, A. (1980). Front-page news and real-world cues: A new look at agenda setting. *American Journal of Political Science, 24,* 16–49.

Erskine, H. (1970). The polls: Opinion of the news media. *Public Opinion Quarterly, 34,* 630–643.

Eysenck, H. J. (1954). *The psychology of politics.* London: Routledge & Kegan Paul.

Eysenck, H. J., & Coulter, T. T. (1972). The personality and attitudes of working-class British communists and fascists. *Journal of Social Psychology, 87,* 59–73.

Eysenck, H. J., & Wilson, G. D. (1978). *The psychological basis of ideology.* Baltimore: University Park Press.

Faludi, S. (1989, November). Where did Randy go wrong? *Mother Jones,* pp. 22–28, 61–64.

Feshbach, S., & Singer, R. (1971). *Television and aggression.* San Francisco: Jossey-Bass.

Festinger, L. (1957). *A theory of cognitive dissonance.* Palo Alto, Calif.: Stanford University Press.

Festinger, L., & Carlsmith, J. M. (1959). Cognitive consequences of forced compliance. *Journal of Abnormal and Social Psychology, 58,* 203–210.

Fishbein, M., & Ajzen, I. (1975). *Belief, attitude, intention, and behavior: An introduction to theory and research.* Reading, Mass: Addison-Wesley.

Fishbein, M., & Ajzen, I. (1981). Acceptance, yielding, and impact: Cognitive processes in persuasion. In R. E. Petty, T. M. Ostrom, & T. C. Brock (Eds.), *Cognitive responses in persuasion.* Hillsdale, N.J.: Erlbaum.

Fishbein, M., & Lange, R. (in press). The effects of crossing the midpoint on belief change: A replication and extension. *Personality and Social Psychology Bulletin.*

Fiske, S. T. (1981). Social cognition and affect. In J. Harvey (Ed.), *Cognition, social behavior, and the environment.* Hillsdale, N.J.: Erlbaum.

Fiske, S. T. (1982). Schema-triggered affect: Applications to social perception. In M. S. Clark & S. T. Fiske (Eds.), *Affect and cognition: The seventeenth annual Carnegie Symposium on Cognition* (pp. 55–78). Hillsdale, N.J.: Erlbaum.

Fiske, S. T., & Dyer, L. M. (1985). Structure and development of social schemata: Evidence from positive and negative transfer effects. *Journal of Personality and Social Psychology, 48,* 839–852.

Fiske, S. T., Kinder, D. R., & Larter, W. M. (1983). The novice and the expert: Knowledge-based strategies in political cognition. *Journal of Experimental Social Psychology, 19,* 381–400.

Fiske, S. T., & Taylor, S. E. (1984). *Social cognition.* Reading, Mass.: Addison-Wesley.

Fowler, F. J. (1988). *Survey research methods* (rev. ed.). Newbury Park, Calif.: Sage.

Free, L. A., & Cantril, H. (1967). *The political beliefs of Americans.* New Brunswick, N.J.: Rutgers University Press.

Freedman, J. L. (1963). Attitudinal effects of inadequate justification. *Journal of Personality, 31,* 371–385.

Freedman, J. L. (1984). Effect of television violence on aggressiveness. *Psychological Bulletin, 96,* 227–246.

Freedman, J. L. (1986). Television violence and aggression: A rejoinder. *Psychological Bulletin, 100,* 372–378.

Friedrich-Cofer, L., & Huston, A. C. (1986). Television violence and aggression: The debate continues. *Psychological Bulletin, 100,* 364–371.

Funkhouser, G. R. (1973). The issues of the sixties: An exploratory study in the dynamics of public opinion. *Public Opinion Quarterly, 37,* 62–75.

Gaertner, S. L. (1973). Helping behavior and racial discrimination among liberals and conservatives. *Journal of Personality and Social Psychology, 25,* 335–341.

Gans, H. J. (1979). *Deciding what's news: A study of CBS Evening News, NBC Nightly News, Newsweek, and Time.* New York: Pantheon.

Garramone, G. M. (1985). Effects of negative political advertising: The roles of sponsor and rebuttal. *Journal of Broadcasting & Electronic Media, 32,* 415–427.

Gaziano, C. (1988). How credible is the credibility crisis? *Journalism Quarterly, 65,* 267–279.

Gelles, R. (1979). Violence toward children in the United States. *Family violence.* Newbury Park, Calif.: Sage.

Georgoudi, M. (1985). Dialectics in attribution research: A reevaluation of the dispositional-situational causal dichotomy. *Journal of Personality and Social Psychology, 49,* 1678–1691.

Gerard, J. B. (1967). Choice, difficulty, dissonance, and the decision sequence. *Journal of Personality, 35,* 91–108.

Gergen, K. J., & Back, K. W. (1966). Communication in the interview and the disengaged respondent. *Public Opinion Quarterly, 30,* 385–398.

Gilens, M. (1988). Gender and support for Reagan: A comprehensive model of presidential approval. *American Journal of Political Science, 32,* 19–49.

Glenn, N. D. (1969). Aging, disengagement, and opinionation. *Public Opinion Quarterly, 33,* 17–33.

Goertzel, T. G. (1987). Authoritarianism of personality and political attitudes. *Journal of Social Psychology, 127,* 7–18.

Gordon, L. (1988). *Heroes of their own lives: The politics and history of family violence.* New York: Viking Press.

Gorkin, L. (1972). *The sensuous doctor: The response to sex-role logic problems.* Unpublished manuscript, State University of New York at Stony Brook.

Graber, D. A. (1980). *Mass media and American politics.* Washington, D.C.: Congressional Quarterly Press.

Granberg, D., Jefferson, N. L., Brent, E. E., & King, M. (1981). Membership group, reference group, and the attribution of attitudes to groups. *Journal of Personality and Social Psychology, 40,* 833–842.

Granberg, D., & Robertson, C. (1982). Contrast effects in estimating policies of the federal government. *Public Opinion Quarterly, 46,* 43–53.

Greenstein, F. I. (1965). *Children and politics.* New Haven: Yale University Press.

Greenstein, F. I. (1975). *Personality and politics: Problems of evidence, inference, and conceptualization.* New York: Norton.

Greenwald, A. G., & Ronis, D. L. (1978). Twenty years of cognitive dissonance: Case study of the evolution of a theory. *Psychological Review, 85,* 53–57.

Griggs, R. A., & Cox, J. R. (1982). The elusive thematic-materials effect in Wason's selection task. *British Journal of Psychology, 73,* 407–420.

Hall, S. (1982). The rediscovery of "ideology": Return of the repressed in media studies. In M. Gurevitch, T. Bennett, J. Curran, & J. Wollacott (Eds.), *Culture, society and the media.* New York: Methuan.

Hamill, R., Lodge, M., & Blake, F. (1985). The breadth, depth, and utility of class, partisan, and ideological schemata. *American Journal of Political Science, 29,* 850–870.

Hamilton, S. B., Knox, T. A., & Keilin, W. G. (1986). The nuclear family: Correspondence in cognitive and affective reactions to the threat of nuclear war among older adolescents and their parents. *Journal of Youth and Adolescence, 15,* 133–145.

Hammen, C., Miklowitz, D., & Dyck, D. (1986). Stability and severity parameters of depressive self-schema responding. *Journal of Social and Clinical Psychology, 37,* 598–608.

Hardy-Brown, K. (1979). Formal operations and the issue of generalizability: The analysis of poetry by college students. *Human Development, 22,* 127–136.

Harrison, B., & Bluestone, B. (1988). *The great U-turn: Corporate restructuring and the polarizing of America.* New York: Basic Books.

Harrison, L. F., & Williams, T. (1986). Television and cognitive development. In T. Williams (Ed.), *The impact of television: A natural experiment in three communities* (pp. 87–138). Orlando, Fla.: Academic Press.

Hart, P., & Teeter, R. (1990). Poll for NBC News and *The Wall Street Journal,* April 11–12, 14, 16, 1990. Results reported in *The Polling Report, 6,* p. 2, May 7, 1990.

Hastie, R. (1980). Memory for behavioral information that confirms or contradicts a personality impression. In R. Hastie, T. M. Ostrom, E. B. Ebbesen, R. S. Wyer, D. L. Hamilton, & D. E. Carlson (Eds.), *Personal memory: The cognitive basis of social perception.* Hillsdale, N.J.: Erlbaum.

Heider, F. (1958). *The psychology of interpersonal relations.* New York: Wiley.

Helmsley, G. D., & Doob, A. M. (1978). The effect of looking behavior on perceptions of communicator's credibility. *Journal of Applied Social Psychology, 8,* 136–144.

Helson, H. (1948). Adaptation-level as a basis for a quantitative theory of frames of reference. *Psychological Review, 55,* 297–313.

Helson, H. (1959). Adaptation-level theory. In S. Koch (Ed.), *Psychology, a study of a science* (Vol. 1) (pp. 565–621). New York: McGraw-Hill.

Hennessy, B. (1981). *Public opinion* (4th ed.). Pacific Grove, Calif.: Brooks/Cole.

Henry, W. A., III (1981). News as entertainment: The search for dramatic unity. In E. Abel (Ed.), *What's news: The media in American society*. San Francisco: Institute for Contemporary Studies.

Herman, C. P., Zanna, M. P., & Higgins, E. T. (Eds.). (1986). *Physical appearance, stigma, and social behavior: The Ontario Symposium* (Vol. 3). Hillsdale, N.J.: Erlbaum.

Higgins, E. T., & King, G. A. (1981). Accessibility of social constructs: Information-processing consequences of individual and contextual variability. In N. Cantor & J. F. Kihlstrom (Eds.), *Personality, cognition, and social interaction* (pp. 69–121). Hillsdale, N.J.: Erlbaum.

Higgins, E. T., Kuiper, N. A., & Olson, J. M. (1981). Social cognition: A need to get personal. In E. T. Higgins, C. P. Herman, & M. P. Zanna (Eds.), *Social cognition: The Ontario symposium*. Hillsdale, N.J.: Erlbaum.

Higgins, E. T., Rholes, W. S., & Jones, C. R. (1977). Category accessibility and impression formation. *Journal of Experimental Social Psychology, 13*, 141–154.

Hill, D. B. (1985). Viewer characteristics and agenda setting by television news. *Public Opinion Quarterly, 49*, 340–350.

Hinsley, D. A., Hayes, J. R., & Simon, H. A. (1977). From words to equations: Meaning and representation in algebra work problems. In M. A. Just & P. S. Carpenter (Eds.), *Cognitive processes in comprehension*. Hillsdale, N.J.: Erlbaum.

Holloway, H., & George, J. (1986). *Public opinion: Coalitions, elites, and masses* (2nd ed.). New York: St. Martin's Press.

Hovland, C. I., Harvey, O. J., & Sherif, M. (1957). Assimilation and contrast effects in reactions to communication and attitude change. *Journal of Abnormal and Social Psychology, 55*, 244–252.

Hovland, C. I., Janis, I. L., & Kelley, J. J. (1953). *Communication and persuasibility*. New Haven: Yale University Press.

Hovland, C. I., Lumsdaine, A. A., & Sheffield, F. D. (1949). *Experiments on mass communication*. Princeton: Princeton University Press.

Hovland, C. I., & Weiss, W. (1951). The influence of source credibility on communication effectiveness. *Public Opinion Quarterly, 15*, 635–650.

Huesmann, L. R. (1986). Psychological processes promoting the relation between exposure to media violence and aggressive behavior by the viewer. *Journal of Social Issues, 42*, 125–139.

Huesmann, L. R., Eron, L. D., Lefkowitz, M. M., & Walder, L. O. (1984). Stability of aggression over time and generations. *Developmental Psychology, 20*, 746–775.

Inhelder, B., & Piaget, J. (1958). *The growth of logical thinking: From childhood to adolescence*. New York: Basic Books.

Iyengar, S., & Kinder, D. R. (1987). *News that matters: Television and American opinion*. Chicago: University of Chicago Press.

Iyengar, S., Kinder, D. R., Peters, M. D., & Krosnick, J. A. (1984). The evening news and presidential evaluations. *Journal of Personality and Social Psychology, 46,* 778–787.

Iyengar, S., Peters, M. D., & Kinder, D. R. (1982). Experimental demonstrations of the not-so-minimal political consequences of mass media. *American Political Science Review, 76,* 848–858.

Jennings, M. K., & Niemi, R. G. (1968). The transmission of political values from parent to child. *American Political Science Review, 62,* 169–184.

Jennings, M. K., & Niemi, R. G. (1974). *The political character of adolescence: The influence of family and schools.* Princeton: Princeton University Press.

Johnstone, J., Slawski, E., & Bowman, W. (1976). *The newspeople.* Urbana: University of Illinois Press.

Jones, E. E., Farina, A., Hastorf, A. H., Markus, H., Miller, D. T., & Scott, R. A. (1984). *Social stigma: The psychology of marked relationships.* New York: W. H. Freeman.

Josephson, W. L. (1987). Television violence and children's aggression: Testing the priming, social script, and disinhibition predictions. *Journal of Personality and Social Psychology, 53,* 882–890.

Joslyn, R. A. (1980). The content of political spot ads. *Journalism Quarterly, 57,* 92–98.

Joslyn, R. A. (1986). Political advertising and the meaning of elections. In L. L. Kaid, D. Nimmo, & K. Sanders (Eds.), *New perspectives on political advertising* (pp. 139–183). Carbondale: Southern Illinois University Press.

Judd, C. M., Krosnick, J. A., & Milburn, M. A. (1981). Political involvement and attitude structure in the general public. *American Sociological Review, 46,* 660–669.

Judd, C. M., & Milburn, M. A. (1980). The structure of attitude systems in the general public: Comparisons of a structural equation model. *American Sociological Review, 45,* 627–643.

Kahneman, D., & Tversky, A. (1984). Choices, values, and frames. *American Psychologist, 39,* 341–350.

Kandel, D. B., & Lesser, G. S. (1972). *Youth in two worlds: United States and Denmark.* San Francisco: Jossey-Bass.

Katz, D. (1960). The functional approach to the study of attitudes. *Public Opinion Quarterly, 24,* 163–204.

Key, V. O. (1967). *Public opinion and American democracy.* New York: Knopf.

Kinder, D. R., & Rhodebeck, L. A. (1982). Continuities in support for racial equality, 1972 to 1976. *Public Opinion Quarterly, 46,* 195–215.

Kinder, D. R., & Sears, D. O. (1985). Public opinion and political action. In G. Lindzey and E. Aronson (Eds.), *Handbook of social psychology* (Vol. 2) (pp. 659–741). New York: Random House.

King, M. L. (1964). *Why we can't wait.* New York: Times Mirror.

Klapper, J. T. (1960). *The effects of mass media.* Glencoe, N.Y.: The Free Press.

Kohlberg, L. (1969). Stage and sequence: The cognitive developmental approach to socialization. In D. A. Goslin (Ed.), *Handbook of socialization theory.* Chicago: Rand McNally.

Kohlberg, L. (1971). From is to ought: How to commit the naturalistic fallacy and get away with it. In T. Mischel (Ed.), *Cognitive development and epistemology*. New York: Academic Press.

Kohlberg, L. (1981). *Essays on moral development: Vol. 1. The philosophy of moral development*. New York: Harper & Row.

Kohlberg, L. (1984). *Essays on moral development: Vol. 2. The psychology of moral development*. New York: Harper & Row.

Kohn, M. L. (1977). *Class and conformity*. Chicago: University of Chicago Press.

Kohut, A. (1988, November 7). Polling: Does more information lead to better understanding? *Boston Globe*, p. 25.

Krech, D., & Crutchfield, R. S. (1948). *Theory and problems of social psychology*. New York: McGraw-Hill.

Krosnick, J. A. (1988). Attitude importance and attitude change. *Journal of Experimental Social Psychology, 24*, 240–255.

Krosnick, J. A., & Kinder, D. R. (1990). Altering the foundations of support for the president through priming. *American Political Science Review, 84*, 497–512.

Krosnick, J. A., & Milburn, M. A. (1990). *Trends in political opinionation in the American public: 1956–1984*. Unpublished manuscript.

Krosnick, J. A., & Milburn, M. A. (1990). The psychological determinants of political opinionation. *Social Cognition, 8*, 49–72.

Kuhn, D., Langer, J., Kohlberg, L., & Haan, N. (1977). The development of formal operations in logical and moral development. *Genetic Psychology Monographs, 95*, 97–188.

Kurkjian, S. (1989, November 5). In contest's fury, issues left behind. *Boston Globe*, p. 1.

Lake, C. C. (1982). *Guns, butter, and equality: The women's vote in 1980*. Paper presented at the annual meeting of the Midwest Political Science Association, Milwaukee.

Lange, R., & Fishbein, M. (1983). Effects of category differences on belief change and agreement with the source of a persuasive communication. *Journal of Personality and Social Psychology, 44*, 933–941.

Langton, K. P. (1967). Peer group and school and the political socialization process. *American Political Science Review, 61*, 751–758.

Langton, K. P., and Karns, D. A. (1969). The relative influence of the family, peer group and school in the development of political efficacy. *Western Political Quarterly, 22*, 813–826.

LaPiere, R. (1934). Attitudes versus actions. *Social Forces, 13*, 230–237.

Larkin, J. H., McDermott, J., Simon, D. P., & Simon, H. A. (1980). Models of competence in solving physics problems. *Science, 208*, 1335–1342.

Lasswell, H. D. (1960). *Pschopathology and politics*. New York: Viking Press.

Lau, R. R. (1986). Political schemata, candidate evaluations, and voting behavior. In R. R. Lau and D. O. Sears (Eds.), *Political cognition* (pp. 95–126). Hillsdale, N.J.: Erlbaum.

Lau, R. R., Coulam, R. F., & Sears, D. O. (1983). *Proposition 2 1/2 in Massachusetts: Self-interest, anti-government attitudes, and political schemas*. Paper presented at the annual meeting of the Midwest Political Science Association, Chicago.

Lau, R. R., & Erber, R. (1985). Political sophistication. In S. Kraus and R. M. Perloff (Eds.), *Mass media and political thought*. Newbury Park, Calif.: Sage.

Lave, C., & March, J. (1975). *Introduction to models in the social sciences*. New York: Harper & Row.

Lazarsfeld, D., Berelson, B., & Gaudet, H. (1944). *The people's choice*. New York: Columbia University Press.

Lemon, N. (1973). *Attitudes and their measurement*. London: Batsford.

Levi, A., & Tetlock, P. E. (1980). A cognitive analysis of Japan's 1941 decision to go to war. *Journal of Conflict Resolution, 24,* 195–212.

Lichter, S. R., Rothman, S., & Lichter, L. S. (1986). *The media elite: America's new powerbrokers*. Bethesda, Md.: Adler & Adler.

Liebert, R. M., & Sprafkin, J. (1988). *The early window: Effects of television on children and youth* (3rd ed.). New York: Pergamon Press.

Likert, R. (1932). A technique for the measurement of attitudes. *Archives of Psychology, 140,* 1–55.

Linder, D. E., Cooper, J., & Jones, E. E. (1967). Decision freedom as a determinant of the role of incentive magnitude in attitude change. *Journal of Personality and Social Psychology, 6,* 245–254.

Lippmann, W. (1922). *Public opinion*. New York: Harcourt, Brace.

Lipset, S. M. (1960). *Political man*. Garden City, N.Y.: Doubleday.

Lodge, M., & Hamill, R. (1986). A partisan schema for political information processing. *American Political Science Review, 80,* 505–519.

Lord, C. G., Ross, L., & Lepper, M. (1979). Biased assimilation and attitude polarization: The effects of prior theories on subsequently considered evidence. *Journal of Personality and Social Psychology, 37,* 2098–2109.

Lowell, A. L. (1913). *Public opinion and popular government*. New York: Longmans, Green.

Machiavelli, N. (1975). *The discourses of Niccolo Machiavelli, translated from the Italian with an introduction and notes by Leslie J. Walker, with a new introduction and appendices by Cecil H. Clough*. London: Routledge & Kegan Paul.

MacKuen, M. J., & Coombs, S. L. (1981). *More than news*. Newbury Park, Calif.: Sage.

Madison, J. (1961). *The Federalist Papers* (No. 10). New York: Mentor Books.

Manktelow, K. I., & Evans, J. St. B. T. (1979). Facilitation of reasoning by realism: Effect or non-effect? *British Journal of Psychology, 70,* 477–488.

Markus, H. (1977). Self-schema and processing information about the self. *Journal of Personality and Social Psychology, 35,* 63–78.

McClosky, H. (1958). Conservatism and personality. *American Political Science Review, 52,* 27–45.

McClosky, H., & Chong, D. (1985). Similarities and differences between left-wing and right-wing radicals. *British Journal of Political Science, 15,* 329–363.

McCombs, M. E. (1981). The agenda setting approach. In D. Nimmo & K. Sanders (Eds.), *Handbook of political communication*. Newbury Park, Calif.: Sage.

McCombs, M. E., and Shaw, D. L. (1972). The agenda-setting function of mass media. *Public Opinion Quarterly, 36,* 176–187.

McGinniss, J. (1969). *Selling of the president, 1968.* New York: Trident Press.

McGuire, W. J. (1964). Inducing resistance to persuasion: Some contemporary approaches. In L. Berkowitz (Ed.), *Advances in experimental social psychology* (Vol. 1). New York: Academic Press.

McGuire, W. J. (1969). The nature of attitudes and attitude change. In G. Lindzey & E. Aronson (Eds.), *The handbook of social psychology* (2nd ed., Vol. 3). Reading, Mass.: Addison-Wesley.

McGuire, W. J., & Papageorgis, D. (1961). The relative efficacy of various types of prior belief-defense in producing immunity against persuasion. *Journal of Abnormal and Social Psychology, 62,* 327–337.

Merritt, S. (1984). Negative political advertising: Some empirical findings. *Journal of Advertising, 13,* 27–37.

Milburn, M.A. (1979). A longitudinal test of the selective exposure hypothesis. *Public Opinion Quarterly, 43,* 507–517.

Milburn, M. A. (1987). Ideological self-schemata and schematically induced attitude consistency. *Journal of Experimental Social Psychology, 23,* 383–398.

Milburn, M. A., Bowley, C., Fay-Dumaine, J., & Kennedy, D. A. (1987, July). An attributional analysis of the media coverage of terrorism. Paper presented at the meeting of the International Society of Political Psychology, San Francisco.

Milburn, M. A., Cistuli, B., & Garr, M. (1988, July 4). *Survey and experimental studies of the effect of television news on individuals' attributions about terrorism.* Paper presented at the annual meeting of the International Society of Political Psychology, Meadowlands, N.J.

Milburn, M. A., & Fay-Dumaine, J. (1988). *The relationship of belief consistency and cognitive complexity.* Unpublished manuscript, University of Massachusetts – Boston.

Milburn, M. A., & Judd, C. M. (1981). Interpreting new methods in attitude structure research. *American Sociological Review, 46,* 675–677.

Milburn, M. A., & McGrail, A. (1990, June 12). *The effect of the dramatic presentation of news events on individuals' cognitive complexity.* Paper presented at the International Society of Political Psychology convention, Washington, D.C.

Milburn, M. A., Watanabe, P. Y., & Kramer, B. M. (1987). The nature and sources of attitudes toward a nuclear freeze. *Political Psychology, 7,* 661–674.

Miller, A. (1983). *For your own good: Hidden cruelty in child-rearing and the roots of violence.* New York: Farrar, Straus & Giroux.

Miller, G. A. (1956). The magical number seven, plus or minus two: Some limits on our capacity for processing information. *Psychological Review, 63,* 81–97.

Miller, N., Maruyama, G., Beaber, R. J., & Valone, K. (1976). Speed of speech and persuasion. *Journal of Personality and Social Psychology, 34,* 615–624.

Mills, C. W. (1956). *The power elite.* New York: Oxford University Press.

Nash, M. C. (1952). A quantitative study of effects of past experience on adaptation-level. *Dissertation Abstracts, 12,* 335–336.

Nel, E., Helmreich, R., & Aronson, E. (1969). Opinion change in the advocate as a function of the persuasibility of his audience: A clarification of the meaning of dissonance. *Journal of Personality and Social Psychology, 12,* 117–124.

Neves, D. M., & Anderson, J. R. (1981). Knowledge compilation: Mechanisms for the automization of cognitive skills. In J. R. Anderson (Ed.), *Cognitive skills and their acquisition.* Hillsdale, N.J.: Erlbaum.

Newcomb, T. M. (1943). *Personality and social change: Attitude formation in a student community.* New York: Holt, Rinehart & Winston.

Newcomb, T. M. (1971). *Persistence and change: Bennington and its students after twenty-five years.* New York: Wiley.

Newton, J. S., Masters, R. D., McHugo, G. J., & Sullivan, D. G. (1987). Making up our minds: Effects of network coverage on viewer impressions of leaders. *Polity, 20,* 226–246.

Nie, N. H., & Anderson, K. (1974). Mass belief systems revisited: Political change and attitude structure. *Journal of Politics, 36,* 540–587.

Nie, N. H., Verba, S., & Petrocik, J. R. (1976). *The changing American voter.* Cambridge: Harvard University Press.

Osgood, C. E., Suci, G. J., & Tannenbaum, P. H. (1957). *The measurement of meaning.* Urbana: University of Illinois Press.

Oskamp, S. (1977). *Attitudes and opinions.* Englewood Cliffs, N.J.: Prentice-Hall.

Page, B. I., Shapiro, R. Y., & Dempsey, G. R. (1987). What moves public opinion? *American Political Science Review, 81,* 23–43.

Parenti, M. (1986). *Inventing reality: The politics of the mass media.* New York: St. Martin's Press.

Patterson, T. E., & McClure, R. D. (1976). *The unseeing eye.* New York: Putnam.

Petty, R. E., & Cacioppo, J. T. (1981). *Attitudes and persuasion: Classic and contemporary approaches.* Dubuque, Iowa: William C. Brown.

Petty, R. E., & Cacioppo, J. T. (1986a). *Communication and persuasion: Central and peripheral routes to attitude change.* New York: Springer-Verlag.

Petty, R. E., & Cacioppo, J. T. (1986b). The elaboration likelihood model of persuasion. In L. Berkowitz (Ed.), *Advances in experimental social psychology* (Vol. 19). New York: Academic Press.

Petty, R. E., Cacioppo, J. T., Sedikides, C., & Strathman, A. J. (1988). Affect and persuasion. *American Behavioral Scientist, 31,* 355–371.

Pfau, M., & Burgoon, M. (1988). Inoculation in political campaign communication. *Human Communication Research, 15,* 91–111.

Piaget, J. (1978). *The development of thought: Equilibration of cognitive structures.* London: Blackwell.

Pichert, J. W., & Anderson, R. C. (1977). Taking different perspectives on a story. *Journal of Educational Psychology, 69,* 309–315.

Poole, K. T., & Zeigler, L. H. (1985). *Women, public opinion, and politics: the changing political attitudes of American women.* New York: Longman.

Ray, J. J. (1984). Alternatives of the F scale in the measurement of authoritarianism. *Journal of Social Psychology, 122,* 105–119.

Reder, L. M., & Anderson, J. R. (1980). A partial resolution of the paradox of interference: The role of integrating knowledge. *Cognitive Psychology, 12,* 447–472.

Reich, S. S., & Ruth, P. (1982). Wason's selection task: Verification, falsification and matching. *British Journal of Psychology, 73,* 395–405.

Robinson, M. J., & Kohut, A. (1988). Believability and the press. *Public Opinion Quarterly, 52,* 174–189.

Robinson, W. V. (1989, September 29). Tax-cut showdown looms on Capital Hill. *Boston Globe,* pp. 1, 21.

Roddy, B. L., & Garramone, G. M. (1988). Appeals and strategies of negative political advertising. *Journal of Broadcasting & Electronic Media, 32,* 415–427.

Rokeach, M. (1954). The nature and meaning of dogmatism. *Psychological Review, 61,* 194–204.

Rokeach, M. (1960). *The open and closed mind.* New York: Basic Books.

Rokeach, M. (1973). *The nature of human values.* New York: Free Press.

Rokeach, M., & Fruchter, B. (1956). A factorial study of dogmatism and related concepts. *The Journal of Abnormal and Social Psychology, 53,* 356–360.

Rosenberg, M. (1968). *The logic of survey analysis.* New York: Basic Books.

Rosenberg, S. W. (1987). Reason and ideology: Interpreting people's understanding of American politics. *Polity, 20,* 114–144.

Rosenberg, S. W. (1988a). *Reason, ideology, and politics.* Princeton: Princeton University Press.

Rosenberg, S. W. (1988b). The structure of political thinking. *American Journal of Political Science, 32,* 539–566.

Rosten, L. (1937). *The Washington correspondents.* New York: Harcourt, Brace.

Rousseau, J. J. (1913). *The social contract and the discourses* (G. D. H. Cole, Trans.) New York: Dutton.

Ruehlman, L. S., West, S. G., & Pasahow, R. J. (1985). Depression and evaluative schemata. *Journal of Personality, 53,* 46–92.

Sabato, L. (1981). *The rise of political consultants: New ways of winning elections.* New York: Basic Books.

Santrock, J. W. (1990). *Adolescence* (4th ed.). Dubuque, Iowa: William C. Brown.

Schoenberger, R. A. (1968). Conservatism, personality and political extremism. *American Political Science Review, 62,* 868–877.

Schroder, H. M., Driver, M. J., & Streufert, S. (1967). *Human information processing.* New York: Holt, Rinehart & Winston.

Schuman, H., & Presser, S. (1981). *Questions and answers in attitude surveys: Experiments on question form, wording, and context.* New York: Academic Press.

Sears, D. O., & Citrin, J. (1982). *Tax revolt: Something for nothing in California.* Cambridge: Harvard University Press.

Sebert, S. Z., Jennings, M. K., & Niemi, R. G. (1974). The political texture of peer groups. In M. K. Jennings & R. G. Niemi (Eds.), *The political character of adolescence: The influence of family and schools.* Princeton: Princeton University Press.

Segal, Z. V. (1988). Appraisal of the self-schema construct in cognitive models of depression. *Psychological Bulletin, 103,* 147–162.

Sharp, C., & Lodge, M. (1985). Partisan and ideological belief systems: Do they differ? *Political Behavior, 7,* 147–168.

Sherif, M., & Cantril, H. (1947). *The psychology of ego-involvements.* New York: Wiley.

Sherif, M., & Hovland, C. I. (1961). *Social judgment.* New Haven: Yale University Press.

Sherif, M., & Sherif, C. W. (1967). Attitudes as the individual's own categories: The social judgment-involvement approach to attitude and attitude change. In C. W. Sherif & M. Sherif (Eds.), *Attitude, ego-involvement, and change.* Westport, Conn.: Greenwood Press.

Sherman, S. J., & Gorkin, L. (1980). Attitude bolstering when behavior is inconsistent with central attitudes. *Journal of Experimental Social Psychology, 16,* 388–403.

Sigall, H., & Helmreich, R. (1969). Opinion change as a function of stress and communicator credibility. *Journal of Experimental Social Psychology, 5,* 70–78.

Sigelman, L., Roeder, P. W., Jewell, M. E., & Baer, M. A. (1985). Voting and nonvoting: A multi-election perspective. *American Journal of Political Science, 29,* 749–765.

Singer, D. G. (1982). Television and the developing imagination of the child. In D. Pearl, L. Bouthilet, & J. Lazar (Eds.), *Television and behavior: Ten years of scientific progress and implications for the eighties* (Vol. 2) (pp. 39–52). Washington, D.C.: Government Printing Office.

Sinnott, J. D. (1975). Everyday thinking and Piagetian operativity in adults. *Human Development, 18,* 430–443.

Smith, E. E., Adams, N., & Schoor, E. (1978). Fact retrieval and the paradox of interference. *Cognitive Psychology, 10,* 438–464.

Smith, M. B., Bruner, J. S., & White, R. W. (1956). *Opinions and personality.* New York: Wiley.

Smithers, A. G., & Lobley, D. M. (1978). The relationship between dogmatism and radicalism/conservatism. In H. J. Eysenck and G. D. Wilson (Eds.), *The psychological basis of ideology.* Baltimore: University Park Press.

Snyder, M., & Swann, W. B. (1976). When actions reflect attitudes: The politics of impression management. *Journal of Personality and Social Psychology, 34,* 1034–1042.

Stendler, C. B. (1950). Sixty years of child training practices. *Journal of Pediatrics, 36,* 122–134.

Stewart, C. J. (1975). Voter perception of mud-slinging in political communication. *Central State Speech Journal, 26,* 279–286.

Stone, W. F. (1980). The myth of left-wing authoritarianism. *Political Psychology, 2,* 3–18.

Stone, W. F. (1983). Left and right in personality and ideology: An attempt at clarification. *Journal of Mind and Behavior, 4,* 211–220.

Stone, W. F. (1988, July 1–5). *Left-wing authoritarianism; yet to be demonstrated.* Paper presented at the Eleventh Annual Meeting of the International Society of Political Psychology, Secaucus, N.J.

Suedfeld, P., & Tetlock, P. E. (1977). Integrative complexity of communications in international crises. *Journal of Conflict Resolution, 21,* 168–178.

Taylor, S. E., & Fiske, S. T. (1981). Getting inside the head: Methodologies for process analysis. In J. Harvery, W. Ickes, & R. Kidd (Eds.), *Advances in experimental social psychology* (Vol. 11) (pp. 249–288). Hillsdale, N.J.: Erlbaum.

Tedin, K. L. (1980). Assessing peer and parental influence on political attitudes. *American Journal of Political Science, 24,* 136–154.

Tetlock, P. E. (1979). Identifying victims of groupthink from public statements of decision makers. *Journal of Personality and Social Psychology, 37,* 1314–1324.

Tetlock, P. E. (1981a). Pre- to post-election shifts in presidential rhetoric: Impression management or cognitive adjustment? *Journal of Personality and Social Psychology: Attitudes and Social Cognition, 41,* 207–212.

Tetlock, P. E. (1981b). Personality and isolationism: Content analysis of senatorial speeches. *Journal of Personality and Social Psychology, 41,* 737–743.

Tetlock, P. E. (1983). Cognitive style and political ideology. *Journal of Personality and Social Psychology, 45,* 118–126.

Tetlock, P. E. (1984). Cognitive style and political belief systems in the British House of Commons. *Journal of Personality and Social Psychology, 46,* 365–375.

Tetlock, P. E. (1986). A value pluralism model of ideological reasoning. *Journal of Personality and Social Psychology, 50,* 819–827.

Thurstone, L. L. (1928). Attitudes can be measured. *American Journal of Sociology, 33,* 529–544.

Tomkins, S. S. (1964). Left and right: A basic dimension of ideology and personality. In R. W. White (Ed.), *The study of lives: Essays on personality in honor of Henry A. Murray.* New York: Atherton.

Tomkins, S. S. (1965a). The psychology of being right—and left. *Transaction, 3,* 23–27.

Tomkins, S. S. (1965b). Affect and the psychology of knowledge. In S. S. Tomkins & C. E. Izard (Eds.), *Affect, cognition, and personality.* New York: Springer.

Tomkins, S. S. (1987). Script theory. In J. Aronoff, A. I. Rabin, & R. A. Zucker (Eds.), *The emergence of personality.* New York: Springer.

Tomkins, S. S., McCarter, R., & Peebles, A. (1965). Reactions to the assassination of President Kennedy. In S. S. Tomkins & C. E. Izard (Eds.), *Affect, cognition, and personality.* New York: Springer.

Tourangeau, R., & Rasinski, K. A. (1988). Cognitive processes underlying context effects in attitude measurement. *Psychological Bulletin, 103,* 299–314.

Tversky, A., & Kahneman, D. (1974). Judgment under uncertainty: Heuristics and biases. *Science, 185,* 1124–1131.

U.S. Bureau of the Census. (1989). *Statistical Abstract of the United States: 1988* (108th ed.). Washington, D.C.: Government Printing Office.

Vallone, R. P., Ross, L., & Lepper, M. R. (1985). The hostile media phenomenon: Biased perception and perceptions of media bias in coverage of the "Beirut Massacre." *Journal of Personality and Social Psychology, 49,* 577–585.

Walster, E., Aronson, E., & Abrahams, D. (1966). On increasing the persuasiveness of a low prestige communicator. *Journal of Personality and Social Psychology, 2,* 325–342.

Walster, (Hatfield) E., & Festinger, L. (1962). The effectiveness of "overheard" persuasive communications. *Journal of Abnormal and Social Psychology, 65,* 395–402.

Ward, D. (1982). *Genetic epistemology and the structure of belief systems: An introduction to Piaget for political scientists.* Paper presented at the American Political Science Association convention, Denver, Colo.

Watanabe, P. Y. (1987). Religion and politics: The rise of the new Christian right. In P. J. Davies & F. A. Waldstein (Eds.), *Political issues in America today* (pp. 106–121). Manchester, England: Manchester University Press.

Wicker, A. W. (1969). Attitudes vs. actions: The relationship of verbal and overt behavioral responses to attitude objects. *Journal of Social Issues, 25,* 41–78.

Wicklund, R. A., & Brehm, J. W. (1976). *Perspectives on cognitive dissonance.* Hillsdale, N.J.: Erlbaum.

Wolfinger, R. E., & Rosenstone, S. J. (1980). *Who votes?* New Haven: Yale University Press.

Wurf, E., & Markus, H. (1983). *Cognitive consequences of the negative self.* Paper presented at the annual convention of the American Psychological Association, Anaheim, Calif.

Zadny, J., & Gerard, H. B. (1974). Attributed intentions and information selectivity. *Journal of Experimental Social Psychology, 10,* 34–52.

Zimbardo, P. G. (1960). Involvement and communication discrepancy as determinants of opinion conformity. *Journal of Abnormal and Social Psychology, 60,* 86–94.

Index

Abelson, Robert, 89–90, 95–97, 103, 104, 154
Abortion, views on, 27–28, 28, 32, 41–42, 60
Abrahams, D., 108
Adams, N., 76
Adaptation level theory, 111
Adorno, T. W., 43, 45, 46, 54
Affect (*see* Emotions)
African-Americans (*see* Race)
Age, 22–23, 24–25, 34
Agenda setting, 142
Agnew, Spiro, 134
Ajzen, Icek, 2, 7, 8–13, 16, 72, 89, 106, 113, 119–123, 154
Allende overthrow, 136–137
Allport, Gordon, 8, 27–28
Altheide, David, 147
Altruistic democracy, 133
Anchoring, 111–112, 116, 133
Anderson, J. R., 76, 77
Anderson, K., 59
Anderson, R. C., 73
Aranberg, D., 117
Aronson, E., 94, 108, 118, 123
Attitudes, 4, 7, 8, 13, 16 (*see also* Cognitive consistency; Persuasion; Public opinion)
  intensity of, 112–113, 129
  mass media effects on, 139–140, 146–147
  measurement of, 8, 126
  reasoned action theory, 2, 7, 8–13, 16, 72, 89
Attribution theory, 65–70
Auerbach, Y., 103
Authoritarian personality, 43–49, 126–127, 154
  left-wing authoritarianism, 45–49
Availability heuristic, 83

Back, K. W., 25
Baer, M. A., 25
Bagdikian, B. H., 132

Bainbridge, W. S., 17
Balance theory, 90–92, 154
Bargh, J. A., 76
Bartlett, F. C., 72, 73
Beaber, R. J., 109
Beck, A. T., 75
Behr, R. L., 142, 143
Belief dilemmas, 95–104, 154
Beliefs, 16 (*see also* Reasoned action theory)
Belief systems approach, 58–61
Bem, D. J., 59
Bem, S. L., 75
Bennett, W. Lance, 2, 7, 14, 15, 16, 41, 60, 85, 129, 132, 137, 152
Berelson, B., 141
Biden, Joseph, 102
Blacks (*see* Race)
Blake, F., 75
Bluestone, Barry, 33
Bluhm, W. T., 58
Bochner, S., 107
Bolstering, 97, 101
Bottomore, T. B., 47
Bowen, G. L., 40, 60
Bowles, S., 39
Bowley, C., 147
Bowman, W., 135
Bradburn, N. M., 17
Bradshaw, J., 39
Breckler, S. J., 13
Brehm, J. W., 94
Brent, E. E., 115–116
Brewer, M. B., 77
Brincka, J., 53
Broadbent, D., 73
Brody, R. A., 129
Bruner, J. S., 112–113
Buckley, John, 74
Burgoon, M., 145
Burnham, Walter Dean, 2, 4, 15, 32–33, 64, 133, 138, 156

Bush campaign, 1988, 34, 129, 146
  and gender gap, 29, 30
  and political nonparticipation, 155, 156
  and schemas, 73–74, 83–85
Busing, 60, 136

Cacioppo, J. T., 106, 108, 110, 123–129, 154
Campbell, A., 58–59
Campbell, B. A., 37
Cantril, H., 59, 74, 112
Carlsmith, J. M., 93, 94, 118
Carlson, R., 53
Carter, Jimmy, 41, 108
Chaiken, S., 82, 108
Charters, W. W. Jr., 23–24
Chase, W. G., 76, 77
Cheng, P. W., 69, 70, 72, 82, 95
Chi, M. T. H., 77
Child rearing, effects of (see Socialization)
Chong, D., 48–49
Chunking, 76–77
Cistuli, B., 67–68, 147, 149
Citrin, J., 31, 32
Class (see Income)
Cognition, 3–4 (see also Cognitive complexity;
    Cognitive consistency; Political ideology)
  attribution theory, 65–70
Cognition, need for, 126–127, 154
Cognitive complexity, 61–70, 72, 80–81, 117,
    153 (see also Schemas)
  and explanation for terrorism, 68–69
  reduction of, by mass media, 147–148,
    149–150, 157
  and schema activation, 80–82
Cognitive consistency, 4, 89–90, 104–105,
    153–154
  balance theory, 90–92, 154
  belief dilemma resolution, 95–104, 154
  dissonance theory, 92–95, 97, 103–104,
    117–119, 154
  and schemas, 68, 78–79
Cognitive development, 61–62
Cognitive dissonance, 92–95, 97, 103–104,
    117–119
Cognitive heuristics, 72, 82–85
Cohen, Bernard, 142
Cohen, C. E., 75, 78
Commoner, Barry, 136
Commons, B., 62
Conservatism, 43–45 (see also Liberalism;
    Political ideology)
Converse, P. E., 7, 13, 58–59, 60, 63, 76,
    112
Cooper, J., 94
Corbett, M., 26
Corteen, R. S., 150
Coulter, T. T., 46
Cox, J. R., 69
Credibility of source (see Source credibility)
Crotty, W., 16

Crutchfield, R. S., 112
Cumming, E., 25

Dawson, K. S., 38
Dawson, R. W., 38
Dempsey, G. R., 146
Denial, 39, 52, 96–97, 101
Dennis, J., 38
De Tracy, Destutt, 58
Dialectical thinking, 65–70, 148
Differentiation, 97, 101, 103
  for belief dilemma resolution, 97
  component of cognitive complexity, 63
Dissonance, 92–95, 97, 103–104, 117–119,
    154
  personal responsibility and, 94–95
  physiological effects, 93
Dogmatism, 46–49
Domhoff, G. W., 138
Doob, A. M., 108–109
Dornbusch, S., 76
Dramatic presentation of news, effects of, 148–
    150
Driver, M. J., 63
Dukakis, Michael (see Bush campaign, 1988)
Dulit, E., 62
Dull, V., 77
Duncan, G., 58
Dyck, D., 75
Dyer, L. M., 77–78

Eagly, A. H., 109
Easton, D., 38
Ebbesen, E. B., 78
Ebbinghaus, H., 72–73
Economic issues, views on, 25–26, 28, 31,
    34, 35–36
Edelman, M., 60
Educational levels, 22–23, 25–26, 29, 34, 35,
    143–144
Educational system (see Socialization)
Elaboration likelihood model (ELM), 123–129,
    130, 154
Emotions, 42, 80, 127, 155
Engels, Friedrich, 65–66
Epstein, E. J., 132
Equal Rights Amendment (ERA), 29
Erber, R., 77
Erbring, L., 144
Eron, L. D., 140
Erskine, H., 150
Ethnocentrism, 132
Evans, J. St. B. T., 69
Eysenck, H. J., 45–46, 47, 153

Faludi, Susan, 42
Family (see Socialization)
Fay-Dumaine, J., 80–82, 147, 148
Feshbach, S., 140
Festinger, Leon, 89, 92–95, 103, 108

Fishbein, Martin, 2, 7, 8–13, 16, 72, 89, 106, 113, 119–123, 154
Fiske, S. T., 73, 74, 77–78, 80
Fowler, F. J., 17
Frank, Reuven, 149
Free, L. A., 59, 74
Freedman, Jonathan, 93, 140
Frenkel-Brunswick, E., 43
Freud, Sigmund, 42
Friedrich-Cofer, L., 140
Fromm, Erich, 47
Fruchter, B., 47
Fundamentalism, 27, 35–36
Funkhouser, G. R., 142

Gaertner, S. L., 49
Gans, Herbert, 132–133, 136, 138, 139
Garr, M., 67–68, 147, 149
Garramone, G. M., 145
Gaudet, H., 141
Gaziano, C., 150
Gelles, R., 52
Gender, 29–30, 34, 35
George, J., 32, 33–34
Georgoudi, M., 57, 65–66, 67, 68, 70, 147, 148, 153
Gerard, H. B., 73
Gerard, J. B., 93
Gergen, K. J., 25
Gilens, Martin, 30
Gintis, H., 39
Glenn, N. D., 25
Goldenberg, E., 144
Goldwater, Barry, 47
Gordon, L., 52
Gorkin, L., 103–104
Graber, D. A., 132
Granberg, D., 115, 116
Greenstein, F. I., 3, 38
Greenwald, A. G., 94
Grenada invasion, 60, 137
Griggs, R. A., 69

Haan, N., 62
Hall, Stewart, 138
Hamill, R., 75, 79–80
Hamilton, Alexander, 15
Hamilton, S. B., 37
Hammen, C., 75
Haphazard sample, 17
Hardy-Brown, K., 62
Harrison, Bennett, 33
Harrison, L. F., 150
Hart, Gary, 29, 102
Hart, P., 91
Harvey, O. J., 113–114, 115, 116
Hastie, R., 77
Hastorf, A., 76
Hayes, J. R., 77
Hegel, Georg, 65

Hegemony, ideological (see Ideological hegemony)
Hegemony, uncontested (see Ideological hegemony)
Heider, Fritz, 65, 89, 90–92, 104
Helmreich, R., 94, 108
Helmsley, G. D., 108–109
Helson, H., 111
Hennessey, B., 16
Henry, W. A., III, 137, 139
Henry, W. E., 25
Herman, C. P., 78
Hess, R. D., 38
Higgins, E. T., 76, 78
Hinsley, D. A., 77
Hispanics (see Race)
Hitler, Adolf, 47, 52
Holloway, J., 32, 33–34
Holyoak, K. J., 69, 70, 72, 95
Hovland, Carl I., 106, 107, 109, 110–119, 141
Huesmann, L. R., 140
Huston, A. C., 140

Ideological consistency, 59–61
Ideological hegemony, 33, 64, 117, 138–139, 151
Income, 26, 29, 31–34, 35–36, 51–52
Inhelder, B., 62
Inoculation theory, 110, 145–146
Insko, C. A., 107
Integration
    component of cognitive complexity, 63
Iran-Contra scandal, 91–92, 97–102, 133, 144, 154
Iyengar, Shanto, 142, 143, 144, 146

Janis, I. L., 106
Jefferson, N. L., 115–116
Jennings, M. K., 37
Jennings, Peter, 137
Jewell, M. E., 25
Johnstone, J., 135
Jones, C. R., 78
Jones, E. E., 78, 94
Josephson, Wendy, 140
Joslyn, R. A., 110, 144
Judd, C. M., 59

Kahneman, D., 72, 82–85, 95, 112
Kandel, D. B., 37
Kant, Immanuel, 65
Kao, C., 126
Katz, D., 112
Keilin, W. G., 37
Kelley, J. J., 106
Kennedy, D. A., 147
Kennedy, John F., 108, 109
Key, V. O., 15–16
Kinder, D. R., 59–60, 77, 129, 141, 142, 143, 144

King, G. A., 76
King, M., 115–116
King, Martin Luther, Jr., 42
Klapper, J. T., 141
Knox, T. A., 37
Koeske, R., 77
Kohlberg, L., 62
Kohn, Mel, 52
Kohut, A., 151
Kohut, Andrew, 18–19
Krech, D., 112
Krosnick, Jon, 59, 103, 113, 129, 144
Kuhn, D., 62
Kuiper, N. A., 78
Kurkjian, S., 129

Lake, C. C., 29
Lange, R., 122
Langer, J., 62
LaPiere, R., 8
Larkin, J. H., 77
LaRouche, Lyndon, 69
Larter, W. M., 77
Lasswell, Harold, 41–42, 45, 54, 107
Lau, R. R., 75, 77
Lave, C., 22
Law of small numbers, 82
Lazarsfeld, D., 141
Lefkowitz, M. M., 140
Lemon, N., 8, 112–113
Lenin, V. I., 47
Lepper, M. R., 134, 141
Lesser, G. S., 37
Lev, A., 63
Levels of conceptualization, 58
Levinson, D. J., 43
Levy, N., 53
Liberalism, 26, 28, 34, 36 (see also Conservatism; Political ideology)
    public perceptions of, 73–74, 116–117
Libya raid, 60
Lichter, L. S., 134–136
Lichter, S. R., 134–136, 137, 138, 139
Liebert, R. M., 140
Liebling, A. J., 131
Likert, R., 8
Lindblom, Charles, 39
Linder, D. E., 94
Lippmann, Walter, 14
Lipset, S. M., 32
Lobley, M. D., 48, 49
Lodge, M., 75, 79–80
Lord, C. G., 141
Lowell, Abbott Lawrence, 14
Lui, L., 77
Lumsdaine, A. A., 109, 141

McCarter, R., 52–53
McClosky, H., 44–45, 48–49
McCombs, Maxwell, 142
McDermott, J., 77

McGinniss, J., 108
McGrail, A., 149–150
McGuire, W. J., 8, 13, 110, 145
Machiavelli, Niccolo, 13–14
McHugo, G. J., 147
Madison, John, 15
Manktelow, K. I., 69
March, J., 22
Markus, H., 74, 76
Maruyama, G., 109
Marx, Karl, 65–66
Mass media, 4, 131–132
    and cognitive complexity, 147–148, 149, 157
    effects of, 139–151, 154–155
    and ideological hegemony, 33, 138–139, 151
    negative effects, 139–140, 146, 150
    and political ideology, 33, 133–139, 151, 154
    and political nonparticipation, 143–144
    values of, 132–133
Masters, R. D., 147
Merritt, S., 145
Miklowitz, D., 75
Milburn, M. A., 59, 67–68, 75, 76, 78, 79, 80–82, 127, 129, 141, 147, 148, 149–150
Miller, Alice, 39, 52, 144
Miller, G. A., 73
Miller, N., 109
Miller, W. E., 7, 58–59
Mills, C. W., 138
Multiple regression analysis, 34–36, 148
Muzzy, R., 76

Nash, M. C., 111
Need for Cognition Scale (NCS), 126
Negative campaign advertising, 144–146, 157
    (see also Bush campaign, 1988)
Nel, E., 94
Neves, D. M., 77
Newcomb, T. M., 23–24, 26
Newton, J. S., 146–147
Nicaragua, 40, 60, 137
Nie, N. H., 59, 116
Niemi, R. G., 37
Nisbett, R. E., 69, 72, 95
Nixon, Richard M., 108, 109
Nonattitudes, 59–60
Nuclear energy, 135, 139
Nuclear war, views on, 28, 29, 30, 34

Oil industry, 135–136
Oliver, L. M., 69, 72, 95
Olson, J. M., 78
Operation Rescue, 41–42
Opinion polling, 2, 11, 13, 14, 16–20 (see also Public opinion)
Osgood, C. E., 8
Oskamp, S., 8, 16

Page, B. I., 146
Papageorgis, D., 110
Parenti, Michael, 136–137
Pasahow, R. J., 75
Peebles, A., 52–53
Peers, 37
Peitromonaco, P., 76
Personality, 3, 40–54
    authoritarian, 43–49, 126–127, 154
    Lasswell's theory, 41–42
    and persuasion, 130
    polarity theory, 49–53, 155
    and political ideology, 43–54, 155
Persuasion, 4, 104, 106–130, 141, 154
    and belief dilemmas, 98–104, 154
    and dissonance, 117–119
    elaboration likelihood model, 123–129,
        130, 154
    Fishbein-Ajzen model, 119–123, 154
    social judgement theory, 110–119, 129
    source characteristics, 100, 107–109, 150–
        151
    Yale model, 107–110
Peters, Mark, 143
Petrocik, J. R., 59, 116
Petty, R. E., 106, 108, 110, 123–129, 154
Pfau, M., 145
Piaget, Jean, 61–62, 69
Pichert, J. W., 73
Plato, 65
Poincare, Henri, 51
Poisonous pedagogy, 52, 96–97
Polarity theory, 49–53, 155
Political ideology, 3, 36, 57–61 (see also Con-
        servatism; Liberalism; Political cognition;
        Schemas)
    limited range of, 33, 64, 117, 138–139,
        151
    and mass media, 33, 133–139, 143–144,
        151, 154
    and personality, 43–54, 155
Political nonparticipation, 2, 4, 15, 25
    and Bush campaign, 155, 156
    and mass media influence, 143–144
    and social factors, 32–34
Political psychology, 1, 152, 155
Political socialization (see Socialization)
Poole, K. T., 29
Pragmatic-reasoning schemas, 70, 72
Presser, S., 19–20
Prewitt, K., 38
Priming, 7, 78
Probability sample, 17
Public opinion,
    definitions of, 15–16
    instability of, 14, 59–60
    origins of concept, 13–14

Question wording, 19–20
Quota sampling, 17

Race, 28–29, 34, 35–36
Random survey, 17
Rasinski, K. A., 13, 20
Reagan, Ronald,
    Iran-Contra scandal, 91–92, 97–104, 133,
        144, 154
    "Morning in America" campaign, 41, 157
    Nicaragua policy, 40, 60
    popularity of, 29, 30, 33–34, 40–41, 60
    Trade Bill veto, 137–138
Reasoned action theory, 2, 7, 8–13, 16, 72,
        89, 113
Reasoning (see Political cognition)
Reder, L. M., 76
Reference group, 23–24
Reich, S. S., 69–70
Religion, 22–23, 27–28, 35–36, 126–127
Representativeness, 82
Response rate, 17–18
Responsible capitalism, 133
Rhodebeck, L. A., 60
Rholes, W. S., 78
Richards, A., 62
Richardson, S. A., 76
Rigidity (see Personality)
Robertson, C., 116, 117
Robinson, M. J., 151
Robinson, W. V., 74
Roddy, B. L., 145
Rodriguez, R., 126
Roeder, P. W., 25
Rokeach, M., 46–49, 63, 153
Ronis, D. L., 94
Rosenberg, Morris, 22
Rosenberg, S. W., 38, 57, 61, 62–64, 66, 67,
        68, 76, 80, 148, 153
Rosenstone, S. J., 25
Ross, L., 134, 141
Rosten, L., 135
Rothman, S., 134–136
Rousseau, J. J., 14
Ruehlman, L. S., 75
Rush, A. J., 75
Ruth, P., 69–70

Sabato, L., 144, 145
Sanford, R. N., 43
Santrock, J. W., 38
Schemas, 3, 4, 70, 72–85, 153
    accessibility of, 76–80
    and cognitive complexity, 64, 80–82
    and cognitive consistency, 68, 78–79
    and emotion, 80
    and mass media, 149
    and persuasion, 127–128
    priming of, 78
Schoenberger, R. A., 45
Schoor, E., 76
Schroder, H. M., 63
Schuman, H., 19–20
Sears, D. O., 31, 32, 59–60, 129, 141

ACA - 5274

Sebert, S. Z., 37
Sedikides, C., 127
Segal, Z. V., 75
Selective exposure, 141
Self-interest, 23, 31–32, 140
Self-schemas, 74–75, 126–127
Semantic differential scale, 8
Sex (see Gender)
Shapiro, R. Y., 146
Sharp, C., 79
Shaw, B. F., 75
Shaw, Donald, 142
Sheffield, F. D., 109, 141
Sherif, C. W., 113
Sherif, M., 106, 110–119
Sherman, S. J., 103–104
Sidera, J., 127
Sigall, H., 108
Sigelman, L., 25
Simon, D. P., 77
Simon, H. A., 76, 77
Simple random sample, 17
Singer, D. G., 150
Singer, R., 140
Situational influences, 7, 10–11, 152
   and attitude change, 154
Situational perspective on public opinion, 15,
   16, 60
   and ideological consistency, 60
Slawski, E., 135
Smith, E. E., 76
Smith, M. B., 112–113
Smithers, A. G., 48, 49
Snyder, M., 104
Social factors, 2–3, 21–32, 152 (see also
   Socialization; specific factors)
   interrelatedness of, 21–23, 24–25, 29, 34,
      153
   multiple regression analysis, 34–36, 148
   and political nonparticipation, 32–34
Socialization, 36–39, 50, 51–53, 96–97, 153,
   155, 156
Social judgement theory, 110–119, 129
Social psychology, 1–2, 16
Social welfare programs, views on (see Eco-
   nomic issues)
Source credibility, 107–108, 120–121, 123
Sprafkin, J., 140
State of consciousness fallacy, 14, 60
Stendler, C. B., 51
Stereotyping, 44, 75, 80, 82, 104
Stewart, C. J., 145
Stokes, D. E., 58–59
Stone, W. F., 49
Strathman, A. J., 127
Stratified random sample, 17
Streufert, S., 63
Subjective norms (see Situational influences)

Suci, G. J., 8
Sudman, S., 17
Suedfeld, P., 63
Sullivan, D. G., 147
Surveys, 16–20
Swann, W. B., 104

Tannenbaum, P. H., 8
Taxes, views on, 23, 31–32
Taylor, S. E., 73, 78
Tedin, K. L., 37
Teeter, R., 91
Television (see Mass media)
Terry, Randall, 41–42
Tetlock, Philip E., 45, 57, 63–64, 66, 67, 68,
   80, 81, 117, 153
Thein, R. D., 76
Thurstone, L. L., 8
Tomkins, Sylvan, 49–51, 52–53, 155
Tourangeau, R., 13, 20
Trade Bill veto, 137–138
Transcendence, 97, 102
Turner, J. A., 118
Tversky, A., 72, 82–85, 95, 112

Uncontested hegemony of liberal capitalism (see
   Ideological hegemony)
Utley, Garrick, 133

Vallone, R. P., 134
Valone, K., 109
Value pluralism model, 46–49
Verba, S., 59, 116
Voting behavior, 1, 11–13 (see also Political
   nonparticipation)
Vreeland, R. S., 76

Walder, L. O., 140
Walster, (Hatfield) E., 108
Watanabe, Paul, 27
Weiss, W., 107
West, S. G., 75
White, R. W., 112–113
Wicker, A. W., 8
Wicklund, R. A., 94
Williams, T., 150
Willie Horton case, 83–85, 146, 155
Wilson, G. D., 45
Wolfinger, R. E., 25
Women (see Abortion, views on; Gender;
   Women's position, views on)
Women's position, views on, 24, 26, 32, 35,
   60
   and race, 28–29, 34, 35
Zadny, J., 73
Zanna, M. P., 78
Zeigler, L. H., 29
Zimbardo, P. G., 118

EMERSON COLLEGE LIBRARY
150 Beacon Street
Boston, MA 02216